URBAN GROWTH IN COLONIAL RHODE ISLAND

Urban Growth in Colonial Rhode Island

NEWPORT AND PROVIDENCE IN THE EIGHTEENTH CENTURY

LYNNE WITHEY

State University of New York Press / *Albany*

Published by
State University of New York Press, Albany

©1984 State University of New York

All rights reserved

Printed in the United States of America

For information, address State University of New York
Press, State University Plaza, Albany, N.Y., 12246

Library of Congress Cataloging in Publication Data

Withey, Lynne.
Urban growth in colonial Rhode Island.

Bibliography: p.
Includes index.
1. Urbanization—Rhode Island—History. 2. Rhode
Island—History—Colonial period, ca. 1600–1775.
3. Newport (R.I.)—Economic conditions. 4. Providence
(R.I.)—Economic conditions. 5. Newport (R.I.)—Social
conditions. 6. Providence (R.I.)—Social conditions.
I. Title.
HT123.5.R4W55   1983   307.7′64′097452   83-438
ISBN 0-87395-751-2
ISBN 0-87395-752-0 (pbk.)

10 9 8 7 6 5 4 3 2 1

For Florence Maxfield, Mary Mason, and Grace Withey

Contents

Illustrations and Tables

Preface

It has been twelve years since the first of a spate of books about New England towns was published suggesting an entirely new way of looking at early American history. More concerned with ordinary people than with leaders, with everyday life rather than with what Perry Miller called the "life of the mind," these pioneering books sparked a generation of followers. The close study of a single town or small group of towns continues to appeal to historians because of the opportunity it presents for understanding the intricate web of family and social life in the seventeenth and eighteenth centuries.

And yet there are persistent frustrations in this form of history. As all historians who have written about individual towns are quick to point out, no town or colony can be called "typical." The innate caution of most scholars leads many to conclude their work with the familiar call for more studies of the same sort; but historians, of course, are not scientists, despite the best efforts of the quantitative methodologists, and their work is never exactly replicable. The result has been a fascinating, idiosyncratic array of books and articles describing enough variations in family structure, community organization, political behavior—whatever the precise topics under discussion—to make one despair of drawing any general conclusions about life in the colonies.

On the brighter side, however, are the trends in recent studies toward comparison, whether of two or three towns or of an entire region, and toward placing the towns studied firmly in the context of time and place. Both trends have encouraged ways of systematically understanding not only the variety of the colonial experience but also the changes in that experience over time. Whereas the pioneering works were essentially static—snapshots of life in specific towns at specific times—the emphasis more recently has been on growth (or, in some cases, decline), on a recognition that towns changed and matured, and that the social patterns so fascinating to recent historians were inextricably linked to the process of change.

It is not surprising, therefore, that this interest in understanding social change as well as social structure has been accompanied by a renewed interest in studying colonial cities. Though cities were undoubtedly the least typical of all colonial communities—only a tiny fraction of Americans lived in urban places in the eighteenth century—nevertheless, as centers of economic and political activity and of social change, they were important out of proportion to their share of the colonies' population.

This book is an effort to understand the relationship between economic growth and the nature of society, the dynamics of urban growth and decline, and the effects of the Revolution on this process in two cities. Newport, the colonies' fifth largest city, and the much smaller Providence offer the opportunity of looking at two interdependent cities in a restricted region and at the ways in which they developed, competed with each other, and eventually traded places as major and secondary centers within the region.

When I began studying colonial Rhode Island, many years ago, I was more interested in its peculiarities than in its potential usefulness as a means of illustrating general trends. The smallest of the colonies, it had perhaps the most colorful early history. Its founders, a small band of passionate religious idealists, were an unlikely lot for community building: Roger Williams, a man who thought even the Puritans were not pure enough in their religion; Anne Hutchinson, who defied both religious doctrine and social convention to preach, in her home, to men and women who shared her antinomian views; the fanatic Samuel Gorton, whose views were too extreme even for Williams or Hutchinson to tolerate. With their followers, they created communities in the wilderness against all odds, not least their near-complete inability to get along with each other. Indeed, it is hardly accurate even to speak of Rhode Island as a colony for the first decades of its existence, for much of its territory was claimed by Massachusetts and Connecticut, and it was only the threat of takeover by one of their despised neighbors that induced Rhode Islanders to unite their villages into a single colony.

Rhode Island's early economic history was equally peculiar, if less chaotic. Religious idealism did not prevent many of the early settlers from grabbing as much land as they could. Some held their acres purely for speculation, while others raised livestock for market on a substantial scale; by the early eighteenth century, a few men had carved up much of southern Rhode Island's land into "plantations"—the term commonly in use—of several thousand acres. At the same time, the citizens of Newport were well on the way to establishing their town as a major commercial center, despite a limited selection of products for export and serious competition from Boston and New York.

But despite its oddities—even partly because of them—Rhode Island offers the possibility of a useful case study of urban development. The ambitions of many of the early settlers, coupled with their self-imposed isolation from the rest of New England, encouraged early commercial development; the political independence of the two major towns, Providence and Newport, combined with the natural geographic barriers separating the regions around the towns, planted the seeds of later urban rivalry. By the early decades of the eighteenth century, Rhode Island had developed a commercial economy with two competing economic centers. As a result it is possible to examine at close range not only the process of urban growth and the social changes accompanying it, but also the increasing competition between two cities and the effects of changing economic conditions on the growth of one and the decline of the other. And, although the fact of urban competition at such close range may be unique to Rhode Island, the economic and social conditions of urban growth and decline were common to other cities and other regions as well.

*   *   *   *   *

This book has been a long time in the making, and I have benefitted from the advice and criticism of many people along the way. The germ of the idea began as an undergraduate thesis, and I continue to be grateful to my adviser, Michael Mullin, for insisting that serious research is not solely the province of graduate students and professors. For their help with the dissertation version, I thank Winthrop Jordan, William S. Simmons, and especially Robert Middlekauff, who was then and continues to be a source of inspiration.

I owe a particular debt of appreciation to Nathaniel Shipton, Albert Klyberg, and Nancy Chudacoff at the Rhode Island Historical Society, for their help over the years; I am grateful also to the staffs of the Rhode Island State Archives, the Newport Historical Society, the John Carter Brown and John Hay Libraries at Brown University, the Providence and Newport County Courthouses, and the Providence City Hall. Financial support came from a University of California traveling fellowship and summer fellowships from the University of Iowa and the National Endowment for the Humanities.

Among the fringe benefits of spending months in the same small group of archives are the friendship and advice of others doing the same thing. I was fortunate in meeting, and learning from, Edward M. Cook, Jr., Jay Coughtry, Gary Kornblith, Sheila Skemp, and Elaine Crane. Other friends and colleagues helped in a variety of ways, from solving problems in the quantitative analysis to reading one or another version of the manuscript; I thank especially James Henretta, Michael Hindus, Sydney James, John Kolp, William Silag, and Bruce Daniels. And Elizabeth Pleck, at a critical moment, suggested a new way of looking at the subject and organizing the book. Without her, I am certain it would never have been published.

Finally, I thank my Rhode Island family—my grandmothers and aunt, to whom this book is dedicated—for making a home for me on countless research trips, for their continuing interest in my work, and most of all for inspiring an interest in New England history in the first place.

L. W.
Berkeley, California
December 1982

1
Urbanization in Colonial New England

PROVIDENCE AND NEWPORT were born out of conflict over religion, but also out of conflict over the social and political realities of Puritan society. Roger Williams and Anne Hutchinson wanted to create a more perfect religion, and their ideas about religion influenced the kinds of communities they helped create. The people who followed them, however, often cared less about a more perfect religion than about their own economic opportunities. The results were towns often riddled with conflict and lacking the shared values of early Massachusetts Bay towns; they provided fertile soil for schemes of economic aggrandizement.

The towns created by these religions rebels were, from the beginning, fundamentally different from the agricultural villages elsewhere in New England. A combination of locale, economic necessity, and individual motivation turned them into commercial towns and later into cities. Their experiences, while unique at first, help illustrate some of the patterns of urbanization that would gradually overtake the whole of colonial New England.

Roger Williams founded Providence in 1636 as a community dedicated to religious toleration and governed by mutual consent. But he soon found himself confronted with land-greedy associates who opposed his notion of holding most land in common for the future use of the town, pressuring him instead to deed huge tracts to them as original settlers. When Anne Hutchinson and her sympathizers were forced out of Boston two years later, they followed Williams to the shores of Narragansett Bay, and with his assistance obtained Aquidneck Island—which they called Rhode Island—from the Wampanoag Indians. Their town, called Pocasset (later changed to Portsmouth), soon split over religious and political issues. The dissident group established the town of Newport on the southern end of the island. As it turned out, Newport had a better harbor and the lion's share of the wealthy and influential men among the original group of exiles; it quickly out-stripped Portsmouth in political and economic influence.

Portsmouth and Newport patched up their disputes by 1640 and joined in a common government, although each town retained local autonomy—a colony in miniature. But neither the island town residents nor those of Providence had any great desire to join in a single colony; and neither group had any use for the fourth town, Warwick, founded in 1643 by Samuel Gorton, who had previously been banished from all three of the other towns. It was largely political necessity—none of the towns wanted to be swallowed up by Massachusetts—that finally united the four towns in the colony of Rhode Island and Providence Plantations under a charter obtained by Williams in 1644.[1]

The early Rhode Islanders had something more in common than religious eccentricity and animosity to Massachusetts, however. Their early settle-ments were dominated by men with an acquisitive mentality—men who chafed at the economic, as well as religious, restrictions of Puritan soci-ety—who wanted to build prosperous towns and personal fortunes out of the wilderness. From the beginning, the towns of Rhode Island were different from most seventeenth-century New England towns because their early resi-dents abandoned utopian, communal goals in favor of re-creating the pros-perous English society they had left. To be sure, the first Rhode Islanders left Massachusetts for religious reasons, but, for Anne Hutchinson and her followers, the dispute with the Boston leaders had economic overtones as well.

William Hutchinson and William Coddington, along with others among the antinomians, were merchants who resented the tight control of John Winthrop and the other magistrates. Their religious views, which stressed the primacy of the individual's relationship with God, by their very nature discouraged the creation of communities based on religious principles, which was so important to the Bay Colony founders. Only Roger Williams, alone among the first Rhode Islanders, cared about creating a more perfect society, and he found little support for this utopian impulse among his fel-low settlers. And even William's religious beliefs, although very different from Anne Hutchinson's or William Coddington's, were essentially individ-ualistic. He wanted strict separation of religious and civil authority and com-plete freedom of religious belief, a far cry from the highly structured, church-centered society of Massachusetts towns. William's belief in reli-gious toleration was not widely shared as a point of principle, but it was eventually adopted throughout the colony as an expedient, because no one could agree on a common set of beliefs. The combination of beliefs that encouraged individualism and discouraged institutional organization, the wide range of religious beliefs, and the early-established policy of toleration ensured that there would be no common set of religious beliefs or social goals shaping these settlements.

The absence of such ideals and goals permitted immediate, unrestrained attention to economic advancement. The backgrounds of the early settlers, many of whom were middle-class merchants and artisans, also encouraged early attention to economic matters. Even the practical problems of the first settlements—their isolation from Massachusetts and desire to remain independent of the other New England colonies—made the residents think from the very beginning about exportable commodities and the establishment of trade routes. All of these conditions helped produce a commercial mentality in Rhode Island from the earliest years of settlement.[2]

At first the men of Newport and Portsmouth devoted themselves to raising livestock for market, encouraged by the quality of grazing land and protection from wild animals on their island. William Coddington sold sheep to John Winthrop, complete with instructions for their care and breeding. Roger Williams ran a fur trading post a few miles south of Providence, and his early companions set about acquiring as much land as possible by redefining the initial Indian deeds. Some Newporters also got into the land speculation business by the 1670s, when they laid claim to much of the southern Rhode Island mainland. Limited trading with other colonies began very early; Williams noted the arrival of a ship bound for Virginia in 1638, and Newporter Peleg Sanford was trading with the West Indies by the 1660s.[3] By the end of the seventeenth century, Newport's economic leaders had shifted their attention almost entirely from agriculture to commerce, and there was some indication of a similar trend in Providence. This interest in trade was rooted in the earliest efforts of the initial settlers, however, for even as farmers they had always had one eye on wider markets.

The story of Rhode Island—and particularly of Newport and Providence, which quickly emerged as the colony's two major towns—illustrates the importance of entrepreneurial and commercial impulses in the settlement of New England. More broadly, their history illuminates the emergence of urban society in a region that historians have long characterized as one of communal villages and subsistence farmers.[4] Most colonial New Englanders were, of course, farmers living in or near small villages. Few persons could be called urban dwellers; as late as 1770, only 7 percent of the American population lived in urban centers.[5] Even so, cities and commercial towns dotted the entire region by the eighteenth century and were important far out of proportion to their size. The cities' importance lay principally in their function as economic centers. From Portsmouth, New Hampshire, to New Haven, from Boston inland to Springfield and Hartford, commercial towns and cities served as market and communications centers for rural villagers. These towns controlled the region's economy and linked it with other parts of the colonies and Europe.

More broadly, cities influenced the nature of society and politics in New England as well. Cities had a disproportionate share of both the wealthiest and poorest people—a consequence of commercial expansion, which created opportunities for some men to increase their fortunes substantially while squeezing others under the pressures of fluctuating wages, cyclical unemployment, and inflation characteristic of a maritime economy. Wealthy merchants exerted enormous political influence, not only locally but also at the colony level, asserting political as well as economic dominance over their regions. And even the lower-class city dwellers exercised their share of political influence in the years just before the Revolution; the mob protests that helped dramatize the American cause and spur the colonists toward independence were almost exclusively centered in cities. In short, as one historian of colonial cities put it, "cities were the cutting edge of economic, social, and political change."[6]

Cities in colonial New England, like those anywhere else, owed their existence primarily to economic growth. They were usually seaports, or less often inland centers strategically located in well-populated agricultural areas convenient to port towns. The survival and growth of these cities were intimately linked not only to continued economic expansion, however, but also to population growth; cities required a certain level of population within their regions to provide agricultural supplies and markets for imported goods. New England was the most highly urbanized region in the colonies, both because it was densely populated and could therefore support a large number of cities and commercial towns, and also because the nature of its economy encouraged urbanization. A region of poor soil, harsh climate, and small farms, New England's agricultural production was inadequate as an economic base. Fish, furs, shipbuilding, and lumber at various times helped fill the gap, but by the eighteenth century the shipping industry itself—exporting goods from regions outside New England—had become a major part of the economy. The combination of population growth, rising demand for imported goods, and the increasing complexity of the regional economy, all encouraged the growth of cities in New England.

An adequate definition of a city, however, involves more than a cluster of people engaged in trade; and an adequate explanation of the process of urbanization must take into account conditions beyond economic and population growth. Cities of the eighteenth century resembled more the agricultural village of their own time than the metropolis of today, but still they differed substantially in physical appearance, in social structure, and in way of life from most New England towns. In the minds of the people who lived there, it was the quality of life, not their place in a regional economic system, that marked their cities as distinctive. Decisions made by urban dwellers also influenced the growth of their cities, within the limits set by economy and demography. Such human efforts were especially important in Newport and Providence; they prospered despite Rhode Island's small population and area, which made a poor base for a commercial economy and required merchants to exercise exceptional ingenuity in developing trade.

Using economic function as the sole definition of a city would elevate every trading outpost and every town with a harbor and a sloop or two to urban status.[7] Even in less extreme cases, there is a fallacy in calling every trading center a city. This question of definition is not mere hair-splitting, but goes to the heart of two important issues in urban development: differences among types of commercial centers—or, put another way, among degrees of urbanization—and the importance of social characteristics in making cities distinctive. It is obvious that Newport was a city, and that a hamlet with a general store was not, even though it might be a trading center of sorts for surrounding farmers; but what of Providence in the first half of the eighteenth century? It had a few ships, a few men who called themselves merchants and traded with the West Indies; but most of its residents were at least part-time farmers, and its population density was relatively low. It is these medium-sized, secondary trading centers—borderline cities, perhaps—which help pinpoint exactly what it was that made a town into a city in the eighteenth century.

Historians who have tackled the problem of classifying and defining types of towns, though they differ on specifics, have all relied on the notion of a hierarchy based on economic function, ranging from the major seaport cities to the simplest agricultural towns. Whether one employs a three-part hierarchy, a five-part hierarchy, or the notion of a continuum without discrete types, the concept of ordering towns into types is linked to their specific role in their regional economy. Joseph Ernst and Roy Merrens describe a chain of trading centers in the South, from small inland towns collecting local agricultural produce, to larger regional centers transferring that produce to seaports, to the major seaports themselves. Jacob Price identifies three major types of traders—country storekeepers, wholesale-retail traders, and import-export merchants—and argues that types of towns can be distinguished according to the types of traders that predominated in them.[8] Bruce Daniels uses a similar scheme in classifying eighteenth-century Connecticut towns, dividing them into three types: major entrepôts engaged in export trade; secondary centers engaged in limited, if any, export trade but serving as commercial centers for other towns; and country towns involved in neither internal nor external trade. Daniels, following James Lemon's work on Pennsylvania, also draws on central-place theory to help explain the location and growth of towns of different types.[9]

Whatever the specific terminology employed, two important distinctions can be made: one between commercial towns or trading centers, on the one hand, and towns devoted primarily to agriculture, on the other; and a second, between major seaports engaged in import-export trade and smaller centers serving limited, local regions. These smaller towns were sometimes seaports engaged in limited intercolonial and West Indian trade; others were inland towns serving primarily as collection points for agricultural produce and as providers of goods and services. Regardless of location, they remained dependent on the major seaports—in New England, on Newport and Boston.

Newport and Providence are examples of major and minor trading centers and illustrate the complexity of New England's regional economic system. Newport, the major seaport for southern New England, engaged in extensive foreign trade by the 1740s. But in large measure, it remained dependent on larger cities—Boston, and to an even greater extent, New York—for reshipment of some cargoes arriving from Europe, for insurance, and for other financial services. Providence was largely an agricultural town until the 1720s and 1730s, with a very limited amount of trade conducted by a handful of merchants. As northern Rhode Island became more heavily settled after 1730, however, it increasingly became a commercial center for this region. Providence remained dependent on Newport for European products, although its merchants expanded their trade to the West Indies. But despite its increasing commercial development, a substantial proportion of Providence's residents continued to earn all or part of their living through agriculture.

These two towns illustrate something of the pattern of regional interdependence in New England—and, for that matter, throughout the colonies. Both Newport and Providence, in their function as local markets, served fairly restricted areas—the Narragansett Bay islands, southern Rhode Island, and southeastern Massachusetts for Newport; northern Rhode Island, parts of southern Massachusetts, and eastern Connecticut for Providence. Patterns of local trade, migration, even marriage show that there was little overlap of these local regions.[10] But while Providence served primarily as a local center, Newport filled some regional functions. Its merchants provided the European goods that Providence shopkeepers then sold to northern

Rhode Island farmers. On this level, Newport's trading network extended to all of Rhode Island, most of Connecticut, and Massachusetts south of Boston and east of Worcester.

At times, however, even this larger region came within the economic sphere of Boston and New York. Thus, for some purposes, small areas in New England were self-contained; but, for other purposes, they were part of larger regions. In practical terms, for Newport and Providence, this meant that most people rarely, if ever, ventured more than about thirty miles from their homes; but shopkeepers and merchants had contact with their counterparts in the other town. And merchants operating on a large scale had extensive contact in other major seaports throughout the colonies and in England.

One of the weaknesses of hierarchical explanations of colonial towns is their static quality; in fact, the pattern of towns and cities changed over the course of the eighteenth century, as part of the process of economic expansion and population growth. A larger population and increased demand for goods required more trading centers, and shifts in population changed the location of those centers.

Newport, for example, was largely a local center dependent on Boston or New York for European goods, up to about the 1730s. Only its rapidly expanding trade with the West Indies indicated the possibility that it would develop into a seaport of major importance. The growth of Rhode Island's population in the early eighteenth century, combined with the accumulation of capital in the West Indian trade and the slave trade, finally propelled Newport out of Boston's orbit and into the status of a major city.

Providence, meanwhile, was clearly a local center in the early years of the eighteenth century, and it remained economically dependent on Newport almost to the time of the Revolution—in much the same way that Newport had once been dependent on Boston. By the late 1760s and early 1770s, however, Providence merchants also tried to develop more extensive trading networks and, in particular, direct trade with Europe. To a considerable extent they succeeded, and by the time of the Revolution the two towns were engaged in economic rivalry almost as equals. Nonetheless, Providence did not expand at Newport's expense, at least before the Revolution; its growth was linked to the extraordinary growth of its local region, aided by a few energetic merchants' efforts to expand Providence's local trading networks into larger areas of Massachusetts and Connecticut.[11] The two towns' respective trading areas still did not overlap very much. After the Revolution, however, Providence continued to expand while Newport declined, owing in part to the ravages of war, and by the end of the eighteenth century it was Providence, rather than Newport, that dominated the southern New England region.

The growth of Providence as an urban center in the second half of the eighteenth century illustrates the relationship between determinative factors, such as economic change and population growth, and individual initiative. Its emergence as a major city would not have been possible without the population growth of northern Rhode Island and the region's development as a manufacturing center. The once secondary center benefitted not only from the shift of population from southern to northern Rhode Island, but also from the beginnings of an important economic change that would make manufacturing, rather than trade, the basis for Rhode Island's economy. Yet the process of change was not always smooth, nor was the eventual outcome obvious. The expansion of Providence's trade from the 1730s to the end of the Revolution was spurred by the energetic efforts of a few merchants, especially the members of the Brown family, who were the town's richest and most aggressive businessmen. Obadiah Brown first attempted to initiate direct foreign trade from Providence in the 1750s, but found it unprofitable and dropped it; his nephews did not make serious efforts in that direction again until the 1770s, when Providence's economy was better able to sustain foreign trade. Several merchants in Connecticut seaports had similar experiences, as they tried to sustain direct foreign trade and found it financially unfeasible.[12]

These experiences indicate both the role of individual merchants in promoting their towns' economic growth and the limitations imposed on them by basic economic and demographic constraints. Obadiah Brown and his nephews were instrumental in transforming Providence into a major seaport; but in the 1750s, even the shrewdest efforts would not turn it into another Newport. The same was true for Connecticut towns. Ten to twenty years later, however, Providence had reached such a point that its merchants could more realistically hope to compete with Newport. The years immediately before and after the Revolution were years in which the relationship between these two cities was changing, and it was unclear what the outcome would be. At this point merchants played a critical role in shaping the future of their cities; here the Browns' experiments in manufacturing, their efforts to control sources of exports, their skill as politicians, and even their ability to manipulate a decision on the location of Rhode Island College foreshadowed the future dominance of Providence.[13]

An understanding of regional economies and their interdependence in the colonial period is essential in explaining urbanization in the eighteenth century. Classification of towns according to a hierarchy of types—whatever its precise form—is important both in defining the nature of cities and in showing the close connections between economic and urban growth. An examination of the social characteristics of commercial towns and cities, however, can expand and clarify the explanations of urbanization based on purely economic conditions. Not only were commercial towns, in general, vastly different from small rural towns, but major cities were different in some significant ways from smaller commercial centers. These social differences help demonstrate what made eighteenth-century cities distinctive.

Above all else, cities were distinctive in population. They not only had more people, but more different kinds of people—people who, whether rich or poor, were attracted to cities because of the economic opportunities they offered. Although Newport and Providence did not have the ethnic diversity of New York or Philadelphia, Newport had Huguenots from France and Jews from Portugal among its inhabitants, along with a steady stream if immigrants from England and other colonies. These people came to Newport because of its commercial opportunities; many of the city's most important merchants were born elsewhere. The slave trade added to population diversity by bringing hundreds of Africans to Rhode Island; both Newport and Providence had substantial black populations.

Diversity of wealth was perhaps the most striking characteristic of the urban population. Both the wealthiest and the poorest Americans tended to live in cities, and this skewed distribution of wealth increased over the course of the eighteenth century as the colonies' economy expanded. The trend was more pronounced in the major cities, but it was apparent in the smaller ones, too—and in fact differences in the degree of wealth stratification form one of the clearest distinctions between major and minor urban centers.[14]

The presence of great wealth, in turn, influenced the politics of commercial towns. Unlike rural villages, in which most adult men participated in government and political offices were widely distributed, commercial towns were characterized by clearly defined elites, with the same small group of men dominating the important positions over a long period of time.[15] Newport and Providence were no exception to this rule. Why this situation existed has never been adequately explained; but undoubtedly this too was related to the fact of greater social stratification. The towns' economic leaders were interested in political policies that would aid commercial development, and, to that end, they dominated positions of political authority. The very existence of sharp distinctions of wealth and occupation in these towns encouraged political distinctions as well.

In physical appearance, Providence and Newport were also set apart from rural towns. Providence's settlement in the 1630s followed the classic pattern of small house lots clustered at the center of town, with fields on the perimeter; by the end of the seventeenth century, many residents preferred to move out of the village center and build homes on their farms. Providence was different from other towns, however, in that its central area continued to be built up as merchants built wharves and warehouses; they too preferred to live near their work and built town houses along the waterfront opposite their warehouses. A similar pattern developed in Newport.[16]

What really distinguished Providence and Newport physically, however, was not so much this parallel development at the centers and fringes of town as the increasing tendency, after the beginning of the eighteenth century, for the bulk of the population to cluster at the centers, especially in Newport. And as the centers became more crowded, with all the accompanying problems of muddy streets, stray animals, and threats of fire, the towns' boundaries grew progressively smaller.[17] Residents of the rural sections of these towns recognized that they had little in common with the merchants and tradesmen living in the "compact parts," as they were called. Providence, which once covered a huge area, was whittled down in the 1730s, and again in the 1750s; in these instances it was clear that people living in the distant parts of the townships could not be expected to remain part of a single town.[18] But when North Providence was separated from Providence in 1765, a major controversy erupted. Similarly, when Newport was divided in 1743, conflict ensued between residents of the "woods" part and those living in the "compact" part. In both instances, the farmers living on the periphery resented paying high taxes that they felt went primarily to support the expenses generated by growing commercial towns. Residents of the central section, on the other hand, opposed the loss of agricultural territory, apparently because they were concerned about getting an adequate food supply for themselves.[19]

This conflict was evidence that Providence and Newport became distinctive in a variety of ways during the eighteenth century. Residents of the rural parts of these towns recognized the changes and wanted to separate themselves from the growing commercialism which dominated the towns. As a result, by the time of the Revolution, these towns were small in area, densely populated, and focused around their waterfronts, the scenes of commercial activity.

Commercial towns like Newport and Providence were clearly very different from agricultural villages, but they were also different from each other. In part, these differences were a matter of timing; Newport developed faster economically than did Providence, and consequently experienced a series of social changes earlier. But some of the differences were qualitative in nature and illustrate the fact that, until after the Revolution, Providence and Newport were essentially different types of towns. Take, for example, the matter of town divisions and the "compact" versus "woods" sections. Newport's final division occurred in 1743, during a period of major commercial expansion. The equivalent action did not take place in Providence until 1765 —two decades later, but also during an important period of growth. In effect, it took Providence twenty years to catch up to Newport. Even after this final division, however, Providence retained a more rural atmosphere than Newport. In 1774, when a census was taken in Rhode Island, Newport was nearly twice as densely populated as Providence.[20] Even after the division of 1765, the heavily settled part of Providence remained very small and the majority of its area was devoted to farms. Some of the major merchants themselves maintained farms along with their commercial activities.[21]

The same kinds of differences between Newport and Providence were reflected in other areas, too. In some ways, social change in Providence paralleled Newport's experience, twenty to thirty years later. Wealth became increasingly concentrated in the hands of the rich in both places, but to a lesser degree in Providence. Poverty was a greater problem in Newport, but Providence had the same kinds of problems later—Newport, for example, built an alms house in 1720, but Providence waited until 1753. Newport had proportionately more blacks, but Providence's black population gradually increased.[22] In both towns, the timing of these kinds of social changes coincided with periods of economic expansion; as Providence lagged behind Newport in commercialization, so it also lagged behind in the social changes that accompanied commercialization.

In other respects, however, Providence and Newport remained completely different. During the eighteenth century, Providence was never as complex demographically as Newport—it had fewer immigrants from distant areas, fewer blacks, fewer religious denominations. Most important, it had a different sort of leadership. Both Newport and Providence differed from the average rural community in having well-defined elites characterized by wealth, economic leadership, and political power. In Providence, this elite consisted of a handful of men and was dominated by a single family. These men controlled most of the town's wealth, were largely responsible for its commercial development after mid-century, and held most of the important political positions. Newport, on the other hand, did not really have a single elite, but a series of overlapping elites. The innovative commercial leaders had little to do with politics. The political leaders were usually well-to-do merchants, but were neither especially wealthy nor particularly innovative in trade. And some of the town's richest residents were neither merchants nor politically active, but were members of prestigious old families.[23]

In part, this complex elite in Newport was the result of its greater diversity in population. The men who were chiefly responsible for the expansion of trade in Newport, for example, were immigrants who arrived in the early eighteenth century and later. Some of them were denied citizenship, because they were Jewish; they could not be active politically, but were extremely important leaders economically. This diversity of population, in turn, was related to the higher degree of economic development in Newport, since at several times in its history the opportunities it seemed to offer attracted men of various backgrounds.

Comparative evidence is slight, but it seems likely that these differences observed between Newport and Providence were not coincidental. To take one other example, Springfield, another secondary center, was dominated by a single family even more strikingly than Providence.[24] All the major cities in the colonies, including Newport, were sufficiently complex economically and socially to require a complex elite structure, while secondary centers like Providence were small enough to be dominated by a small, unified group or even a single family. Ironically for Providence, and perhaps similar towns as well, the success with which a handful of men controlled the town contributed to its economic growth. Willing to take risks, aggressive enough to take on Newport's merchants, and wealthy enough to finance their adventures, they built fortunes that not only enriched themselves, but also pushed Providence as a whole into more extensive commercial activity. And their continued strength after the Revolution helped Providence make a successful transition from a primarily commercial to a primarily industrial economy.

2

The Growth of a Commercial Economy, 1680–1760: The Pre-eminence of Newport

FROM THE VERY BEGINNING of Newport's settlement—even when it was barely more than a hamlet of a few exiled families from Massachusetts—its residents had visions of creating an important commercial city. Although their initial impetus for settlement was the desire for religious freedom, Newport's first residents were just as strongly committed to economic freedom. The antinomian crisis, which spawned Newport and its neighboring town, Portsmouth, involved economic issues as well as religious ones. Most of the men who left Boston for Rhode Island were merchants, including Anne Hutchinson's husband William, and William Coddington, the leader of the group that founded Newport. These men did not get along with the political leaders of Massachusetts, and their support for Anne Hutchinson's teachings was in part an attack on those leaders.[1]

This combination of religious and economic motives for leaving Boston resulted in a new community committed to religious toleration, but also carefully planned and located in a place well-suited to the development of a commercial economy. The land of Aquidneck Island was exceptionally fertile and free of wild animals that might prey on livestock. The harbor at the southern end, where Newport was located, was excellently situated for trade, protected from the elements, and warm enough so that it rarely froze during the winter. Both the religious tolerance and the economic sagacity of Newport's founders paid off in later years. Men of various religions were attracted there, drawn by both its religious and economic climate, and these men were largely responsible for developing Newport's economy at several key periods in its history.[2]

Providence's first settlers, too, left Massachusetts in search of fortune as well as freedom of conscience, but they were less successful in establishing their town on a firm economic footing. Providence lacked the natural advantages of Newport—it was more isolated, was located in a region with poorer soil, and did not have as good a harbor. Its earliest settlers were not so wealthy as Newport's, nor did they have a clear plan for the economic success of their town. Their leader, Roger Williams, was not blind to the advantages of encouraging trade—he established a fur trading post south of Providence—but his goal for Providence was to create a community based on toleration, love, and mutual consent. He wanted Providence to remain small and to be governed by consensus, without formal government officials or coercion of any sort.[3] His companions, for the most part, did not share his idealism, and the town very quickly became embroiled in a series of controversies over land allotments, which lasted through most of the seventeenth century.[4] As with Newport, these circumstances of location and early settlement had a lasting influence on the nature of Providence's economy. It was not until the second quarter of the eighteenth century that the growth of new towns around Providence and the efforts of a later generation pointed the way towards enlarging the role of Providence in a regional economy.[5]

Until about the middle of the eighteenth century, Newport dominated Rhode Island's commerce. From modest beginnings in the seventeenth century, its trade expanded rapidly during the first three decades of the eighteenth century. During these years, a small group of merchants—most of them recent arrivals from other colonies—established the basic trading patterns and methods that remained the essential framework of Newport's commerce until after the Revolution. The volume of Newport's trade leveled off in the 1740s but spurted upwards again in the 1750s, as a new generation of merchants undertook the first sustained efforts at direct trade with Britain. This expansion marked Newport's emergence as a major port, no longer completely in the shadow of Boston and Newport. At about the same time, Providence began to develop significant intercolonial trade, although its merchants remained dependent on Newport for imported goods. Both cities suffered seriously from a depression in the early 1760s, but then recovered and grew rapidly during the ten years before the Revolution. During this period Newport consolidated its position as a center of international trade, and Providence became firmly established as a regional trading center—with the potential to challenge Newport's commercial dominance.

The reasons for Newport and Providence's commercial growth in the eighteenth century, and for the differences in the timing of the two cities' growth, are complex and interrelated, but they can be divided into two general types: those dependent on environmental conditions and those dependent on the actions of individuals. Newport's favorable location and fertile land were obvious natural advantages, but were not sufficient to give it a long-term edge over Providence or, for that matter, other potential port towns in Rhode Island. Providence's harbor was adequate for the small ships used in most eighteenth-century trade, and Newport's agricultural advantages ceased to be significant as soon as trade expanded to the point that local produce no longer sufficed as a source of exports.

More significant was the relationship between population growth and the expansion of trade. As with all commercial towns, Newport and Providence owed their existence to the demand for goods that were not produced locally. Population growth created new demand for the goods merchants imported and also increased their supply of labor. Rhode Island's population grew very rapidly in the late seventeenth and early eighteenth centuries, roughly coinciding with the colony's initial period of economic expansion. From slightly more than 2,000 people in 1670, the colony grew to about 7,000 at the turn of the century and to just under 17,000 in 1730[6] (table 1). The majority of these people lived in Newport and surrounding towns; at the time of the first Rhode Island census in 1708, nearly a third of the colony's population lived in Newport alone, with another 28 percent living in the surrounding towns.[7]

Providence's population was only about 20 percent of the colony's total, although at this time its boundaries included the entire northern half of the colony. By 1731, when three new towns were created out of what had been Providence, this area still constituted only about 22 percent of Rhode Island's total. Thus, in the initial period of rapid economic growth for Rhode Island, from about 1680 to 1730, the largest proportion of the population was concentrated around Newport.

By 1730, Rhode Island's population was sufficient to support a stable, relatively high level of trade, with the bulk of both population and trade concentrated in and around Newport. The colony's growth rate slowed down during the next twenty years, as did the rate of commercial expansion. After 1750, however, the rate of population growth in Providence and surrounding

TABLE 1
POPULATION OF NEWPORT AND PROVIDENCE BEFORE THE REVOLUTION

YEAR	NEWPORT	PROVIDENCE	TOTAL RI
1708	2,208	1,446	7,181
1730	4,640	3,916	16,950
1748	6,508	3,452*	32,773
1755	6,753	3,159*	40,576
1774	9,208	4,321	59,706

SOURCES: See Appendix A.
*Reduction in population attributable to the creation of new towns from Providence's original land area in 1731, 1747, 1754, and 1759.

towns spurted upwards, while Newport's growth rate continued to decline.[8] At the same time, the rural area around Providence also grew much more rapidly than the area around Newport. While the southern part of the colony achieved its most important growth in the seventeenth and early eighteenth centuries, the major period of growth for Providence and its region occurred in the last quarter century before the Revolution.

These growth patterns help to explain the particular pattern of expansion in Rhode Island's trade. The first burst of trade activity, during the early years of the eighteenth century, took place almost entirely in Newport and was part of a general period of growth there, both in population and in economy. Newport's trade continued to grow, particularly in the 1760s and 1770s, but a large part of the rapid rise in Rhode Island shipping around mid-century must be attributed to the emergence of Providence as a shipping center. Not only population growth, but the shipping statistics themselves suggest this conclusion. In the mid-1740s, Providence's shipping was no more than about one-fifth the volume of Newport's; by the late 1760s and 1770s, its share had risen to about one-third.[9]

Expansion of trade in Rhode Island depended on population growth and on the general development of the colonial economy, but the process of developing trade required the initiative of merchants seeking new commodities and new markets. Each new generation of merchants worked out new techniques for expanding the volume of Rhode Island's shipping. They had major obstacles to overcome. The limited agricultural area around Newport and Providence meant that merchants could not draw on a steady supply of farm products for export, as could their counterparts in New York or Philadelphia. This situation not only created problems in getting export cargoes, it also caused chronic shortages of currency.

Newport and Providence merchants helped solve these problems at various times by developing new trade routes, by taking the risks involved in privateering and wartime trade, and by encouraging local manufactures as a source of commodities for export. The slave trade, for example, first undertaken in the 1720s, gave a substantial impetus to Newport's trade during the middle years of the century. And the growth of the 1770s was made possible largely by an enormous expansion of the coastal trade and by the export of locally manufactured whale oil, candles, and rum. Providence merchants expanded their trade and finally achieved a measure of commercial independence, in part by pushing their markets into rural areas to the north and west, and by developing the manufacture of candles, iron, lime, and potash.

Geographical advantages and the early pattern of settlement in Rhode Island provided the initial impetus to establish Newport as a trading center. Those geographical advantages were not significant enough to give Newport a long-term edge over potential rivals, however, and population growth in the northern part of the colony, particularly after 1750, provided a base for Providence's growth as a trading center as well. Geographical conditions, settlement pattterns, and demographic trends were all part of the preconditions for economic expansion in Newport and Providence, but the initiatives of merchants—in establishing trade routes, seeking export commodities, and developing markets for both their exports and imports—helped consolidate their towns' positions as important seaports. Newport enjoyed a near monopoly on entrepreneurial capital and talent in the first half of the eighteenth century, a fact critical to its early economic growth. Significant commercial leaders began to emerge in Providence by mid-century, however, and in the post-Revolutionary years they displayed considerably more unity and ingenuity than their Newport counterparts, which had a major effect on Providence's long-term economic growth.

The merchant leaders in both Newport and Providence did more than accumulate capital and establish trade routes and markets. They also pressed for political and institutional changes that would support their commercial efforts; they helped consolidate their influence as a group—although perhaps not consciously—by forming organizations and sponsoring civic projects; they banded together to control the lower classes, who, as laborers and seamen, were necessary to their economic endeavors but were also potentially disruptive. In all these ways, the merchants helped create in Newport and Providence those social and political characteristics often described as typically "urban," as well as establish the basis for urban growth.

Newport's first settlers began immediately to establish trade. Out of sheer necessity they were too small a group to be self-sufficient, and they could not count on much help from neighboring Massachusetts. "I heare of a Pinnace to put in to Newport bound for Virginia," Roger Williams wrote to John Winthrop at the end of 1638."[10] During the 1640s and 1650s, small ships from Newport carried on trade with Boston, Connecticut, and occasionally New Amsterdam. By the 1660s, local traders ventured farther afield, building up trade with the West Indies to obtain products that could be exchanged for English goods, which were then shipped back to Newport by way of Boston. By the end of the seventeenth century, this trade was well established, if still limited in scope.

A report sent by Rhode Island's governor, Peleg Sanford, to the Board of Trade in 1680 illustrates the limited nature of Newport's trade in the seventeenth century. Rhode Island's shipping was limited to "a few sloopes." The colony's principal exports were horses and provisions; their imports were a "small quantity of Barbadoes goods for supply of our familyes." No individuals conducted trade on a large scale. "We have severall men that deale in buyinge and selling;" Sanford noted, "although they cannot properly be called Merchants." This absence of merchants—men with enough capital to undertake more elaborate trading ventures—was the chief obstacle to Rhode Island's commercial expansion, according to Sanford, although he thought that the potential for such expansion in the future was considerable.[11]

Sanford may not have fit his own definition of a merchant; but he, perhaps more than anyone else, helped to launch Newport's trade in the 1660s and 1670s. Along with men like Walter Newbury, who was active in trade in the 1680s and 1690s, Sanford helped establish the basic trading methods that Newport merchants continued to use over the next several decades. Sanford was born in Portsmouth, just north of Newport; but Newbury was an immigrant to Newport from London, arriving in Rhode Island sometime around 1670. In this respect he helped establish a pattern, since few Newport merchants were natives at any time during the period before the Revolution. Both Sanford and Newbury were Quakers, as were most Newporters engaged in trade during the seventeenth century; they were able to build up trade in part by taking advantage of contacts with men of their faith in other ports. Here, too, they set a precedent, for throughout the colonial period religious and family ties were the most important means of developing business contacts for Rhode Island merchants.[12]

Sanford's and Newbury's major innovation was the development of trade between Newport and the West Indies. Before about 1660, Newport's economy had been based primarily on agriculture; raising livestock, especially sheep, for market was the principal activity. Newport's shipping industry had its small beginnings in marketing this livestock.[13] Most trade was confined to the coastal area between Boston and New Amsterdam. There was a limit to the volume of trade that could be based on the products of Rhode Island's land, however; the land was fertile, but in short supply. It was the West Indian trade, instead, that supplied Newport merchants with the commodities needed to expand shipping and pay for European goods.

Sanford learned the West Indian trade first-hand by spending two years in Barbados. When he returned to Newport in 1665, he began a regular trade with the island. His principal exports to Barbados were Rhode Island agricultural products, including beef, port, butter, and livestock; he traded them for molasses, sugar, and rum, which were shipped to Boston where they could be exchanged for English goods. This arrangement indicated the primitive state of Newport's commerce in the 1660's, when European goods had to be purchased from Boston merchants rather than imported directly. Sanford attempted to break this dependence on Boston by initating a direct correspondence with a London merchant, who sent goods to Boston on Sanford's account. This procedure eliminated the Boston merchant as a middleman, but goods still had to be reshipped from Boston to Newport since Newport's demands for imported products were still too small to justify direct shipments from England. Even this limited arrangement did not work well, however, and Sanford eventually dropped these efforts. In addition to helping establish the basic trade routes to the West Indies, Sanford set an example in using family members as his principal business contacts. He sent his brother William to Barbados to look after his interests there. In Boston, his cousin Elisha Hutchinson took care of most transactions. Two uncles and his father-in-law, William Brenton of Newport, were also involved occasionally in trading ventures.[14]

Sanford had many problems: trade was often slow; he frequently received inferior goods, both from Barbados and London; he was disappointed in his London correspondent; and he was involved in a serious lawsuit in Boston, even spending some time in debtors' prison. But he helped establish a pattern of trade which was, on the whole, profitable for him and used successfully by other merchants who followed him. Its elements were relatively simple: shipping agricultural products from Rhode Island and neighboring areas to Barbados, in return for molasses, sugar, and rum, which were then shipped to Boston to exchange for English goods. Cargoes were consigned to resident merchants in both locations, preferably family members. Later merchants would add many variations, including widening the range of West Indian ports, consigning cargoes to ship captains as well as local merchants, trading with other colonies to obtain more types of products for trade, and dealing directly with European merchants rather than relying on Boston connections. But the basic patterns changed little.

Walter Newbury's record of his shipments in the years 1673–89 shows business methods similar to Sanford's, but more varied. The limited scale of the Newporters' trade is apparent from the rather small size of the shipments. He branched out somewhat from Sanford's trading patterns of the 1660s, although Barbados was still the most frequent port of call; his ships also visited Jamaica, Nevis, and Antigua, all of which would become popular destinations for Newport cargoes in the eighteenth century. He still relied heavily on merchants in other cities, but dealt with New York men as well as Boston traders. He also sent an occasional ship farther south, and one directly to London. Newbury, too, employed family members on the other end of his voyages when possible, notably in his ventures to Jamaica.[15]

A new generation of merchants came to Newport between 1700 and 1720, from places as diverse as Massachusetts, Virginia, the West Indies, and Europe. Under their leadership, Newport's commerce changed from a sporadic, limited trade with a handful of ports to a complex trade involving hundreds of voyages annually to ports throughout the West Indies and continental colonies. During this period Newport shipping achieved its fastest rate of growth, and efforts began to reorganize and stabilize Rhode Island's government—efforts that secured Newport's position as an important trading center.

When Thomas Richardson moved from Boston to Newport in 1712, he was already an established merchant. He moved to Newport because he saw opportunity in a port that was growing rapidly, but was still dependent on Boston for imports and lacked any merchant with the capital and experience to break this dependence. As a Quaker, he undoubtedly also found Newport's religious climate preferable to Boston's. At about the same time that Richardson was setting up shop in Newport, younger men, who would become important merchants in the 1720s, also settled there.[16] Daniel Ayrault, a French Huguenot, first emigrated to North Kingstown, Rhode Island, but settled in Newport around 1700; his sons, Daniel Jr. and Stephen, both became prominent merchants. Godfrey Malbone moved to Newport from Virginia at about the same time. William and John Wanton, shipbuilders from Massachusetts, arrived a few years later and soon shifted their interests to trade. Abraham Redwood, another Quaker, came to Newport from Antigua.[17]

The promise of Newport's future growth attracted these men to this small port. In 1708, Governor Samuel Cranston reported to the Board of Trade that the number of ships belonging to Rhode Island had increased from four or five to twenty-nine in the previous twenty years. Almost all of them were owned by Newporters. From the occasional voyages to Barbados, trade had expanded to include several other islands in the West Indies, most of the continental colonies, and the Wine Islands. Provisions were still the major export, but were supplemented with lumber, candles, rum, molasses, and iron.[18] By 1720, trade had continued to increase to the point that more than 600 ships passed through Rhode Island's ports yearly. This volume of shipping remained stable throughout the 1720s and 1730s[19] (figure 1).

Expansion of trade during the first decade of the eighteenth century involved several kinds of changes. The West Indian trade was expanded to include more islands, including French and Dutch islands, which were technically off limits to American traders. The War of the Spanish Succession (1702–13) provided lucrative opportunities for trading with enemy forces in the West Indies, and Newport merchants used these opportunities to acquire capital and establish trade relations with foreign islands.[20] Increased demand for exports for the West Indian trade forced merchants to develop trade with other continental colonies, since Rhode Island could not produce a sufficient quantity of agricultural products for export. Rhode Islanders also

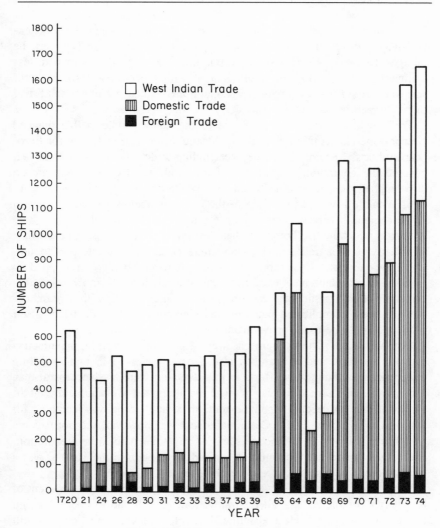

FIG. 1. Rhode Island shipping, 1720–1774

began distilling rum, the first of several experiments in manufacturing products for export. During the 1720s, Newporters discovered that rum was an
extremely profitable commodity on the African coast, thereby launching
themselves in the slave trade. Ultimately this trade provided the largest
source of capital for further commercial expansion.[21]

Thomas Richardson's career illustrates some of these changes. His major
goal was opening direct trade between Newport and London, something that

Peleg Sanford had attempted unsuccessfully. Richardson counted on his experience in the Boston-London trade to ensure his success in Newport; he thought that being the first to begin this trade, in a smaller town with less competition than in Boston, would guarantee his profits. By 1716, Richardson was trading regularly with five London merchants, but imports still had to be shipped by way of Boston.[22]

Trade with London introduced one of the major problems that plagued Newport merchants throughout the eighteenth century: how to pay for European imports. Receipts from the West Indian trade was one way, and that ensured the continuing importance of this trade for Newport. Richardson also shipped rice, turpentine, pitch, tar, whale oil, and whale fins to London. Whale oil proved to be one of the most satisfactory exports; to obtain it, he became involved in trade with Nantucket. He supplied whalers there with salt, which he had bought in the West Indies, in exchange for the whale oil.[23] This kind of trade pattern—obtaining products from one port to supply a second port, to get the products that would finally be shipped to London—was elaborated over the next several decades and became the principal characteristic of Newport's trade. Direct trade with Britain demanded these complicated patterns, since nothing that Rhode Island itself produced could be used for payments there.

Complex trade patterns were one way of generating exports; manufacturing was another, and Richardson also became involved in manufacturing experiments, although his efforts in this direction were less successful than his innovations in trade routes. In 1712, he attempted to manufacture cloth. He apparently succeeded to some extent, since in 1716 he was searching for a skilled weaver and dyer.[24] Cloth manufacturing, however, did not become a significant industry in Rhode Island at any time before the Revolution. Richardson found that shipbuilding, an industry begun in the 1640's, was a much more dependable source of remittances to England.[25]

Richardson was in many ways a transitional figure in the development of Newport's commerce. For all his innovation, he still had to operate within traditional constraints. He had initiated direct trade with England, but still depended on Boston merchants for reshipment of goods. The West Indian trade remained the mainstay of his business, and, as earlier merchants had, he depended on a relative there to manage his affairs. Like both earlier and later merchants, he dealt with other men of his religion when possible.[26] And he still needed local agricultural produce for export, even though he had taken the lead in developing new exports.[27] His efforts were not without their disappointments; his English trade was not as profitable as he had hoped, and obtaining return cargoes was not as easy as he had expected when contemplating the move from Boston to London.[28] But he also made some gains in trying to solve this problem of the return cargoes by developing trade with other mainland colonies that had products in demand in Europe. His inclusion of such products as whale oil, pitch, tar, and turpentine, in addition to sugar and molasses, foreshadowed the much greater trade in commodities produced in mainland colonies later in the eighteenth century.

The merchants who established themselves in the 1720s—the Wantons, Malbones, Ayraults, and Redwoods—generally lacked Richardson's advantage of experience as a merchant before arriving in Newport. But most had experience in some aspect of trade; their achievements were in expanding markets and export commodities along the lines developed by Richardson.[29] They continued to conduct the bulk of their trade with the West Indies, but increasingly favored French and Dutch ports, rather than the English islands.[30] Trade during the war years had introduced Newport merchants to the foreign islands; the higher quality and lower price of sugar there encouraged them to continue. Abraham Redwood was an exception, but his circumstances were unusual; he had inherited a sugar plantation in Antigua in 1726. He paid an overseer to run the plantation, and used it as his main trading base. He could not escape the general decline of the English sugar islands, however, as the profitability of his plantation dropped considerably during the 1730s.[31]

As the West Indian trade expanded, it became more complex. Direct voyages to and from the islands remained the most common practice, but increasingly merchants made stops along the way, or made a series of shorter voyages in order to obtain goods to send to the islands. And it became more common to send ships to several islands, rather than to a single port, as in Peleg Sanford's day. The need for larger and more diversified cargoes for the West Indian trade sent merchants to Newfoundland for fish, to Long Island and Connecticut for grains and other agricultural products, and to Philadelphia and Baltimore for flour. Sometimes ships traveled to the Mediterranean with fish, picking up wine or salt there to exchange in the West Indies. Merchants increasingly ordered their ship captains to travel from port to port in the islands in search of the best prices, rather than consigning their cargoes to a single individual. The multiplicity of ports, the absence of merchants in many of them, and the growing competition among North American merchants encouraged this speculative system of trade in the islands.[32]

Products obtained in the West Indies changed relatively little from the seventeenth century; the one major exception was the increasing importation of molasses. Sugar had been the most valued West Indian product in the seventeenth century, but early in the eighteenth century, Rhode Islanders discovered that molasses, when distilled into rum, became an extraordinarily useful commodity in trade. Merchants became interested in a few other West Indian products too, especially dye woods from Central America. But molasses became, and remained, the most important West Indian commodity for Rhode Island merchants.[33]

One of the major reasons for the importance of locally distilled rum was Newport's increasing involvement in the slave trade after 1720. The trade had been initiated in Newport in 1700, when three ships, partly financed by Barbadians, sailed for the African coast. Their cargoes of slaves were sold in Barbados. By 1723, Rhode Island sea captains had introduced local rum on the coast of Africa; it proved very profitable as a trading commodity. Throughout the 1720s and 1730s, several ships a year sailed to Africa, usually selling their return cargoes in the West Indies. This trade became increasingly important over the course of the eighteenth century, particularly as the price of slaves rose in the West Indies between 1720 and the Revolution.[34] It was attractive to Newport merchants because slaves commanded cash in the West Indies, and because the principal export commodity— rum—was locally manufactured and therefore easily available in large quantities.

Always looking for reliable sources of exports and ready cash, and willing to take the kind of risks associated with the slave trade, Newport merchants dominated the American slave trade by mid-century. For them, Africa became the critical third point in the famous "triangle" of eighteenth-century trade. Rhode Island rum bought slaves, who were sold in the West Indies for cash, which then paid for English goods. Along with the shuttle trade between New England and the West Indies, which yielded other kinds of commodities to be traded for English goods, the slave trade became a mainstay of Newport's commerce.[35]

This reliance on the slave trade fit into the overall pattern of commerce that Newport merchants had developed during the early years of the eighteenth century, one based on risk-taking, diversity of exports, and the creation of a complex network of shipping. They readily undertook voyages that would have been considered marginal by merchants in cities larger than Newport, or blessed with a better supply of local exports, and used such voyages as the basis for a profitable—if often unstable—economy.[36]

During the first thirty years of the eighteenth century, Newport merchants built the foundation of their city's commercial economy. During the same period, they helped strengthen that foundation with legislation and political reorganization designed to support the growing shipping industry and consolidate Newport's position as the capital and leading city of the colony.

As early as the 1660s, trade was important enough to require special legislation for commercial interests. In 1663, the General Assembly authorized special courts to be held for the convenience of merchants and seamen, so that their ships would not be delayed while waiting for court sessions. By 1679, it became necessary to establish some regulation of shipping. Ships of more than twenty tons were required to report to the governor before leaving port, a regulation that was superseded by the appointment of naval officers in each port in 1682. Because masters of ships occasionally found that their hard-drinking seamen accumulated debts to the local tavern keepers while in port and consequently were detained for debt when their ships were ready to set sail, the General Assembly limited the amount of credit that tavern owners could extend to sailors. And, by the end of the century, competition from outsiders who came into the colony to trade was sufficient to warrant passing a law to restrict such activity.[37]

Legislation enacted in the early eighteenth century extended these initial efforts to regulate trade and improve the business climate for merchants. A system of fees for vessels entering and clearing Newport was established in 1719 as the principal means of regulating shipping. Efforts were also made to control the retail sale of goods in Newport, primarily to prevent outsiders from reaping a share of the profits without paying taxes. And subsidies were provided for people who produced goods that could be useful in trade.[38]

Most important, however, was the legislation that introduced paper money. First printed in 1710, the paper was a boon to merchants trying to expand their trade. Currency shortage was always the merchants' number one problem; paper money was designed to remedy it. At first, most of them thought that paper money was largely responsible for their prosperity. The first bills of credit, issued to pay for extraordinary wartime expenses, were intended to be redeemed within five years and paid for by increased taxation. A second issue was voted in 1715, followed by fairly regular issues over the next thirty years. By 1740, about £340,000 in bills of public credit were in circulation, and they suffered from a high rate of depreciation. Merchants still generally supported the paper money policy, however. Not until 1750 did they come to view the steady depreciation of Rhode Island currency as a problem outweighing the advantages of plentiful currency. As creditors, they had the most to lose from continued depreciation.[39]

Significant political and administrative changes in the first three decades of the eighteenth century, while not so obviously linked to the needs of Newport's growing commercial economy, nevertheless also played an important role in its development. Through most of the seventeenth century, Rhode Island existed in a state of political and religious chaos. The colony's original four towns (Providence, Newport, Portsmouth, and Warwick) had little in common other than their antipathy towards Massachusetts and any form of religious coercion. As a consequence, the towns fought among themselves and guarded their autonomy jealously, tolerating only the weakest form of colony government. Even within the individual towns, squabbles over land allotments and religious practices were commonplace. This political chaos had to end before Rhode Island could achieve any significant commercial growth, for several reasons. At the most basic level, the colony's very survival was threatened by neighboring Massachusetts and Connecticut, both of which eyed Rhode Island's land and laid claim to various parts of it. In addition, rational laws to regulate business dealings, fundamental guarantees of the validity of deeds and boundaries, and a functioning court system to enforce contracts and payment of debts were all needed if commerce was to be expanded beyond the most primitive level. Rhode Island's early seventeenth-century government could guarantee none of these prerequisites to economic stability and growth.

During the early years of the eighteenth century, however, many of these problems were remedied. A stronger colony government reduced the political powers of the towns and imposed some uniformity of government on them. Many of the old land disputes were finally settled. And, while religious diversity continued to flourish and even to increase, theological disputes faded and the churches became stable institutions with well-defined social characteristics, rather than hotbeds of contention. Although these changes affected the entire colony, they had a particular impact in Newport. Not only did Newport stand to benefit most from political and administrative changes that would protect the colony's autonomy and rationalize its commerce, but its leaders took control of the reorganized colony government and used it as a means of consolidating their power within the colony. In the long run, Rhode Island's quirky beginnings worked to the merchants' advantage, since it remained an independently governed colony throughout the colonial period. Not subject to royal control, Rhode Island's merchants had an easier time evading taxes and importing illegally obtained goods, tactics that often meant the difference between profit and loss.

The man primarily responsible for instituting administrative reorganization and increasing political stability was, not surprisingly, a Newporter —Samuel Cranston, who served as governor of the colony from 1698 to 1727, an unusually long term by Rhode Island standards. Cranston, a Newport native, launched his career first as a ship captain and later as a merchant, but he devoted most of his energies to politics. During his tenure as governor, he was responsible for several kinds of changes, including settling the land squabbles between the various towns, a feat largely accomplished by 1710; strengthening the General Assembly, which became more of a legislature and less of an all-purpose judicial tribunal; establishing uniform procedures for town government; and codifying laws and expanding the court system.[40] In the process, towns lost much of their autonomy and became primarily administrative units regulated by the General Assembly. They lost their power to regulate common lands, were limited in their judicial powers, and had their discretion in admitting inhabitants and freemen reduced as uniform standards for such status were prescribed. Even more significant for the life of the towns was the increasing delegation of town business to Town Councils and to a growing list of specialized town officials. Town meetings became less important as governing bodies and centers of debate; even the timing of meetings became fixed, rather than flexible according to the demands of local business. Most of these changes were accomplished by the end of the Cranston administration.[41]

Shortly after he left office, in 1730, another major administrative reorganization was accomplished in the spirit of Cranston's work, when the colony was divided into five counties. The counties were established primarily for judicial purposes; the town remained the basic unit of local government for all other matters. The single, colony-wide Court of Trials, which could no longer reasonably handle all the colony's judicial business, was replaced by county-level courts, with a colony-wide Superior Court to hear appellate cases.[42] As a result, it became much easier to have a case heard in the courts, and the volume of civil cases expanded enormously.[43]

The largest single group of men using the courts in Newport County were merchants from the town of Newport, and their proportion of the total number of litigants increased steadily in the decades before the Revolution.[44] In a time when there were no financial institutions to speak of and no regularized system of billing and debt collection, the court played a critical role in merchants' attempts to enforce contracts and collect their debts.[45]

This expansion of the court system completed the basic framework of Rhode Island's colonial government. The administrative changes initiated by Cranston and completed by his successors strengthened the colony government at the expense of individual town governments, but, significantly, these changes benefitted Newport even though it lost some of its autonomy as a town—in part because its economic growth depended to a considerable extent on the establishment of a stable political system in Rhode Island, and also in part because Newport effectively controlled the colony government, a situation that more than made up for any reductions in local autonomy. Not only was Newport the colony capital, but it also dominated the governorship until the 1760s. The lone Providence man elected governor in the first half of the century, Joseph Jenckes, felt compelled to move to Newport for the duration of his term.

Newport's dominance within the colony had symbolic importance, but offered practical advantages as well. Not only did the Newport merchants' control of the government allow them considerable freedom in violating English trade laws, but it also offered opportunities to profit from the activities of government itself. The faction that controlled the colony government could reward its supporters with political jobs, influence the way taxes were levied, and elect friendly judges to the courts.[46] These kinds of practical, economic accompaniments to political power were extremely important in the Newport merchants' efforts to establish their town as a commercial center.

Their goal was accomplished, to a considerable extent, by 1730. After a period of rapid expansion, Newport's commerce was well-established, based on a foundation of trade with the West Indies and Africa. Administrative reorganization and expansion had helped eliminate the sort of religious and political bickering that threatened Rhode Island's integrity as a colony, and a much strengthened, Newport-dominated colony government passed laws intended to help support commerce. The next two decades—the 1730s and 1740s—were a period of consolidation in commerce, a time when merchants refined already established business practices, extended their activities to some new domestic ports, and experimented with direct trade to Europe. Trade levels remained relatively stable in the 1730s and 1740s, and the same group of merchants dominated the town's economy, with a few notable additions like John Banister and Samuel and William Vernon.[47] They helped pave the way for another period of major commercial expansion in the 1750s.

The most significant development in Newport's commerce during the mid-century years was the beginning of sustained, direct trade with Europe. Earlier merchants, notably Thomas Richardson, had attempted such trade sporadically, but remained dependent on Boston and New York for imported goods. John Banister was the pioneer in this trade. He made a trip to England in 1738 to initiate direct trade between Newport and English ports, and managed to convince several English merchants to invest in his voyages. Samuel and William Vernon followed Banister's lead in the early 1740s, along with some of the older and more established merchants, notably Daniel Ayrault, Jr.[48]

A number of conditions made it possible for Newport merchants to establish and maintain European trade in the 1740s, where they had been unable to do so before. A certain basic level of population and commercial development was a prerequisite. How large a population and how elaborate a commercial system is impossible to specify precisely—though the primitive state of transportation and communication in the eighteenth century limited the geographical range of any single commercial center and made it easier for small cities like Newport to establish and maintain international trade.

Richardson, in the first decade of the eighteenth century, had perceived Newport as a growing town offering opportunities to the merchant who would move in and establish trade; he misjudged the situation, for Newport could not at that time sustain the European trade that he attempted to initiate. Sometime between 1715 and 1740, however, Newport reached that critical level of size and importance.

It was significant also that young merchants, relative newcomers to the economic scene in Newport, were the ones to initiate trade with Europe. Like the merchants of a generation earlier, they had fresh ideas and were willing to take risks. They also needed capital, however, and Banister was able to convince English merchants to give him the financial backing—and the lines of credit—that he needed. His success undoubtedly owed something to his powers of persuasion, but the English investors had to be convinced that both Banister and Newport could support the kind of trade he proposed—something that even the most persuasive of men would have had difficulty doing ten or twenty years earlier. Finally, Banister and his colleagues faced the time-honored problem of finding suitable exports to exchange for English goods, or sources of cash to pay for them. The West Indian trade and the slave trade remained critical, but were no longer sufficient to sustain Newport's level of trade by the 1740s and 1750s; merchants were forced to seek more diversified exports. As a result, they expanded trade with other continental colonies, especially those in the South, to obtain cargoes of flour, tobacco, rice, and naval stores. This new emphasis is apparent in the trade statistics. Sixty to 75 percent of Newport's shipping was directed to the West Indies in the 1720s and 1730s, with 15 to 30 percent directed to the continental colonies and the remainder to foreign nations; by the 1760s, however, about 65 percent went to the continental colonies and only 25 to 30 percent to the West Indies[49] (figure 1). Merchants sought new markets in the continental colonies partly as a source of exports to the West Indies, there to be exchanged for other exportable commodities—creating a complicated and many-layered trading network.

In keeping with their efforts to expand commerce and transform their town into a major trading center, Newport's leading merchants undertook civic projects that were both practical and symbolic of their vision of Newport as an urban center. The most ambitious project of the mid-century merchant group, aside from organizing direct trade with England, was expanding and remodeling the town's waterfront. In 1739, Newport's principal merchants, organized as the Long Wharf Proprietors, undertook the expansion of the "Town Wharf," which had been constructed in 1702. Town residents granted them a large parcel of land along the waterfront, apparently agreeing with the merchants that the wharf would benefit Newport as a whole by providing employment and improving the town's appearance. The larger wharf was designed to accommodate the larger ships entering Newport's harbor; it also included shops and warehouses which were rented to tradesmen by the proprietors to help defray the wharf's cost. In addition to their practical motives, the Long Wharf proprietors saw their project as part of an effort to give Newport the status of a major seaport. They boasted that theirs would be the grandest wharf in New England. And by the end of the 1750s, plans were under way to build a market house on the wharf, a structure that would also be important in both practical and symbolic ways. This building, the Brick Market designed by Peter Harrison, was not completed until 1763, but it fulfilled both expectations.[50]

Many of the same merchants also joined forces to organize the American colonies' first library, in 1747. Abraham Redwood made the initial contribution to start the library, and Peter Harrison designed the building in 1748. The actual work of organizing the library was undertaken by the Philosophical Club, an elite organization of merchants and professionals who met regularly to discuss philosophical and moral issues. They formed the core of the membership of the new library and adopted articles of incorporation that ensured it would remain an organization of the wealthy: members paid an initial fee of £100 and were taxed yearly to pay for the upkeep of the building.[51]

Rebuilding the town wharf and establishing a library were two outward manifestations of Newport's increasing importance as an urban center. In different ways, they reflected the city's economic prosperity: it took a certain level of growth to justify a new wharf and to support the sort of wealthy upper class that had the money, time, and inclination to establish libraries. Other manifestations were the building of churches—here, too, Peter Harrison was active, designing the Touro Synagogue in 1761—the grand houses of wealthy merchants, the increasing congestion in the center of town as population increased, and the volume of ships sailing in and out of the harbor. A painting of Newport's waterfront in 1730 shows a harbor dotted with ships, a string of wharves, and houses lined up close to each other along the waterfront and several blocks inland, punctuated occasionally by church steeples. In the background, beyond the compact, congested area, are fields, meadows, and occasional farmhouses—a sharp juxtaposition of urban and rural.[52]

As commerce came to dominate Newport, the people who lived in the rural parts of the town—outside the central, urban area but within the town's legal boundaries—felt increasingly alienated from the business of trade and the people who worked in it. Arguing that their taxes were increasing as a result of commercial growth that offered no direct benefits to them, in 1743 the farmers living in the outlying parts of Newport petitioned to be set off as a separate town. The petition caused a certain amount of controversy, as some residents of the central part of town feared that they needed the farmers to supply food for the nonagricultural population; but the petition was granted with a minimum of rancor, and the new town of Middletown was incorporated. This division, perhaps more than any other single event, illustrated the changes that had taken place in Newport during the previous decades—changes that clearly set it apart as an important urban center.

While Newport expanded its commerce and consolidated its position as Rhode Island's major city in the first half of the century, Providence remained primarily a rural community. A major division of the town in 1731, necessitated by the expansion of population into the northern and western parts of the colony, created three new towns; but even so, Providence remained far larger in area than Newport, and its residents were still primarily farmers.[53] Only a few men ventured into trade, and then only on a small scale.

By the 1750s, however, this situation began to change; and Providence began, in a very limited way, to challenge Newport's commercial dominance. Providence's commercial growth was almost single-handedly the work of the Brown family. Unlike Newport's leading merchants, most of whom came to the city as adults, the Browns were descended from one of Providence's original settlers.

James Brown, a sailor and shopkeeper, made his first voyage to the West Indies in 1721, and continued to make an occasional voyage while maintaining a shop in Providence. During the 1720s and 1730s, he built up contacts with farmers in southern Massachusetts and eastern Connecticut, as well as with merchants in Newport and Boston. Through these efforts, he developed a regular trade with the West Indies, eventually spending all his time in Providence while his younger brother Obadiah took over as captain of their voyages. James died in 1738, leaving four young sons; Obadiah trained them to continue the family business.[54]

By the 1750s, Obadiah Brown was prepared to expand his family's trade substantially, working with his nephews, John, Nicholas, Joseph, and Moses. Together they were responsible for Providence's increasing share of Rhode Island's trade around mid-century. Obadiah began trading directly with London, although that trade was never extensive and ended in 1759; he explored new ports in the coastal and West Indian trade; and, most important for the future of the Brown enterprises, he began experimenting with manufacturing. His first effort in this direction was a chocolate mill, built in 1752, which served customers in Newport as well as Providence. Shortly thereafter, along with some of his fellow merchants in Newport, he began manufacturing spermaceti candles.[55] When he died in 1762, his nephews were prepared to take over the family business, which they vastly expanded in the 1760s and 1770s.

In many respects, Providence's commercial growth paralleled Newport's, although it was compressed into a shorter period of time. The Browns and the handful of other Providence merchants began with the West Indian trade and gradually expanded, increasing their contacts in other North American ports; Obadiah Brown made some forays into the European trade, but was unable to sustain it, just as the first Newport merchants to attempt it were also unsuccessful. Expansion of Providence's trade in the 1750s and later depended on a combination of population growth and merchants' initiative. And these merchants tried to enhance their economic power by increasing their political power, challenging Newport's long control over the colony government in the late 1750s and 1760s.

In other ways, however, Providence's growth was different, and some of these differences had significant implications for the later growth and decline of the cities. Providence's economy was controlled by a much more tightly knit elite group, a group dominated by a single family. Newport's leaders, in contrast, were more numerous and varied. During the formative years of Newport's economy, this frequent influx of new talent was a source of strength; but in the long run, the stability and power of Providence's elite group would prove to be critical to the city's growth. Providence's merchants, on the whole, adopted business methods similar to those of Newport's merchants, although they never depended heavily on the slave trade, and began, at a very early stage, to develop local manufactures as a source of exports. Both variations, while minor at first, later became very important.

3
Rhode Island's "Golden Age," 1760–76: The Rise of Providence

THE 1760s AND 1770s—the "Golden Age" of trade for Newport and Providence—were paradoxical years. During the early 1760s, these towns, along with the rest of the American colonies, suffered the worst depression of the century, which exacerbated all the traditional difficulties of conducting trade in Rhode Island. But the merchants recovered from this depression to enter the most significant period of commercial expansion in the towns' histories. During the 1770s, the volume of trade peaked, the range of markets broadened, and the ingenuity of merchants in developing products for export reached its height. For Newport, these years represented its most important period as a commercial port; after the Revolution, both its population and its trade dropped markedly. For Providence, this period was one of brief commercial significance, before its economic leaders turned to manufacturing in preference to trade. Commerce during the Golden Age exemplified all the methods of trade developed over the course of the eighteenth century. The men who were responsible for its development in these years were for the most part the men who were just establishing themselves in trade in the 1750s—Aaron Lopez, Jacob Rivera, and Christopher Champlin in Newport, and the four Brown brothers in Providence; some older merchants, notably the Vernons, were also important.

The depression which preceeded these years of prosperity illustrates the continuing problems that Newport and Providence merchants had to overcome in their quest for profits. To the Rhode Islanders' perennial problems—scarcity of currency and of products for export—was added the effect of England's first serious effort to regulate American trade more closely. The Sugar Act of 1764, which provided for strict enforcement of the tax on molasses, was potentially devastating to Rhode Islanders because molasses was a critical item in their trade and because they had long avoided paying duty on it by smuggling. The adverse effects of this tax were complicated by the general downturn in trade and by continued inflation in paper money, which reached dire proportions by the 1760s.

A remonstrance protesting the Sugar Act sent from the colony to the Lords of Trade, in 1764, summed up Rhode Island's postwar problems; in the process, the petitioners outlined Rhode Island's economic position in terms very similar to those used by Governor Cranston nearly sixty years earlier. The colony's major problems, they explained, were a limited amount of land and a lack of any "staple commodity for exportation." These deficiencies were mitigated by a favorable location for trade, which "with the spirit and industry of the people hath in some measure supplied the deficiency of its natural produce, and provided the means of subsistence to its inhabitants." As a result, a large proportion of the colony's residents lived in its two major ports. The fundamental purpose of this trade was importing British products; the colony annually imported goods worth at least £120,000. The lack of a staple commodity and a chronic shortage of currency made discharging the debt a constant problem for merchants, and consequently most of their efforts were directed to that end. In the words of the petitioners, "It can . . . be nothing but commerce which enables us to pay it." They further explained that the products which could be raised for export by Rhode Island merchants were marketable largely in the West Indies, and consequently the islands were "the foundation of all our commerce.[1]

This was precisely the situation that had governed Rhode Island's economy from its earliest days: lack of land, dependence on trade, focus on the West Indies—all for the purpose of importing English goods. But if Rhode Island could claim any staple commodity at all, it was rum; and the increasing importance of rum as a basic export was one of the most important developments in the colony's trade in the eighteenth century. It was rum, distilled from molasses, that had aided the expansion of trade in the early eighteenth century, and it was rum that sparked the colony's protest against the Sugar Act. "Molasses," the petitioners stated, " . . . serves as an engine in the hands of the merchant to effect the great purpose of paying for British manufactures." Rum was shipped to New York and Philadelphia, to help pay for British imports; to the West Indies, as one of the basic components of cargoes sent there; and to other colonies in exchange for commodities that could be sold in Britain. Most important, it was the principal medium of exchange in the slave trade. Rum had first been traded on the coast of Africa in 1723, the petitioners stated; since then the slave trade had grown to the point that they estimated it to be responsible for about one-third of all remittances to England.

The manufacture of rum had secondary benefits, as it employed "many hundreds of persons," in thirty or more distilleries throughout the colony. A tax on molasses, if enforced, would, in the minds of the petitioners, be disastrous for Rhode Island's trade. They painted a gloomy picture:

> These distil houses . . . must be shut up, to the ruin of many families, and of our trade in general; . . . two-thirds of our vessels will become useless, and perish upon our hands; . . . our mechanics, and those who depend upon the merchant for employment, must look for subsistence elsewhere; . . . and as an end will be put to our commerce, the merchants cannot import any more British manufactures. . . ."[2]

The rhetoric was exaggerated, but the message was clear: the entire Rhode Island economy depended on the sea, just as surely in 1764 as in 1700. The patterns of trade, and the problems the merchants faced, were similar; the differences between Rhode Island in its Golden Age and Rhode Island a half-century earlier were differences of degree, not of kind.

Coming just after the postwar depression, the efforts to tax molasses were seen as particularly critical. The remonstrance and other correspondence to England stressed the reduction in value of local produce, the shortage of specie, and the indebtedness of the merchants. These woes were only increased by the fact that "commerce is so checked by the regulations since made, that it is daily declining."[3] What was not reported to English authorities was the fact that continued inflation of Rhode Island's paper money contributed to economic problems, along with the weight of British regulation. In 1760, £6 in paper money had been equivalent to one Spanish milled dollar; by 1763, it took £7 to equal one dollar, but after the war, in 1764, paper money had inflated to the point that £23.5 were equivalent to one dollar. This inflation took place despite efforts to legislate the value of paper currency.[4]

So the Golden Age began somewhat inauspiciously; but the rate of inflation slowed after 1764, the tax on molasses was dropped to a nominal one pence in 1766, and the economy in general began to recover by the late 1760s. The commercial development of the next several years may be attributed to a variety of conditions, including the general growth of the colony and increased demand for imported goods, the ability of a new generation of merchants, and the cumulative effect of decades of trade during which generations of merchants had worked out methods that were used to great advantage by younger men.

The remonstrance against the Sugar Act had described trade with England as the basic goal of commerce, and it was in this branch of commerce that the most important developments came in the 1760s and 1770s. The volume of trade with Europe, both in absolute and proportional terms, began to rise in the late 1730s, and it rose again in the 1760s. Roughly half of all European voyages were directed to Britain (including an occasional trip to Ireland); most of the others went to Spain, Portugal, or the Wine Islands, although occasional trips were made to Holland. The African trade increased even more sharply, bearing out the Rhode Islanders' contention that the slave trade was an important component of their trade with England. The number of voyages involved, however, was small, and the increase in volume consequently less dramatic than the increase in trade as a whole.[5]

What was most significant about the growth in foreign trade was the establishment of regular trade relationships with England that were much more secure than those existing in earlier years. Whereas occasional merchants like John Banister and Obadiah Brown had traded directly with England in the 1740s and 1750s, that trade had not always been frequent or extensive. They continued to rely on Boston, New York, and Philadelphia as sources of imported goods. By the mid-1760s a few merchants became regular importers of English products. Most direct importing was done by Newport men who in turn supplied Providence merchants, although the Browns reopened direct trade with London in 1766.[6] In Newport, Aaron Lopez and Christopher Champlin dominated the European trade.[7]

The two major problems in establishing and maintaining a regular English trade were obtaining a regular source of imports and finding ways of paying for them. The first problem was solved by maintaining regular business relationships with English merchants; establishing these relationships was one of the most important developments of the 1760's, one that enabled Rhode Islanders to import directly from England on a regular basis. Christopher Champlin began a correspondence with William Stead in the years 1756–59; Lopez traded with Stead regularly from 1763 to 1775. Lopez also traded with George Hayley, starting in 1767; Samuel and William Vernon, Christopher Champlin, and Nicholas Brown & Co. all eventually entrusted most of their English business to Hayley.[8]

The English merchants' principal services to their American correspondents were selling goods shipped to them and procuring appropriate assortments of English goods for the return voyages, tasks which required considerable discretion. In addition they provided financial services, including insurance and bills of exchange. Extending credit to specie-poor Rhode Islanders was an inevitable part of these services. Colonial merchants generally consigned cargoes to their English correspondents, who then sold the produce and credited the proceeds to their accounts. English goods shipped to Rhode Island were charged against these accounts; almost invariably the Rhode Island merchants were indebted to the London men. Twelve months' credit without interest was standard.[9]

Lopez's relationship with William Stead illustrates some of the workings of this trade. He began a regular correspondence with Stead in 1763. After some disagreement over the terms of credit, Stead kept up a constant flow of letters to Lopez, reporting on sale of his cargoes in London, getting insurance, and filling orders for manufactured goods. From January to October, 1764, for example, Stead reported that he had arranged insurance on the Brig Sally and the Ship Hope; honored Lopez's draft on him; noted the arrival of the Brig Sally and sold some of its cargo of oil, tar, and turpentine; collected the goods Lopez ordered; sent the goods to him via New York; noted the arrival of a ship from Carolina; held its cargo to wait for higher prices; and sold the Ship Hope.[10]

Lopez attempted to regularize his London trade and take maximum advantage of his position as a major manufacturer of spermaceti candles by proposing to Stead that Lopez maintain one ship constantly in the London trade, with his spermaceti candle works providing the bulk of the cargo. It would never be difficult to make a profit on the return cargoes from London, he pointed out, since relatively few ships traveled between London and Newport.[11] In another attempt to increase the profitability of a high-risk trade, Lopez set up trade with Bristol, a market as yet unexplored by Rhode Islanders. He expected prices of English goods to be lower there than in London, and endeavored to get Henry Cruger, Jr., his correspondent there, to agree to an exclusive trade.[12]

Imports from England were the ultimate goal of Lopez's and Champlin's trade, but paying for those imports required them to continue and extend their trade with the West Indies and the continental colonies. Only a small proportion of Rhode Island's ships traveled to and from Europe; but many of the coastal voyages were linked to the European trade, since their purpose was obtaining exportable commodities or cash to pay for English goods. To oversimplify somewhat, they traded with continental colonies to obtain cargoes for the West Indies, and to a lesser extent, London; traded with the West Indies to get molasses to distill into rum used in the African trade; and bought slaves to get cash for English imports. In all branches of trade, local manufactures became increasingly important—candles for the West Indies, rum for Africa, potash and iron for England.

In this respect, Newport and Providence's trade differed from that of most other American cities. New York and Philadelphia sent about one-third of their ships on European voyages in the late 1760s and 1770s, compared with only 6 percent for Rhode Island. They devoted relatively less of their shipping to the West Indies and far less to the other continental colonies —around one-third of their ships compared with over half of Rhode Island's ships. Among the major cities, only Boston, which suffered from some of the same problems as Newport and Providence, had a similarly high proportion of shipping in the coastal trade and a low proportion of European voyages (although Boston's involvement in European trade was still considerably greater than Rhode Island's—about one-fifth of all voyages.)[13] New York and Philadelphia merchants could get marketable products from their immediate countryside for shipment to England, while New England merchants had to travel just to get many of the commodities for European export. This situation helps explain why Newport dominated the slave trade; in the long run, the slave trade, despite its complexities, was a device to obtain hard money to pay English debts.[14]

Rhode Island's exports in the 1760s and 1770s indicate the nature of changes in trade since the seventeenth century. The most frequent export to Britain, measured in terms of total value, was whale oil, obtained partly from the local whaling industry but in greater quantities from Nantucket and New Bedford, New England's major whaling centers. The second most common product was potash, which was manufactured in Rhode Island, particularly around Providence, and in Massachusetts as well.[15] Among the other major commodities exported to England were iron, naval stores, and cotton, the latter two items obtained from the southern colonies. Thus, from a heavy reliance on West Indian sugar as an export to England, Rhode Island merchants by this time were able to draw also on their own local manufactures. This development of manufacturing, along with the growth of direct European trade, were the major changes in Rhode Island's economy after mid-century.

The West Indian trade continued to be important, but its function in Rhode Island's overall pattern of trade became more complex. The primary virtue of the West Indian trade, from a Rhode Island merchant's point of view, was that payments were commonly made in cash or bills of exchange, which could be remitted to London immediately. Slaves, in particular, brought good returns in hard money. But the West Indies also supplied molasses, necessary for the rum that was the principal export to Africa. So, the West Indian trade served a dual purpose: as a source of supply of molasses, which was then converted into rum; and as a market for the slaves, bought with the rum, who were then sold for cash to be sent to England.[16] The principal export to the West Indies was spermaceti candles, a by-product of the whaling industry, which also produced the oil sent in large quantities to England. Other major exports to the islands were fish, obtained in part from local fishing expeditions but more commonly from Maine and Canada; flour from New York and Pennsylvania, and horses, one of the last remaining Rhode Island agricultural products exported in significant quantities.[17]

In all branches of trade, local manufactures became increasingly important in the 1760s and 1770s. These products included rum, spermaceti candles, iron, potash, and lime.[18] Interest in manufacturing had begun, in a limited way, earlier in the eighteenth century, especially with the distilling of rum. Efforts were also made, as early as Thomas Richardson's day, to manufacture linen cloth, a natural development since flaxseed was grown in Rhode Island. Linen manufacturing never became a particularly successful industry, however, despite a series of colony subsidies for it.[19] The manufacture of spermaceti candles, Rhode Island's most important export (along with rum) did not begin until the 1750s; it became a major operation by the mid-1760s. This industry started in Massachusetts and was almost exclusively a New England business.[20]

Of all merchants in both Newport and Providence, the Browns had the greatest interest in developing manufacturing. They exploited locally produced products, especially rum and spermaceti candles, in expanding their trade; in turn, they used capital from their commercial ventures to finance further experiments in manufacturing. Welcome Arnold, a protege of the Browns who established himself as a merchant in the early 1770s, also followed their example in linking trade and manufacturing; he pursued lime manufacturing as a principal source of capital for his trading activities. This concern with manufacturing was the principal difference between Providence and Newport merchants' trade, and it proved to be a very significant one in the long run. While the Browns and Arnold devoted much of their attention to manufacturing, Lopez, Champlin, the Vernons, and their cohorts in Newport relied more heavily on the carrying trade as the principal basis of their commerce.

The Browns first undertook candle manufacturing in 1753. Lopez and Jacob Rivera also went into the candle business sometime in the 1750s, using it in part to launch their careers as merchants. At first, Rhode Island whalers provided some of the headmatter, the basic material used in making candles, but the local whaling industry was not extensive enough to keep up with the demand, and it became necessary to secure a regular supply of headmatter from New Bedford and Nantucket whalers.[21] Obtaining a steady supply of headmatter at reasonable prices and limiting competition to protect the price of candles became increasing problems for the manufacturers. Displaying a spirit of cooperation rather uncharacteristic of Rhode Island merchants, candle manufacturers in Newport and Providence, along with two in Boston, undertook an early effort at monopoly and price fixing. This effort began, in 1760, with informal agreements between the Browns and several Newport manufacturers to establish the maximum price of headmatter. Without such an agreement, the increasing demand for headmatter allowed whalers to charge ever-higher prices, to the point that the manufacturers feared the candles would become prohibitively expensive. In 1761, the Browns, four

Newport firms (Collins & Rivera, Isaac Stelle & Co., Naphtali Hart & Co., and Aaron Lopez), and two Boston firms formed the United Company of Spermaceti Chandlers; they fixed both the maximum price of headmatter and the minimum price for candles.[22]

The union suffered from a series of accusations that various members were not abiding by the terms of the agreement. A new union, formed in 1763, was still unable to overcome this fundamental problem. The group also attempted to prevent the establishment of new manufacturing plants, because they feared that expanding the business would create an intolerable demand for headmatter. They were, however, even less successful in this scheme than in their price-fixing agreements. By 1770, there were three manufactories in Providence in addition to that of the Browns, and thirteen in Newport. To make matters worse, the Nantucket whalers themselves went into the business.[23] By this time, therefore, candle manufacturing had become less profitable than it had been in the 1760's, although candles continued to be an important export up to the time of the Revolution, and the development of this industry provided an example for other kinds of manufacturing.

The Browns began manufacturing iron in 1765, building on the profits from their candle enterprise. To work out the technical problems, they employed Israel Wilkinson, the same man who had handled the technical side of their candle business. Iron manufacturing was ultimately less significant than candles as a source of exports, aiding Rhode Island's balance of payments problems only indirectly. The Browns shipped some of their iron to England as an experiment to test its quality, but most of it was sold to refiners in the colonies, especially in New York.[24] Iron manufacturing was important for other reasons, however. A more complex operation than candle manufacturing, it had a significant economic impact on the whole region. The iron furnaces required an enormous amount of wood for fuel; to fill this need, the Browns contracted with farmers in the surrounding countryside to provide timber. The furnace itself was a major source of employment, with a labor force of around seventy-five men. Local iron manufacturing, however, provided no significant source of exports.

Welcome Arnold, even more than the Browns, used manufacturing as a means of supporting and expanding his trade. He achieved a remarkably successful mercantile career by the early 1770s almost entirely on the strength of marketing lime, manufactured principally in his native Smithfield, outside Providence. His career illustrates some of the reasons for Providence's rapid economic rise in the 1770s—particularly in his ability to link manufacturing and trade and in his development of local markets.

Arnold did not initiate the lime burning business in Rhode Island, but he exploited it to a far greater extent than earlier manufacturers. Lime manufacturing began as early as the 1730s, but, like other branches of Rhode Island manufacturing, it became much more highly developed by the 1760s, when its manufacturers began to employ tactics strikingly similar to those of the spermaceti candle manufacturers. David Harris, a Smithfield distiller who was employed by the Browns, became one of the principal limeburners in the Providence area. His family controlled extensive limestone deposits —more than he could burn himself—so he began to lease rights-of-way and kiln rights to other Smithfield and Providence residents. by 1762, he moved to Providence and established himself as a merchant on the strength of his success as a limeburner.[25] Beginning in 1767, the major limeburners made a series of agreements in which they, like the candle manufacturers, tried to limit production. They agreed to maintain four kilns unless they decided that the market would bear more; they also determined the selling price of lime. Any new burners had to sign a covenant agreeing not to undersell the major burners.[26]

Arnold, like Harris a Smithfield resident, began working as a limeburner there in the 1760s. After a few years' experience, he set himself up as an agent for all the limeburners, and in 1772 he moved to Providence, having made an agreement with the limeburners to represent them. Anyone wanting to purchase lime had to make arrangements with Arnold, who thus put himself in an excellent position to control prices. With the profits from his work as an agent, and with some financial backing from the Browns, he set himself up as a retailer in Providence.

Arnold made good use of his connections in Smithfield and other neighboring towns, building up his retail trade by supplying country shopkeepers. He did not limit himself to the area immediately surrounding Providence, but cooperated with a Boston firm to supply parts of western Massachusetts as well. His marriage, to the daughter of a mercantile family from the East Greenwich-Warwick area, south of Providence, further increased his Rhode Island contacts. By 1777, Arnold traded with sixty towns in Rhode Island, Massachusetts, Connecticut, and New Hampshire. Arnold made effective use of his combination of interests in lime manufacturing and the retailing of imported goods by using lime as a medium of exchange and by catering to his country friends in his retail trade. He also used his position as a marketer of lime to establish commercial connections with other colonies, where demand for lime was considerable.[27]

This combination of manufacturing and retailing interests was far less common in Newport, where merchants placed greater emphasis on trading with other areas as a means of obtaining exports and cash to pay for British goods. Aside from rum and candles, there was little interest in manufacturing among Newport merchants. A few minor enterprises were attempted, usually beginning with an effort to secure a monopoly on the business. Moses Lopez was granted a monopoly for ten years to manufacture potash in 1753, and James Rogers received a similar monopoly on pearlash in 1754; James Lucena received exclusive permission to manufacture castile soap in 1761.[28] None of these enterprises was particularly successful. Potash did become an important export from Rhode Island, but its manufacture centered in Providence, not Newport, despite Lopez's monopolistic efforts. David Harris began producing potash as an outgrowth of his lime manufacturing by 1755, taking advantage of the fact that the ashes produced by lime-burning could be converted into potash. He undertook to convert crude potash, which was made throughout the countryside, into an exportable product, in agreement with Thomas Vernon and Daniel Singer of Newport. Vernon and Singer were to do the actual manufacturing, but leased land from Harris and bought ashes from him.[29]

These various efforts at manufacturing were never sufficient to supplant those products that had to be obtained from other colonies; in fact, most of these manufactures were sent to other colonies, not England, in exchange for products that would sell in England. And some of this manufacturing depended on raw materials from other colonies, a dependence that sometimes caused problems—notably for the candle business. So Rhode Island's attempts at manufacturing did not eliminate its dependence on a complicated trade network and even to some extent reinforced it. Before the Revolution, it was impossible to separate manufacturing from mercantile interests; all the major manufacturers were merchants as well. These men differed in the relative degree of their involvement in manufacturing and trade, however, and Providence became much more of a manufacturing center than did Newport. In part, this situation may have been the smaller city's way of trying to compete effectively with the already established trading center of Newport; certainly it also had something to do with the fact that the Browns, who dominated Providence's economy, had a particular interest in manufacturing. In the short run, the Providence merchants' manufacturing enterprises helped them build up a supply of exports and expand their trade; in the long run, they helped establish the ground work for significant economic change.

Throughout the colonial period, Newport and Providence existed in a strangely competitive-cooperative relationship. The origins of their competitiveness go back to the seventeenth century; the towns were founded independently of each other, joined forces in a colonial government more out of expediency than conviction, and remained distrustful of each other throughout the eighteenth century. Both geography and inclination kept the towns, and the regions around them, separate. Most people from the region around Providence (roughly speaking, the northern half of Rhode Island and contiguous towns in Massachusetts and Connecticut) obtained whatever goods and services they needed in Providence and rarely, if ever, traveled to Newport. They generally married within the region and, if they moved, stayed in the same general area. The same held true for people in the Newport region.[30] Only in trade and colony-level politics was there much contact between Newport and Providence. On this level, the relationship between the towns was one of dominance for Newport and dependence for Providence until just before the Revolution. The signs of change were apparent in two ways: Providence merchants began to develop their own trade independently of Newport, and Providence politicians began to challenge Newport men for the colony's highest offices. In both areas, the Providence men were successful.

Providence's economic dependence on Newport through most of the eighteenth century was, on the surface at least, a mutually beneficial relationship. Before the Browns began importing English goods in large quantities, they obtained most of their imports from Newport, and in exchange provided agricultural products from the area around Providence.[31] Even after they began extensive importing in the 1760's, some other Providence merchants still depended on contacts in Newport. Samuel Nightingale, Jr., for example, bought dry goods from Aaron Lopez, Benjamin Mason, and Joseph Bennett, all of Newport, in exchange for dairy products, lumber, and molasses.[32]

An undercurrent of rivalry between merchants in the two towns lay below this cooperative trading, however. The spermaceti candle manufacturers association, a cooperative agreement that turned into competitive backbiting, was the best example of this situation. And by the 1760s, the Browns were beginning to upset Providence's traditional dependence on Newport. Occasionally they tried to assert their influence as Providence's leading merchants to divert business from Newport; Nightingale, for example, made a trip to Newport to buy hardware but was called back by his brother because the Browns had bought a supply of hardware in Boston which they "Insist on you and the Rest of the Merchants Buying." Otherwise the Browns threatened to undersell the other merchants.[33] In the early 1770s, they cornered the market in Rhode Island tobacco and forced Newport men to pay their price.[34]

Providence's challenge to Newport's dominance was the result of a complex combination of demographic and social circumstances. Without the extraordinary growth of the region around Providence in the second half of the eighteenth century, it would have been impossible for the city to expand as it did. But it would have been equally impossible without the concerted effort of a small group of merchants.

The population of the Providence region jumped 168 percent from mid-century to the time of the Revolution, compared with a growth rate in the Newport area of only 42 percent.[35] Moreover, Providence merchants had a larger territory in which they could build up potential markets—an area that included northeastern Connecticut and much of central and western Massachusetts as well as northern Rhode Island. Newport, on the other hand, was not well located for expansion of retail markets. Hemmed in by water, Newport faced competition from New London and New Haven to the west and Providence to the north. So Newport, geographically, had probably reached the limits of its expansion by the 1770s, whereas Providence was well located for expansion.

Providence merchants were especially effective in exploiting these possibilities for growth. Welcome Arnold's career illustrates their efforts particularly well, as he expanded his commercial trade by establishing contacts and supplying retail goods to country shopkeepers in an ever-widening circle of towns around Providence. Similarly, Clark and Nightingale, another expanding Providence firm, developed contacts with storekeepers in southern and western Massachusetts and much of eastern Connecticut. And, of course, the Browns had long since proven their effectiveness at moving into new markets for retail trade, even to the point of selling some goods to Newport merchants.

Not only were Providence merchants innovative entrepreneurs as individuals, but they worked together extremely effectively as a group. Providence's merchants constituted a small, tightly knit elite group that dominated the city's economic, social, and cultural life. Newport, in contrast, had no single, unified elite, but instead had at least three overlapping groups —one dominating the economy, another controlling the city's politics, and a third made up of old, established, wealthy families who were no longer active in either trade or government. These different types of elite groups appear to have been characteristic of major and secondary cities in the colonial period, but—rather ironically—Providence's more restricted elite, by virtue of its unity and strong leadership, did much to help its city expand to the status of a major center.

The core of Providence's elite was a group of men who were extremely wealthy, dominated the city's commerce, and exercised considerable political power. Led by the Browns, they ran Providence in a way that no single group ran Newport. Nor could any single family in Newport compare with the Browns. They were the only Providence family who conducted trade on the scale of the major Newport merchants, and in many respects by the 1770s they were even more successful than their Newport competitors. By 1775, the four brothers who were the most prominent members of this family—Nicholas, Moses, John, and Joseph—ranked first, second, third, and eighth in assessed wealth. The combination of their extraordinary commercial success, the size of their family, and the relatively restricted nature of Providence's elite allowed them to dominate the town in a way that would not have been possible in Newport. The eight men in this family who ranked in the wealthiest 10 percent all held political office, five of them holding major town or colony positions, or both. In more subtle ways, their influence was felt, too; they gave a substantial amount of money to Rhode Island College and were instrumental in having it located in Providence rather than Newport. Contributions from later members of the family resulted in renaming the college Brown University. Joseph not only designed the college's first building, but was one of its first professors; he also designed the Market House and the Baptist Meeting House. The Browns' presence in Providence was of long standing. James (father of the four brothers) had been one of the first residents to undertake extensive trade, in the 1730s. And the progenitor of the family, Chad, was one of the first settlers in Providence.[36]

Members of the Angell, Field, Greene, and Olney families also traced their ancestry back to the early months of Providence's history, and each was represented by four or five members in Providence's wealthiest group in the 1760s and 1770s. Most of them were merchants, six of them politically active. Along with the Browns, these families constituted about 10 percent of the town's elite. More prominent, if not quite as ancient in background, were Esek, John, and Stephen Hopkins and Daniel, John, and Jonathan Jenckes.[37] Stephen Hopkins was governor of the colony for much of the pre-Revolutionary era; Esek also held colony-level office. He was a ship captain; Stephen and John were merchants. They were closely associated with the Browns in building up Providence's trade after mid-century. The three Jenckes men were also among the town's most active merchants, and all held major political positions.

Along with the Browns, the Hopkins, and the Jenckes, the most important merchants in Providence were John Innes Clark, the Nightingale family, and Joseph and William Russell. These men were more recent arrivals in Providence, and equally wealthy—the Russells ranked just after the Browns in assessed wealth—but less active politically. Samuel Nightingale and Joseph Russell each served briefly on the Town Council, but the others held only minor office, if any at all, and none of them ever served in colony government.[38]

In Newport the wealthiest men were more diverse in background. Most of its economic leaders were members of families who had settled in town around the beginning of the eighteenth century. The Ayraults, Malbones, Redwoods, and Wantons were the families who had been principally responsible for Newport's growth in the early years of the eighteenth century, and members of those families continued to rank among the town's elite in the 1760s and 1770s, even though most of them were less active commercially. Samuel and William Vernon, among the young merchants who came to prominence in the 1760s, were the grandsons of a man who settled in Newport in 1666.[39] And the most prominent merchant of all, Newport's wealthiest resident, was a newcomer, Aaron Lopez, who arrived from Portugal in 1752. He was one of nine Jewish merchants, all immigrants of about the same time, who ranked among Newport's wealthiest men in this period. At every critical point in the eighteenth century, newcomers to Newport were responsible for economic expansion. Of the major merchants in the 1760s and 1770s, only Christopher Champlin came from one of the old families; his ancestor was one of the first settlers of Portsmouth and moved to Westerly in 1655. Most of the family remained centered in Westerly and neighboring Charlestown, and Champlin himself maintained a country estate there.[40]

Members of the old seventeenth-century families were also conspicuous among Newport's elite—but their wealth was concentrated in land, rather than trade. The Brentons, for example (Benjamin, Jahleel, and Jahleel, Jr.), were descendants of William Brenton, one of the founders of Newport, a man who left a sizable estate, including extensive landholdings, at his death. The later Brentons continued to maintain large landholdings along with some commercial activities. Elisha and James Coggeshall were also gentlemen farmers; they and two other members of the family were descendants of John Coggeshall, a Boston silk merchant who was disarmed during the antinomian crisis. He became one of the colony's early presidents. Jonathan and Nicholas Easton, also farmers, were related to another of Newport's founders and one of its spiritual leaders, Nicholas Easton.[41]

Descendants of more humble early residents also achieved elite status by the 1760s, including Samuel Dyre, a ship captain, whose ancestor Mary was the famous Quaker martyr. Mary's husband William was a milliner; most of the men of Samuel's father's generation were artisans as well. Job Bennett, a merchant, and John Bennett, a farmer, were the descendants of a tailor employed by William Coddington. And Caleb Earl traced his ancestry to Ralph Earl, Jr. and his father, both of whom had been in constant trouble with the courts in the mid-seventeenth century.[42]

What most of these men had in common was a tendency to prefer farming rather than trade and the traditional Baptist and Quaker religions, rather than the Church of England, to which most of the merchants belonged. Their ancestors had set out to achieve prosperity primarily through commercial agriculture and secondarily through trade, and although some of them were merchants and some combined farming with trade, the number of farmers among them set them apart from more recently arrived families who made their fortunes entirely through trade. Among all the elite men who were descendants of early settlers, about half were either Quakers or Baptists, compared with only 20 percent among more recent arrivals.[43]

Unlike their Providence counterparts, however, neither the descendants of old families nor the major merchants were politically active. Among the former, Job Bennett and Jonathan Easton served on the Town Council; Nicholas Easton and three of the Coggeshalls held minor town office; George Hazard, a member of another old family, served in colony government; but one finds nothing close to the degree of political participation of the old Providence families.[44] Among the merchants, only the Wantons were politically active; they monopolized the governor's office for much of the first half of the eighteenth century.

Newport's political leaders were distinguished neither by great wealth nor by illustrious ancestry—but family connections were important here nonetheless. The best way to obtain major office was to follow a father, brother, or close relative into office. The Wanton family is a case in point; four members of that family served as governor. Richard Ward, although retired from politics by 1760, is another example. He served as colony secretary and as deputy governor; his son Thomas followed him into the secretary's position, and his younger son Samuel (actually only an occasional resident of Newport) alternated with Providence's Stephen Hopkins as governor in the faction-torn 1760's. Thomas Cranston, another wealthy Newport man who sat in the General Assembly, was the son of the early eighteenth-century governor, Samuel Cranston. The same sort of family connections were important among Providence politicians; but there, the politicians were also the driving force behind the town's economic growth.

The differences between Newport and Providence must be attributed partly to circumstance; the presence of a single large, wealthy and politically influential family like that of the Browns over several generations shaped the whole character of Providence's elite. But these differences also reflect some basic economic and social differences in the towns. Newport, larger, more economically developed, and with a long history as the colony's economic and political center, attracted a more diverse group of people than Providence did. It is no coincidence that Godfrey Malbone in 1700, Abraham Redwood in 1720, and Aaron Lopez in 1750 all chose to live in Newport. Newport was more stratified socially, more diverse in religion, and had more pretensions to intellectual and cultural sophistication. All of these differences were reflected in the character of its elite.

Providence, on the other hand, while it had long been a regional center, was in many ways still a provincial town in 1760. It was growing in size and commercial importance, but was still small enough, and sufficiently homogeneous socially, that a handful of men, mostly interrelated, with long-standing family ties, could dominate both economically and politically.

The same kind of small, cohesive elite and tendency toward single-family dominance has been observed by historians studying other small cities in the colonial period. Springfield, Massachusetts, for example, was overwhelmingly controlled by the Pyncheon family for more than a century; and three cities in Connecticut—Hartford, Norwich, and Fairfield—were each dominated politically by a single family after 1720. Broad studies of both Rhode Island and Connecticut towns have suggested that these observations were not isolated examples, but that small cities in general were dominated by single families or a small group of families, in contrast to the more complex elite patterns of the major urban centers.[45]

Providence's elite, however, though small and closely controlled by one family, was sufficiently flexible and innovative to have a positive effect on the city's growth. Newport, on the other hand, despite the diversity of its elite, was beginning to suffer from a lack of creative leadership by the time of the Revolution.

The changing balance of influence between Newport and Providence—and the importance of Providence's elite in accelerating the change—was apparent in the political arena as well as in trade. By the end of the 1750s, Providence politicians were prepared to challenge Newport's political control of the colony; the result was an annual battle for the governorship between Newport and Providence factions which continued for the next dozen years. The leader of the Newport faction was Samuel Ward, scion of a prominent political family. A farmer and retail merchant, Ward lived in Westerly, on the coast of southern Rhode Island, but he had been born in Newport and had strong business connections there. He began his political career in the General Assembly in 1756 and was elected governor for the first time in 1762. Ward's annual opponent for the governorship was Providence merchant Stephen Hopkins; he was a close business ally of the Browns, who became the principal backers of his election campaigns.[46]

The contest between these two men was very clearly based on regional rivalries. The lines were not rigid; Elisha Brown, uncle of the merchant brothers, supported Ward and once served as his deputy governor, and the Wanton brothers of Newport supported the Hopkins faction. But for the most part, voting followed regional lines. The Newport-Providence political contest developed at a time of economic hardship for the colony—when the economic benefits of political office took on particular significance—and at the moment when Providence's merchants were trying to establish their economic independence from Newport. The rivalry ended in 1770 with the election of Joseph Wanton, Jr., a Newport man who supported the Providence faction. In some sense his election represented a compromise between the two factions, but in reality it signaled the end of Newport's control over the colony government. Wanton's election effectively ended Ward's political career, and the Providence faction remained in control of the colony government through the 1770's.[47]

Symbolic evidence of Providence's new position within the colony came when Rhode Island College (now Brown University) was relocated in Providence, rather than Newport. The college, established in Warren in 1764 by the Baptist Church, needed more space by the end of the decade. Significantly, although there was little doubt that the college would be moved from Warren, it was not assumed that Newport would be the logical new site. Instead, the trustees decided that the county raising the largest sum of money would get the college, and the issue quickly boiled down to a contest between Newport and Providence.[48]

The college controversy became entangled in the general political conflict between the two towns, turning into the major political issue in the election of 1770. It became a political issue because of the financial advantages and the status it would bring to the town where it was located. Promoters of the Newport location pushed for subscriptions by stressing the financial value of the college—students would bring in money, and local residents could educate their sons at low expense. Stephen Hopkins, however, thought that Newport residents were motivated solely by their vindictive desire to defeat Providence. His town, he claimed, had loftier motives. But men outside Newport and Providence thought that both towns' reputations for political conflict should disqualify them as seats of learning.[49]

Providence won the contest for the college, along with the election, despite the fact that Newport residents had raised more money. The college trustees were apparently convinced by Moses Brown's arguments that construction costs would be lower in Providence, along with the generally favorable impression made by Providence merchants. The fact that Providence was a more staunchly Baptist town than Newport, and that several of the town's leading citizens, including the Browns, were Baptists, helped, too.[50]

What is most important about the college controversy is the fact that it was perceived at the time specifically as a contest between Newport and Providence—and that Providence won. Providence's success in both the fight over the college and the battle for the governorship were signs that it had successfully challenged Newport's decades of dominance over Rhode Island. Rivalry between the two towns quieted down in the 1770s, in part because the return of prosperity made it less essential to fight over the crumbs of profit from education and political office. But the change also signified an acceptance of Providence's new position as more nearly an equal to, than a dependent of, Newport. After the Revolution, the trends apparent in Rhode Island's economy and politics would accelerate, finally completing the shift of power from Newport to Providence.

4

The Social Consequences of Economic Growth

COMMERCIAL EXPANSION in the eighteenth century invariably brought with it social change, as a few men amassed great fortunes and many more were attracted to cities in search of jobs and some measure of economic security, if not fortune. The social changes associated with economic growth—occupational and ethnic diversity, increasing stratification of wealth, an influx of transients, a growing poverty problem—have been documented for several of the colonies' cities, and Newport and Providence were no exception.[1]

The growth of trade brought wealth to a small group of merchants in the seaports, but at the same time it helped attract less fortunate men to the cities—artisans, sailors, and laborers looking for work. Commercial expansion benefitted these men, too, by increasing the likelihood of their finding jobs, but the benefits of prosperity were skewed toward those with capital that could be multiplied into even greater wealth. As a result, wealth became increasingly concentrated in the hands of the rich over the course of the eighteenth century; the timing and degree of this concentration were closely tied to the pace of commercial development.[2]

In Newport in 1760, the wealthiest ten percent of taxpayers paid 56 percent of taxes, while the bottom 20 percent paid only 3 percent. By 1775, the situation was even more extreme, with the top group paying 59 percent and the bottom group, only 1 percent. Providence, not surprisingly, had a somewhat less skewed wealth distribution in 1760, but was catching up to Newport by the time of the Revolution (table 2). In reality, the situation was even more extreme than these numbers suggest, because the estates of the wealthy were generally undervalued, and a substantial number of residents

TABLE 2
DISTRIBUTION OF WEALTH IN NEWPORT AND PROVIDENCE

TAX GROUP	PERCENTAGE OF TAX PAID			
	1705	1749	1760	1775
PROVIDENCE				
Lowest 20	7.2	6.0	3.5	3.4
40	12.0	8.0	5.0	3.2
60	16.0	12.7	8.8	7.4
80	24.8	22.6	16.9	15.4
90	17.5	15.0	17.2	15.8
100	22.6	35.8	48.7	55.0
Shutz coefficient	.25	.38	.46	.51
NEWPORT				
Lowest 20			2.8	1.2
40			3.4	2.8
60			7.1	6.0
80			15.0	15.1
90			15.9	15.4
100			55.8	59.0
Shutz coefficient			.58	.63

SOURCES: Newport: Ms. tax lists, 1760, Rhode Island State Archives; 1775, Newport Historical Society. Providence: 1705, in *Early Records of the Town of Providence*, vol. 17 (Providence, 1903), 209–13; 1749–75, ms. lists, Rhode Island State Archives.

were too poor to pay taxes—perhaps as many as 20 percent of the adult male population in both cities just before the Revolution.[3]

The extent to which the increasing wealth of these cities benefitted people below the top is hard to determine. The middle ranks of society—ship captains and the reasonably well-established artisans—saw their interests closely linked with those of the merchants, as increasing shipping and higher profits created more work for them. At the same time, however, the growth of trade attracted an increasing number of transient laborers and seamen, both those who came from rural towns around Newport and Providence and those who came into the colony on board ships from more distant parts. Among the latter group was a growing number of blacks, brought back from Newport merchants' slaving voyages. Both the wealthy and the "middling sort" closed ranks against these more marginal groups, particularly after mid-century, as they perceived the poor and the transient to be increasing in number, costing the cities more money, and creating more disturbances.

Concern about poverty increased steadily during the eighteenth century, and efforts to control it were directed at both the resident and the transient poor.[4] The transients were the principal targets of such efforts, however, partly because diligent control of newcomers without legal resident status was the first line of attack against rising poor relief costs. Transients were also a source of special concern because they did not fit the traditional notions of poverty; they were generally young, able-bodied men and women unable to find steady work. The resident poor, in contrast, were almost always dependent in some way, because they were old, very young, sick, or otherwise unable to care for themselves. Such individuals seemed more clearly deserving of public aid, although they too were affected by increased efforts to control poor relief costs.[5]

After around 1710 in Newport and 1730 in Providence, both towns tried to exert greater control over transients.[6] Before these dates, the numbers of transients examined in both places was negligible, despite the fact that the years before 1730 were a period of extremely rapid population growth (table 3). In the early years, newcomers were allowed to stay, no doubt because there was little sense that the towns were becoming overcrowded. There was plenty of land in Providence before 1730, when most of the northern part of the colony was within the town's bounds. And although Newport was already becoming densely populated by the first decades of the eighteenth century, its developing commercial economy provided opportunities for newcomers. The towns were not disposed to restrict transients in these years, because they wished to encourage growth—up to a point. The few people examined in Providence (there were no examinations recorded in Newport before 1711) were mostly individuals who were clearly deviant—unmarried women with children, cohabiting couples, and persons of both sexes who were considered troublesome or morally reprehensible in some way.[7] However, after about 1710 in Newport and 1730 in Providence, the situation began to change. More transients were examined in both towns, and they were no longer always people who were obviously deviant. Newport did not begin examining transients until the decade after 1710; in Providence, the

TABLE 3

TRANSIENTS EXAMINED BY NEWPORT AND PROVIDENCE TOWN COUNCILS

YEARS	NEWPORT			PROVIDENCE		
	Male	Female	Total	Male	Female	Total
1681–90				6	5	11
1691–1700				9	9	18
1701–10				—	—	—
1711–20	29	6	35	2	4	6
1721–30	62	16	78	5	5	10
1731–40	13	2	15	54	10	64
1741–50	49	27	76	41	16	58
1751–60	32	25	57	30	29	59
1761–70	15	14	29	34	28	63
1771–80	3	0	3	62	46	108

SOURCES: Town Council Records, Newport (Newport Historical Society) and Providence (Providence City Hall).

number of examinations jumped from under twenty per decade before 1730 to around sixty per decade between 1730 and 1770. In both towns, these changes took place at times of major population growth and economic development.

In Providence, the increase in concern over transients occurred just after the town's area had been sharply decreased by the creation of three new towns from its territory, and at a time when commercial interests were beginning to develop in a serious way. Town officials' response was almost invariably to order newcomers to leave. Transients, after 1730, were more commonly men, frequently with families; unlike the earlier years, they were no longer people of doubtful moral character. Their only undesirable characteristic was their poverty, or suspected poverty. In the 1770s, the numbers of transients examined jumped again. These were years of major expansion for Providence's economy, the period when it finally began to challenge Newport for commercial dominance. At the end of the decade, the Revolution forced hundreds of people from southern Rhode Island to flee; many of them went to Providence. These two developments made the Town Councilmen renew their efforts to control the transient problem.

In Newport the situation is far less clear. No case can be made for an increasing number of transients examined through the century, because of gaps in the town records. But a shift in policy occurred sometime around 1710—a period that might be seen as comparable to the 1730s for Providence—the years when Newport reached the point at which unchecked growth no longer seemed ideal. The numbers of transients examined in Newport were greater than those in Providence, not particularly surprising in view of that town's position as the colony's major port.

In both towns, however, it was not so much the absolute increase in numbers of transients which was important, but rather the town authorities' increased awareness of their numbers. There is no way of knowing what proportion of transients were examined; given the size of the towns and the inefficiency of methods of keeping track of their populations, it seems likely that the proportion was small. The numbers examined in Providence did not increase steadily in proportion to population, but jumped at two critical times, the 1730s and 1770s; the numbers remained steady from the 1730s through the 1760s. Changes in the town's capacity for dealing with transients are more important than the actual percentage of transients examined.

The number of resident poor relief cases increased also, although somewhat later than the increase in transiency. The number of poor relief cases in Newport mushroomed after 1740. Providence had far fewer cases than Newport; between 1710 and 1750, the number of cases rose each decade, but they never exceeded an average of about two cases per year. After 1750, the number of cases handled by the Town Council dropped to almost nothing (table 4). This change coincided with the construction of a work house in Providence, suggesting that poor relief was from that point handled by the committee appointed to oversee that institution.[8] Unfortunately, no work house records survive; but both the need for such an institution and the transfer of poor relief responsibility from a governing body to an essentially administrative body suggest that the problem had become too great to leave to the Town Council.

The vast majority of the people who received poor relief were dependent in some way besides being poor. They were single women, widows, women with children, orphans or other children whose parents could not care for them; or they were old, sick, handicapped, or insane. In Newport, only 52 poor relief recipients were adult males, compared with 115 women and 62 children. Another 104 children were bound out as apprentices. Only 5 of the men were heads of families. The records give little information about the circumstances of these individuals; but 18 of the men were listed as sick or handicapped, and 11 were elderly. The situation in Providence was similar. Nine men received poor relief, none of them heads of families; 22 women and 6 children also received town support.[9]

In contrast, young and middle-aged men with families made up a large proportion of the transient poor. In Providence, about half of the transients were men; 64 percent of them were married. Eighty percent were between the ages of 20 and 50. Women were more likely to be single (only 25 percent were married) but, over all, 46 percent of the transients were married, and they were, for the most part, in the prime of life.[10] The proportion of male transients was even higher in Newport than in Providence; more than twice as many men as women were examined. Thus there were two types of poverty in these towns: young and middle-aged men, women, and families,

TABLE 4
POOR RELIEF CASES

YEARS	PROVIDENCE			NEWPORT		
	Poor relief cases	No. individuals involved	Children apprent.	Poor relief cases	No. individuals involved	Children apprent.
1706				2	2	
1714–20	11			21	18	3
1721–30	14	10	7	33	29	15
1731–40	19	15	2	14	14	1
1741–50	22	7	10	109	79	37
1751–60	4	3	29	170	101	28
1761–70	8	6	11	81	44	18
1771–80	5	5	19	1	1	0

SOURCES: Same as table 1.

who were generally not legal residents; and the very young, old, sick, and otherwise dependent people who were legal residents and could legitimately claim town support. The nonresident poor were usually capable of working and, in fact, came to Providence and Newport looking for work. The people who actually received town support were, for the most part, incapable of working. Individuals who could work did not receive poor relief even if they were legal residents.

Transients examined by the town councils and recipients of public poor relief were not the only individuals living in poverty in Newport and Providence; they were simply the only ones to receive official recognition and documentation. Another group of people were too poor to be taxed, but they were not in dire enough straits to receive town relief. Such people would be considered poor by any current definition. They amounted to about 30 percent of the population in Providence, and about 45 percent in Newport, in the 1770s.[11] It is likely that these were precisely the people who were motivated to move to other towns. If work was not to be had in Newport, or if wages were too low for reasonable subsistence, perhaps the situation would be better in another town. This, too, helps explain why the resident and nonresident poor were so different. The able-bodied poor moved frequently in search of work. The result was that such people rarely established a legal residence anywhere except in the place of their birth. Because they were poor, they moved often; and because they moved often, they were never legal residents of the towns where they lived. If such individuals became dependent for any reason, they were likely to be shipped back to their original legal residence—usually their birthplaces.

The methods of poor relief were of two basic types: "warning out" or removing nonresidents; and providing subsistence for the resident poor, usually by boarding them with families. These methods were common to towns throughout the colonies.[12] Towns attempted to minimize the potential number of poor relief cases by eliminating anyone not legitimately entitled to town support, and to provide for the others as cheaply as possible. The most common way of caring for the resident poor was to find them places to live in families; those families then received allowances from the towns for supporting the poor. When the numbers of poor persons were small, this was the most efficient way of taking care of them, and it also had the virtue of reinforcing colonial notions about the importance of the family as the primary social institution. In Providence, all but a handful of adult poverty cases were handled in this way.

In Newport, boarding in another family was also the most frequent method of poor relief, but a substantial proportion of the poor were supported in their own homes. Usually this took the form of providing such necessities as food, clothing, or firewood; sometimes it meant paying the person's rent. Anywhere from about one-tenth to one-fourth of Newport's poor received this type of support in the period before the Revolution. Very infrequently direct cash payments were made to poor individuals, but providing commodities rather than money was preferred. For children old enough to work, the most common means of support was binding them out as apprentices. Sometimes these children were as young as three or four years of age. Younger children were boarded with families. Occasionally adults were bound out also, but usually they were considered worthy of town support precisely because they were unable to work.[13]

Over the course of the eighteenth century, as poverty became an increasing source of concern to the towns, they attempted to strengthen traditional measures of poor relief and added new ones. They made the requirements for legal residence stricter and tried to develop more efficient ways of identifying and examining strangers; made stronger efforts to force family members to support indigent relatives; gave special attention to the problem of poverty-stricken sailors; and, most significant, began to shift the burden of relief from family support to institutions.

Controlling transients was the first line of attack on poverty. In the late seventeenth century, the first steps were taken to allow town councils to examine strangers and either grant them legal inhabitant status or order them to post bond to indemnify the towns from possible future changes. The councils could also forcibly remove anyone considered undesirable.[14] It was not until 1727, however, that specific conditions were established under which individuals could gain legal status as inhabitants. A law passed in that year stated that an individual's legal settlement was presumed to be his birthplace, unless superseded in one of several ways. Strangers were required to notify the town council of their birthplaces, last legal settlements, and size of family, within one month after entering a town. Then if they were not warned out (requested to leave within one year), they could claim legal residence. It was this one-year provision that made towns so anxious to identify and warn out all strangers as quickly as possible; otherwise the towns would become liable for their support. Providence, however, largely ignored this provision of the law, as its Town Council frequently warned out people who had been living in town for several years if they suddenly required poor relief. The only clear-cut ways of gaining legal residence were buying at least £40 worth of real estate or completing an apprenticeship in the town. This law was reiterated and revised several times over the course of the century, in 1741, 1748, and 1765.[15]

Town councils could deal with strangers in one of two ways. They could be allowed to stay, if they posted bond or if they had a certificate from their towns of legal residence stating that town's willingness to take the person back if he or she became a town charge. Or, if the individual seemed likely to require poor relief, the towns had authority to send him back to his legal residence. In fact, however, the councils' powers to remove noninhabitants were even broader, since they could remove any person of "bad Fame and Reputation, or such as the Town Council shall judge unsuitable Persons to become Inhabitants"—regardless of whether they had posted bond, had certificates from other towns, or were likely to require poor relief. This provision was enacted because the General Assembly feared that undesirable individuals sometimes persuaded inhabitants to post bond for them "by their cunning Insinuation," and then proved to be a bad influence on young people and servants.[16] In practice, this provision of the law could be used against anyone that the town councils felt like removing.

Providence and Newport differed in their treatment of strangers. Providence almost invariably ordered strangers to leave, while Newport commonly allowed them to post bond. In 65 percent of the cases of individuals examined by the Providence Town Council, the people involved were ordered to leave. Only 6 percent of them were allowed to stay, and generally only after posting bond or obtaining financial support from their towns of legal residence. In the remaining cases, no action was recorded. In Newport, on the other hand, about equal numbers of individuals were ordered to leave and allowed to post bond, up to 1730. After that date, the number allowed to post bond declined, varying from about one-sixth to about one-third of the total number of people examined. Most of those permitted to post bond were men; women were almost invariably ordered to leave. This differential treatment suggests that Newport was prepared to encourage male transients, because they might be useful as laborers or sailors. By demanding that they post bond, the town received the benefits of their labor while ensuring that the town would not become responsible for their support, should they fall into need. Women, however, were not only less useful as workers but, if they were single or widowed, more likely to require poor relief.

Newport's distinction in treatment of the sexes also suggests a reason for the differences between Providence and Newport in their treatment of strangers in general. Newcomers could be valuable to a growing town in need of labor. The problem was balancing that need against growing expenditures for poor relief. Newport solved this problem by allowing transient males to stay, but asking them to post bond. (In fact, bond was usually posted for individuals by someone else—perhaps their employers.) Providence did not recognize such a need for labor. Its needs may have been lower, but it is also likely that Providence officials did not recognize this need, or thought the risks of increasing poverty outweighed the advantages of newcomers.

Throughout the eighteenth century, Providence exhibited a level of concern about strangers that was never apparent in Newport.

The Providence Town Council periodically published reminders of the residency law in the newspaper, and continually attempted to simplify and routinize the handling of strangers. In 1728, for example, they voted that it was no longer necessary for the Council to meet to discuss all cases of strangers. Any two justices of the peace or assistants could issue a warrant to remove "any such person or persons out of the Town as may be In there Opinions thought to be troublesum to sd Town." Thirty years later the Council directed that the town sergeant automatically order any transients who came to his attention to appear before the Council for examination. The Councilmen often felt, however, that despite their best efforts, the transient problem was being compounded by townspeople's failure to be diligent in reporting strangers to the authorities. In 1770 and 1773, as well as on several occasions after the Revolution, orders were given to remind Providence residents of the law prohibiting them from entertaining strangers for more than a week without giving notice to the Council.[17] The townspeople's apparent reluctance to report strangers to the Town Council may have stemmed from apathy, but it may also have indicated an awareness of the need for labor and an unwillingness to see potential workers summarily dismissed from town.

Efforts to control the problem of poverty among legal residents generally took the form of trying to limit the numbers of people eligible for poor relief. Relatively early in the eighteenth century, Newport had to confront the problem of indigent sailors. While the growing economy demanded men to work as sailors, the work was sporadic, the wages low, and the mortality rate high. In 1729, the town petitioned the General Assembly, saying that they were put to increasing expense for the relief of poor sailors and the families of sailors who died at sea. To solve the problem, they asked that twelve pence per month be deducted from all sailors' wages, to go into a fund for the relief of men and families who fell on hard times. The Assembly passed such a law for the entire colony, though clearly at that time Newport was the primary beneficiary.[18] At the same time, efforts were made to control strangers brought into the colony on board ships. To supplement the existing settlement law, another law was passed requiring captains of vessels to post a £50 bond for all persons brought on their ships from outside the colony.[19]

In a more general sense, efforts were made to find sources of support other than the town treasury for as many people as possible. A series of laws passed in the 1750s placed primary responsibility for support on family members (if possible), on fathers of illegitimate children, and on the individuals themselves, if capable of working. Unmarried pregnant women were required to name the fathers of their unborn children, who then had to post bond and pay a regular sum for the support of the child. Parents and grandparents were made responsible for supporting children and grandchildren, if they had the means, and children were made responsible for their parents. Anyone refusing to support a family member could be fined. And any "idle and indigent person . . . who by his evil course of Life is likely to become a Town-charge" could be bound out to service to pay for his own support, whether or not he had actually requested town assistance. Wives of such men could also be bound out, as could single people, whether man, woman, or child.[20] These laws merely codified practices that were already common, but they showed that, by mid-century, the poor relief problem was assuming significant dimensions in the eyes of Rhode Islanders, particularly those in Newport and Providence.

This concern was also indicated by local efforts to achieve greater efficiency in poor relief expenditures. At a Providence town meeting in 1758, it was reported that poor relief expenses were increasing; a committee was appointed to inspect the accounts and make a list of all persons maintained by the town with their ages, abilities, and amount of money spent on them. They were also directed to suggest methods "for the futur management of such poor Persons as may Save future expences to the Town."[21] Their efforts were, like all the other efforts to limit poor relief, of limited success. A similarly gloomy picture of the poverty problem was painted at a Town Council meeting in 1770; this time it was the issue of support for freed slaves that sparked the concern over the poor relief budget.[22]

Newport went so far as to ask for colony-level relief in 1760, citing the condition of the many "Poor Distressed Inhabitants of this Town."[23] In another case, the Newport Town Council asked one of the churches to help support a woman who was a chronic poor relief case. And although the churches provided relief to their members, they too began to feel financial pressure and turned to the towns for assistance.[24]

At least some of the time, these efforts to crack down on poor relief expenses worked. Even before the law was passed making ship captains post bond for people brought into the colony, the Newport Town Council billed Captain Jonathan Clarke £14 for the care of a man that he brought with him from Jamaica.[25] The strongest efforts, however, were made to get family members to support relatives. The Newport Town Council once went so far as to sue a man for the money they had spent to support his daughter. And both towns were quick to act if it seemed that men were not doing all they could to support their families. Samuel Phillips, for example, was hauled before the Providence Town Council because he was heard to threaten to leave Providence and let the town support his wife and children. As a result of his rash statements, he was sentenced to jail until he posted bond to guarantee that his family would not become town charges. John Aplin, a cooper in Providence, was reported being "very Idle and Negligent in his Business" with the result that he seemed likely "to bring himself and Family to want and Misery and thus render himself and Family chargeable to the Town." Guardians were appointed to manage Aplin's estate for him, to guard against such a possibility.

A similar situation occurred in Newport when George Harris's wife herself appeared before the Council, asking them to take steps because her husband was improvidently spending all his money, leaving his family to suffer. In perhaps the most unusual case of encouraging family members to support each other, Ann Meekins of Newport was given the money to go to Nova Scotia, where her brother-in-law lived, with her two children. The expense was justified on the grounds that, by encouraging her to leave, the town would save the expense of supporting her in the future.[26] When necessary, the county courts were used to shift the burden of poor relief from the towns to individuals. Most common were cases that forced men to support their bastard children; in other cases the courts forced individuals to support indigent relatives and tried to force other towns to support transients.[27]

These efforts to make the traditional poor relief methods more efficient really only succeeded in patching a system that seemed to become increasingly limited as the towns grew larger. The major effort to reduce poverty expenditures was construction of almshouses in both Providence and Newport. Institutions designed for relief of the poor were rare before the nineteenth century, except in cities; warning out strangers and family-centered relief for the resident poor were the preferred methods. But larger towns and cities, because of their greater poor relief problems, commonly built almshouses during the eighteenth century.[28] Newport built its almshouse in 1723, thirty years before Providence took a similar step. In both cases, the decision to build an almshouse came at about the time when the towns' economies were expanding, concern about strangers increasing, and poor relief problems rising. The decision to shift to a primarily institutional means of supporting the poor was part of the general increase in social problems associated with a growing economy and urbanization. To some extent, however, it was also part of the growing concern about poor relief costs, which was not only confined to cities. Kent County built a workhouse in 1762, and the rural towns of West Greenwich and North Kingstown followed suit in 1764 and 1769.[29] Providence actually began debating the matter of building a workhouse in 1737, but no action was taken until 1750 when the town meeting opened negotiations with other towns in Providence County about the construction of a workhouse. When the institution was actually built in 1753, it was a cooperative venture involving the whole county, but was located in Providence and was most heavily used by Providence.[30] By the 1750s, Newport had both an almshouse and a workhouse. The date of the construction of the latter is unclear, but it was apparently intended to house the poor who were able to work, while the almshouse housed those who were unable to work.[31]

The workhouses fulfilled several functions. They housed the poor and were at least intended to provide work for them in order to keep down the cost of their support. They also served as temporary housing for transients who had been ordered to leave. Usually the transients consigned to the workhouse were the intransigent ones, who refused to leave or who returned after having been removed. In this sense the workhouses functioned somewhat like jails for people who had committed no crime. The jail-like atmosphere of these institutions was strengthened by the broad powers given to town councils to commit any "indigent, Idle persons" who seemed likely to require town relief, or any "straggling Persons" not legal inhabitants of the towns, regardless of whether they seemed likely to fall into poor circumstances. They could also commit "idle or drunk" Indians.[32] What the workhouse laws did was give towns broader powers over controlling the poor and the near-poor. Rather than dealing only with those people who requested town assistance, the workhouses provided an opportunity to round up anyone who seemed likely to require relief and confine them in an institutional setting where they would be forced to work at menial tasks.

The workhouses were supervised by the towns' overseers of the poor, and their day-to-day operations run by a man appointed by the town. He and his family were expected to live on the premises, and he contracted with the town to provide food, clothing, and working materials in return for a regular, fixed payment from the town. In Providence, by the 1770s, the master of the workhouse was paid partly by the profits of the labor of his inmates. This system was apparently abused, since in 1776 a complaint was made to the town meeting that the keeper was not taking proper care of the poor under his charge.[33] Nevertheless, the fact that the workhouse masters lived on the premises with their families did not make them merely an extension of the system of family-style poor relief.[34] The workhouse supervisors were called "masters" and "keepers" interchangeably. And the institutional setting marked a significant break with past practice. Not only were workhouse residents expected to work, but their lives were regimented in ways that suggested that they were viewed more as criminals than as the deserving poor. The quasi-family style system itself provided ample room for abuses. By allowing the master a fixed sum for boarding each individual in the workhouse, or by expecting him to make part of his wages through the profits of the labor of the poor, masters were encouraged to provide a minimal level of support and extract the maximum amount of work from their inmates.

The rules adopted by the Providence town meeting for governing the workhouse in 1774 illustrate the character of workhouse life and the expectations set for its residents. Great stress was placed on order and cleanliness. The master was to keep a list of all inmates, with detailed information about them, and maintain precise accounts of all stock and materials sent to the workhouse and all goods manufactured by the poor. Oakum picking was the standard task for residents. They were ordered to work during fixed hours every day; anyone who refused to work, destroyed materials, became involved in fighting, or used abusive language was to be confined to the workhouse "cage" for twelve hours on a diet of bread and water. A second offense brought a whipping of up to twenty lashes. Residents were allowed to leave the workhouse only with the master's permission, even to go to church. Anyone absent without permission was to be deprived of one meal for the first offense; for the second offense, the culprit was to be chained to a block for a week.[35]

Confining people whose only offense was poverty in such a setting was indicative of changes in the nature of poverty and in attitudes toward it. As the poverty problem increased and became more complex in Newport and Providence, individuals unable to support themselves were increasingly viewed as deviants. Without actual workhouse records, it is impossible to know exactly what kinds of people were confined to the workhouse. But the intentions behind the creation of these institutions indicate a growing concern not only about poverty in general, but specifically about poverty among people who were capable of working. The traditional methods of family-style relief were designed to help poor people who were also dependent—people who could not take care of themselves, and so had to be placed in a family for that purpose. But this kind of system no longer made sense when more and more people requiring town relief were not dependent, but merely unemployed. Often such people were not legal residents and could be removed from town. But some were legal residents, and it was difficult for respectable townspeople to reconcile their legal obligation to care for the town's poor with their traditional notion that poverty was a condition that befell only the helpless. The seeds of the belief that poverty equalled laziness were apparent in the construction of workhouses and the routines established for their residents. Increasingly, the poor were labeled as deviants and treated as such.

This change in attitudes towards the poor was apparent also in the changes in treatment of the nonresident poor, at least in Providence. Before the middle of the eighteenth century, the process of examination and removal was used largely against people who were obviously deviant—unmarried women with children, cohabiting couples, men who were labeled as "bad characters." As the century progressed, however, these methods were used increasingly against people who were poor, but not necessarily deviant—especially men with families. But even as examining strangers became largely a means of tightening up poor relief, the people who came under scrutiny became tarred with the brush of deviancy. The Town Council began removing anyone who seemed to be an unsuitable inhabitant—and more and more often, that meant anyone who was poor or seemed likely to fall into poverty. As poverty became a serious problem for these towns, and as it affected able-bodied men and women, rather than merely the very young, old, or ill, being poor became synonymous with being undesirable. The individuals unfortunate enough to fall into this category were treated in keeping with these new attitudes.

Transients in Providence were questioned, often in minute detail, to determine their legal residence. The Newport Town Council, unfortunately, was less diligent in recording more than the barest outline of their dealings with transients. The stories of the Providence men and women, however, provide a rare look at the lives of one segment of the urban lower class before the Revolution.

Virtually all of them were white, although by the 1760s this was beginning to change.[36] They were about evenly divided between men and women. Almost all were young, came from towns within a thirty-mile radius of Providence, and worked as servants or laborers. Poverty and youth were the two characteristics that most transients had in common. About 80 percent were under 40, and over 60 percent under 30; women were generally younger than men, with 70 percent under 30 and about 90 percent under 40. In the 1750s, 60s, and 70s, men and women were approximately equal in numbers, although in the 1730s and 1740s men had outnumbered women by about four to one. Sixty-four percent of the men were married, but only 25 percent of the women. Sixteen percent of the women were unmarried mothers, and another 16 percent were separated from their husbands or widowed. (Only two percent of the men were separated or widowed.) Only a third of the transients had children, and most of those who did had only one or two. On the whole, transient families were very small, owing to youth and poverty. They averaged 2.7 persons, compared with an average of 6.6 for all Providence households in 1774, and 7.0 for taxpayers.[37]

These transients—young, single, or just beginning a family—moved to Providence in search of work. Women forced on their own by the death of, or separation from, their husbands were another important group. In economic terms, the overwhelming fact about them was their poverty. It was their requiring town assistance—or appearing to be in imminent danger of requiring assistance—that usually brought them to the attention of the Town Council in the first place. Only 10 percent owned real estate, and another 25 percent had once owned property, but no longer did by the time they came to Providence.[38] Although occupations are known for only fifty of these people, half of them were servants, with the others scattered among several different types of work. Many who did not specify an occupation lived in families other than their own, suggesting that they, too, were either servants or laborers.

To youth, small families (or no families), and poverty must be added another basic characteristic of this group: mobility. Moving to Providence was only one of a series of moves for most. Only one-fourth of the transients who reported detailed information on their travels had moved just once. Most had made two or three moves; twelve people had moved so often that they lost count of the number of times. Most, however, moved around within a fairly restricted area. Sixty three percent were born within 30 miles of Providence. About 17 percent came from areas 30 to 50 miles from Providence, ten percent from other parts of the colinies, and ten percent from Europe or Africa. Most transients did not move directly from their birthplace to Providence, but the sequence of their moves did not follow a clear pattern. Instead, they seem to have moved from one place to another within a 30-mile radius of Providence; and their migration patterns were more often erratic than direct.[39]

Twenty-one-year-old Pamela Manning, for example, lived in a series of families, all within a limited area, before going to Providence in 1780. Born in Dighton, Massachusetts, about 30 miles southeast of Providence, she left home at the age of 18 and went to the neighboring town of Swansey where she lived with one family for three months and then with another family for over a year. She returned to her parents' home for three months, and then went back to Swansey, living with two families there before going to Providence. She then made a series of moves back and forth between Providence and Swansey, never staying in one place more than a few weeks, until the Town Council sent her back to Dighton.[40] Others had more varied experiences. Comfort Eddy moved from Norton, Massachusetts (about 30 miles east of Providence), to Providence some time in the 1750s or 60s, at about age 10 to 12, working as a laborer "upon small wages" for several years; then he worked for several blacksmiths, went to sea for six years, and returned to Norton. He enlisted in the army at the beginning of the Revolution, fought at Bunker Hill, and returned home immediately. He then bought land in Douglass, Massachusetts, northwest of Providence, stayed there a year, went to North Providence, enlisted in the army again, went back to North Providence for three years, and then went to Providence.[41]

Some moved so often, and so aimlessly, that they could hardly recount all the places they had lived. Even if they remained in one town for months at a time, they moved from family to family within the town. Olive Pero, a free black woman, was one of these. After completing her apprenticeship at the age of 18, in the mid-1760s, she moved to North Providence, where she lived with a series of families, never more than a few weeks at a time. After several months of this, she went to live with an aunt in Smithfield, Rhode Island, for three months, and then returned to North Providence. She lived with two families there, but "then I being Sickly went from House to House." Finally she went back to her home town, Rehoboth, and applied to the overseers of the poor for support, but they refused her request. One of them gave her money for the ferry and ordered her to go back where she had come from. So she returned to North Providence and appealed to the overseers of the poor there. After two days, the overseers ordered her to go to Providence; the Town Council there shipped her back to Rehoboth.[42]

By the time Lydia Shepherd was in her early twenties (in 1769), she had lived in at least fourteen different places, always as a servant in someone else's household. Born in Bristol, she left home at age 12 and spent most of her subsequent life in Newport and Providence, usually staying only a few months with each family.[43] Richard Woodrough also moved around from family to family, as his indentures were sold to a series of people. He lived variously in Lebanon, Andover, and Hartford, Connecticut; and Bridgewater and Dartmouth, Massachusetts. He moved to Providence in 1773, where he worked "from place to place, having no settled place to Live at."[44]

Some transients traveled more extensively. Ten percent were born overseas, and another small group, born in the colonies, traveled widely from one colony to another. James Bourk, for example, followed a common pattern in emigrating from Ireland to Newfoundland, where he worked in the fishing business for seven years. He worked his way south, living at Cape Ann, Boston, and Roxbury. In 1775, he moved to Nantucket; then he moved back to Boston, and later New York and New Haven. He fell sick in New Haven, so the selectmen there removed him and his wife to Massachusetts. In 1785 he went to Providence from Boston with his wife, and was ordered back to Boston.[45]

The transients seldom spoke of their motives for their frequent moves. A few did, however; although their numbers were too small to produce any firm conclusions, they give some idea of the range of motivation among these people. The largest numbers left home as children, with their parents; to begin an apprenticeship; to live with a relative; or simply to live in another family. Grace Records, a young single woman with a child, spent virtually her whole life as a transient. As a child, she moved several times with her father, from her birthplace in Pembrook, Massachusetts (about 40 miles east of Providence), to Easton, Norton, Rehoboth, and Attleboro, Massachusetts; and Johnston and Smithfield, Rhode Island. She then set out on her own, as a servant in a Smithfield family and later in Providence.[46]

Young adults sometimes left home to marry in another town; young men went to sea, sought to buy land or start a trade, or, during the Revolution, enlisted in the army. And when men decided to go to sea, their wives sometimes moved to Providence, probably because it was the port from which their husbands sailed. Deserted wives, too, occasionally moved to the city. These women became a particular target of town authorities, since they were assumed to be likely candidates for poor relief, especially if they had children. At a single meeting in 1757, for example, the Town Council rejected three women who had come to Providence, two from Newport and one from Cumberland, Rhode Island. All were wives of sailors. And, in another instance, a black woman from Worcester whose husband went to sea on a Providence-based ship was ordered to return to her home town.[47]

When Hannah Clements appeared before the Council in 1757, she informed them that she had not lived with her husband for six years, nor had she received any support from him. She had lived in the neighboring town of Cranston for four years working as a servant in various households. The Council called her husband to appear before them in an attempt to force him to support his family, but they were unsuccessful.[48] Abigail Foster's case was more extreme. She married William Foster in Saybrook, Connecticut, but he left her soon after the marriage, taking all her property. She could not learn anything about him for five years, when she heard he was in Providence, living under the name Christopher Stocker. So she too went to Providence, to try to get her husband to support her. At the time that the Council examined her, in August 1786, she had seen her husband but had not reached any agreement with him. The Council also examined Stocker; he admitted using the name William Foster and said he had lived in New London, but denied having been married. The Council ordered him to leave, but the dispute with his supposed wife apparently remained unresolved.[49]

Some transients moved involuntarily because their employers moved. Smaller numbers moved for various idiosyncratic reasons—because they had failed in business elsewhere, wanted to escape punishment in another jurisdiction, were trying to collect a debt, or were forced to leave town because it was determined that their legal settlement was elsewhere. The unspoken implication in many of the transients' stories, however, is that they were looking for work—usually as servants or laborers. They might work for a brief period in one town and then move on to another when their services were no longer needed or, perhaps, when they simply felt like leaving.

Eventually they came to Providence because, for most, it was the nearest city that offered greater possibilities of employment than the rural towns from which they came.

Not all transients took the judgment of the town fathers quietly, however. Several came back after being removed, and one can only guess how many may have returned and managed to escape the notice of the Town Council. A few simply refused to stay away, subjecting themselves to repeated removals and sometimes to fines and whippings as well. The worst offenders were classified as vagrants and were then dealt with under a separate law, which permitted offenders to be whipped and shipped out of town without any determination of their legal residence or any responsibility on the part of the town to deliver them to the officials in their town of legal residence. An occasional bold individual went so far as to complain about his orders to leave and to make a case for being allowed to stay. John Hunt was a case in point. He was removed from Providence in 1735. In September 1738 he returned and was brought before the Council, where he claimed that he didn't know that he had been "Lawfully carried out of Town" or that it was "any crime" to return. He was ordered to pay a fine or be whipped, and then be removed again to Warwick. However, the following February, twenty freemen petitioned the Town Council, complaining against Samuel Ladd for harboring Hunt and preventing him from being removed. They also complained that Warwick had allowed Hunt to stay there without warning him out, but had then "used their Interest" in the General Assembly to have him declared an inhabitant of Providence. They took a particular interest in this case because they feared that the right of removing noninhabitants might be infringed, and they urged the Council not to give up its "ancient privilege of rejecting vagrants." As a result, Hunt and Ladd were called before the Council, along with Sarah Pintset, who was rumored to be cohabiting with Hunt. This development gave the Council a way out of the problem; because cohabitation was a crime, they turned the case over to the justices of the peace, with unknown results.[50]

Refusing to heed the Town Council's orders was one form of protest against harsh policies towards strangers. Christopher Stocker, alias William Foster, the man who refused to acknowledge his marriage or support his wife, decided to confront the Council directly. In 1787 he petitioned the town to allow him to stay in Providence. Stocker said in his petition that he had left Providence, under orders from the Council, about a year earlier and had gone to New York. But, apparently unable to make a living there, he decided to return to Providence. The Council had again ordered him to leave and so he resorted to a petition. Stocker's petition is interesting not only for the light it sheds on his motives for coming to Providence, but also for what it suggests about the motives of others as well. He thought Providence would be the best place for him to make a living, and he hoped to find work there either as a common laborer or as a sailor. No action on Stocker's petition was recorded, but he was not again forced to leave the city.[51]

Robert Gray protested his order of removal in 1751, arguing that he was not likely to become a town charge, and apologizing for any behavior that the Council might have found amiss. He declared his willingness to leave, if that was the only thing that would satisfy the Council, but wanted time to dispose of a mill he had rented for several years and had spent considerable time repairing and improving. Were he ordered to leave summarily, Gray feared he would lose much of the money he had put into this enterprise.[52] Cato Freeman, a black man removed to Cambridge, also thought himself better able to support his family in Providence. The town of Cambridge petitioned Providence on his behalf, asking that he be allowed to return and stating their willingness to support him if he became a town charge.[53]

Not only did individuals sometimes protest their orders to leave Providence, but the towns to which they were sent also occasionally filed complaints. These complaints could mean that an individual was sent back and forth between towns several times. The most serious disputes could be settled only by litigation, an especially complicated process when two colonies were involved and were unable to agree on the appropriate jurisdiction. In April 1775, the Council examined Sarah Matthewson, a black woman, about the legal settlement of herself and her 16-year-old daughter Susannah. They determined that Sarah should be sent to Warwick and Susannah to Rehoboth, where she had been born. By November, Susannah had returned to Providence. She was ordered to be whipped, but when it was learned that she was pregnant, the punishment was suspended and she was sent back to Rehoboth again. In May 1778, however, she was once more back in Providence. They ordered her to return to Rehoboth, but that town now refused to accept her as a legal resident, so a Rehoboth constable brought her back to Providence, where the overseers of the poor strenuously objected to having Susannah left with them. They promptly did the same thing, however, sending the Providence constable with her back to Rehoboth, where the overseers of the poor also raised strong objections to receiving the young woman. By this time, the state of Rhode Island had gotten into the act, signing the warrants for Susannah Matthewson's removal, and the whole case had been referred to the Rhode Island Superior Court. Rehoboth, no doubt skeptical of the judgment they might expect from a Rhode Island court, suggested that the case be arbitrated instead, but the Providence Town Council refused.[54]

From the occasional examination of a wayward young woman or a questionable young man, official concern over strangers increased to the point where poor nonresidents were routinely examined and removed from Providence. Construction of a workhouse indicated a similar concern about controlling the cost of supporting the resident poor. The period of sharp increases in examinations of transients—the 1730's and 1770's—overlapped with efforts to revamp poor relief for residents, including discussions of a workhouse in the late 1730's, its actual construction in the 1750's, and tightening its rules in the 1770's.

As the numbers of transients increased, some of their social characteristics changed as well. Before the 1730s, when removing transients was an occasional practice, the Town Council's chief targets were obviously deviant individuals. The process of examination and removal in these years was a means of controlling poverty, but it was employed principally against those who were not only poor, but also socially deviant. In part this reflected town officials' perceptions about poverty and deviance, but it also reflected reality. Providence as a small town was no more attractive to potential migrants than any other small town. Nor was the town large enough, or its social structure complex enough, to make poverty a serious problem. Instead it was an occasional problem, and its victims were highly visible. Over the course of the eighteenth century, however, as the town grew and its economy diversified, Providence presented more potential opportunities and attracted more transients. These transients posed a different kind of problem for the town authorities. They were no longer commonly people who could be easily classified as troublesome and unfit inhabitants. Their deficiencies were a combination of youth, lack of property, and lack of skills. They came from rural towns around Providence, drawn to the city by opportunities for work. Christopher Stocker stated the plight of many of these individuals; he told the Town Council that "he is unacquainted with farming, and has not any trade whereby he might obtain a living."[55]

The town fathers of Providence feared that Stocker and men and women like him would become town charges, and they would take no risks. Over the course of the eighteenth century they developed more elaborate legal definitions of residence and routinized the examination and removal of all those who could be defined as nonresidents. Clauses allowing town councils to remove anyone considered unfit for inhabitant status were interpreted broadly to allow a town to remove anyone in danger of requiring poor relief. At the same time, they took a new and harsher look at poor persons who could not legally be removed. The result was that poverty itself stamped individuals as unworthy.

The transients' responses to their treatment at the hands of the Providence Town Council were rarely recorded. But a few cases show that they were aware of the greater opportunities that Providence offered, and occasionally resisted the judgment against them. Their resistance, however, when it existed at all, hardly ever took the form of a direct challenge to the towns' policies for dealing with the poor. Instead, they occasionally quietly slipped back into town, sometimes only to be subjected to further humiliation. In the long run, it was the best they could hope for; the transient poor were by their very nature a fragmented, elusive group, with few defenses when confronted by the moral and institutional force of the town of Providence.

To the citizens of Newport, the growing population of black slaves raised even more serious problems than the white poor. Newport had one of the largest concentrations of black slaves to be found in the northern colonies, the result of its active involvement in the slave trade. Providence's black population, on the other hand, was far smaller, although it was still larger than in most parts of the North.[56] Newport's blacks increased substantially in numbers during the first half of the eighteenth century, posing special problems for the town. Most blacks were slaves, and therefore not part of the public responsibility; yet the growth of slavery required some control. And the small number of free blacks were viewed in much the same light as white transients—as people who, almost by definition, threatened to become public charges. As more slaves were manumitted in the years just before the Revolution, the slavery and poor relief problems became intertwined. The towns had no wish to take on more potential poverty cases, but public opinion increasingly urged freedom for slaves.

Blacks in Newport ranged from 10 percent of the total population at the beginning of the eighteenth century to 18 percent by mid-century, a rate of increase much higher than that of the population as a whole[57] (table 5). The most significant increase occurred between 1708 and 1730, the years when Newport was establishing itself as a trading center and particularly as a leader in the slave trade. Slaves who could not be sold in the West Indies or southern colonies were often brought to Newport, where slave ownership

TABLE 5
BLACK POPULATION

Year	Newport nonwhite*	% of total	% increase	Prov. nonwhite*	% of total	% increase
1708	220	10	0	7	1	0
1730	797	17	262	109	5	1,457
1748	1,173	18	47	275	8	152
1755	1,234	18	5	0	0	0
1774	1,292	14	5	371	9	35

SOURCES: See Appendix A for complete citation of censuses.
*Includes Blacks and Indians, but the number of Indians was very small.

became increasingly fashionable. After 1748, the numbers of blacks increased only slightly, and their proportion of the total population actually declined.

Providence's black population was far smaller, never exceeding 9 percent of total population, but there, too, the rate of increase was more rapid than in the total population during the first half of the century. In Providence, white labor was apparently preferred to black labor, however. Servants made up about a quarter of the adult male population in both towns, but the proportions of white and black servants were almost exactly reversed.[58] In both towns most blacks were slaves before the Revolution. Although their legal status was not specified, 86 percent of blacks in 1774 lived in white men's households, and the probability is strong that most of them were slaves.[59]

Town authorities did not usually distinguish between slaves and free men, however, or between blacks and Indians, in attempting to control their behavior. The increasing use of slave labor prompted a series of regulatory measures, but such regulations usually applied indiscriminately to all nonwhites. For example, the first of these laws, passed in 1704, imposed a 9 p.m. curfew on all blacks and Indians in "Newport or any other town." The law also prohibited anyone from entertaining blacks and Indians without their masters' permission. These restrictions formed the basis of the attempts to control blacks and Indians, and were re-enacted, with slight modifications, in 1750 and 1770—in the latter year as part of a law designed specifically to control minorities in Newport. These laws gave constables broad powers to discipline slaves who violated the curfew. The 1704 law provided that offending slaves could be whipped up to fifteen stripes, or more, if they proved incorrigible. In 1756, Newport gave its constables power to arrest and commit to jail any blacks away from their masters' houses on Sundays without sufficient excuse. And the 1770 law, noting that the Newport jail was inadequate, authorized the building of a "cage" for confinement of slaves violating the curfew.[60]

Two other problems inherent in slavery also concerned Rhode Island officials: preventing slaves from running away, and preventing owners from freeing slaves no longer able to earn their keep, thus forcing the towns to support them. The large number of boats and ships in and around Newport made escape relatively easy. In 1714, a prohibition was enacted against transporting any slave by boat without a certificate from the slave's master; in 1757, another law was passed to prevent masters of ships from taking slaves out of the colony.[61] In 1729, the General Assembly thought it necessary to forbid manumission of slaves, unless the owners posted a £100 bond to insure the town that the former slaves would not become town charges.

This restriction was renewed in 1770.[62] By this time, antislavery sentiment was so strong that some blacks were being freed, although manumission did not become common until after the Revolution. Even occasional manumission, however, raised the specter of yet more poor relief costs; the Providence Town Council's increased concern over black transients in the 1760s and 1770s also indicates that the free black poor were being viewed as a potentially serious problem. At the same time, blacks were being partly blamed for increasing poverty among whites—one of the arguments for ending slavery was the belief that slaves were taking jobs away from whites.[63]

Indians were smaller in number than blacks by the eighteenth century, but were apparently viewed as even more threatening than blacks; an effort was made in 1715 to prohibit bringing Indian slaves into the colony because of the belief that they were responsible for "Divers Conspiracies, Insurrections, Rapes, Thefts, and Execrable Crimes"—a charge not borne out by the extant criminal court records. Later legislation concerning Indians prohibited them from being bound out as servants without the consent of at least two justices of the peace, and gave town councils the power to prevent "Disorderly Indian Dances."[64]

Of the blacks themselves, very little is known. Almost all of them were servants of some sort, living in a dependent status in white households. They rarely appear in the records, even on tax lists, since blacks did not pay taxes. They occasionally appeared in court, in civil as well as criminal cases; but because slaves owned no property and most slave crimes were handled by local courts, court records are not a good source of information about them.

Some of Newport's ministers made efforts to convert slaves, with the result that substantial numbers of them worshiped at white churches, though in separate sections. About 100 blacks attended services at Trinity Church in the 1740s, and Ezra Stiles reported about 70 blacks in his congregation around 1760. Of these, only 12 had actually been baptized, but at the time of Stiles' ordination in 1755, there had been no black members at all. The black members, however, not only sat in a separate section of the meetinghouse, but had to build their own pews at their own expense. The minor religious revival of the mid-1760's in Newport affected considerable numbers of blacks, who organized an informal religious group under the spiritual guidance of Sarah Osborn.[65]

The only detailed information about Newport and Providence blacks, however, describes the intransigent members of the black community—those who ran away. As might be suspected, the runaways were predominantly men, young, and frequently skilled tradesmen or sailors. But their characteristics do offer some suggestions about the nature of the black population in these towns. Thirty runaway slaves or servants from Newport were advertised in the pages of the Newport *Mercury*, from 1758 to 1776; only twelve Providence runaways were advertised, in the Providence *Gazette*, in the period 1762–76. Ninety-nine runaways from other areas were also advertised in these newspapers, the bulk of them from the southern Rhode Island towns that had the heaviest concentrations of blacks in the colony. Three-fourths of the runaways were black or mulatto, in Newport, in Providence, and in the group as a whole. The remainder were either Indian, or part Indian and part black. Color was apparently an important distinction among these individuals, since blacks were more likely to be described as slaves, while mulattos and Indians were more likely to be servants.[66] Although the numbers involved were small, this pattern is suggestive for the larger nonwhite population; there is no reason to think that this relationship between color and status was confined to runaways.

Almost all runaways were men. An exception was an indentured servant girl, a teen-ager who left "barefooted and barelegged," presumably trying to return to Providence where her mother lived.[67] Runaways were a youthful group; a third of them were teen-agers, and more than 80 percent were under 30.[68] Most were native-born, with only one recorded as African and nine from the West Indies and non-English colonies.[69] This fact, along with the variety of skills the runaways possessed and their generally good language ability, suggests that they were a relatively well-assimilated group of men who could move around with some hope of escaping detection and had aspirations beyond their menial status, a description that has been confirmed by studies of runaways in other areas as well.[70] Rubent, a Jamaican slave in Newport, was described as speaking good English, and "very artful and insinuating." He ran away well prepared, taking several sets of clothing with him. Another Newport slave managed to get a pass before he ran away; he too spoke "exceedingly good English," and, judging from his description, was dressed quite fashionably, wearing a "new felt hat, a blue cap, red duffil great coat, a green ratteen jacket . . . buckskin breeches, light coloured worsted stockings."[71]

Although descriptions of most runaways were not detailed enough to provide a full analysis of their skills or occupations, it does seem significant that more were sailors than anything else. Such men had the best opportunities for running away because of the extent of their travels and the ease of escaping a master by shipping out on a voyage. The 36-year-old slave York, from Newport, was suspected of going to Nantucket to sail on a whaling voyage; he was a small man, only about 5 feet tall, spoke good English, and was said to be "a nimble, active, complaisant fellow of an insinuating address." Will, another Newport slave, had just returned from a whaling voyage. He was a cooper, and could play the violin. Other slaves or servants escaped from ships in Newport harbor, including two Indians who escaped from the same whaling ship, and a mustee from the East Indies who left a North Carolina ship bound from Newport to New York. And a mulatto named Francisco escaped from a ship at Providence.[72]

Other runaways were artisans of various types or specialized servants, including coachmen and gardeners. Quam, a Providence cooper, was described with unusual praise by his master as a man of "a serious thoughtful Turn of Mind, inclines to talk but little, but speaks pretty good English, is a good workman at his Trade, and . . . uncommonly neat and precise in his Dress." He was subject to fits of delirium, which was assumed to be the reason for his escape.[73] In a lighter vein, nine men were reported to be good fiddlers, one a fortune teller, and another a medium. Most spoke English well. Caesar, slave to John Banister of Newport, was said to speak "good English for one of his color."[74] Several had scars or other physical marks which suggested a history of intransigent behavior or harsh masters. Joseph Brown's 14-year-old slave had many scars "occasioned by his having been severely whipped in Surinam"; and a Newport slave named London had lost the toes of both feet.[75] Others had been branded, had broken teeth, problems with their eyes, and difficulty walking.[76]

Even more than most runaways, urban blacks were likely to be skilled and to be fluent in English. This is hardly surprising, just as it seems logical that a disproportionate number of the runaways came from Newport and Providence. Urban blacks were in general more likely to be employed at trades or as specialized house servants; they also probably had more opportunities to escape, and more places to hide. They could sign up on a voyage, a practice that was apparently so common that almost all fugitive slave advertisements included a warning to masters of ships in port. They could slip away from Newport on one of several ferries, which occasioned legislation forbidding ferrymen from taking blacks as passengers unless they had passes from their masters. Or they could stay in town, trying to vanish among a population of several hundred other blacks. The runaways were undoubtedly younger, probably more highly skilled and more aggressive than the average black slave or servant in Newport or Providence. Nevertheless, the presence of these kinds of slaves, along with the evidence of blacks building their own pews in churches and holding their own religious meetings, and white men's legislation against unauthorized gatherings of blacks, suggests the existence of a black culture, despite the fact that most blacks lived in white households, singly or in very small groups.[77]

Controlling the lower classes—whether they were black or white, slave or free—was an increasing preoccupation in Newport and Providence throughout the eighteenth century. The magnitude of the increase in size of these groups is less important than upper- and middle-class perceptions that social conditions were changing and that these changes required new attitudes and new methods for dealing with potentially threatening groups of people. Equally important, but more elusive to the historian, is the evidence that lower-class men and women responded to efforts to control them in the only ways that seemed open to them—by avoiding public scrutiny, forming their own groups in the case of the blacks, and moving around when necessary.

Most of the efforts to control the lower classes in Newport were concentrated in the first thirty years of the eighteenth century, the years of most rapid population growth and of the first important period of commercial expansion. Efforts to place limits on slaves, on the poor, on transients, and on other undesirables were part of a general preception on the part of Newport's leaders in the first decades of the eighteenth century that the town was changing in ways which were perhaps inevitable, but which required closer supervision of its inhabitants.

In Providence the concern about controlling the lower classes came somewhat later and was concentrated almost entirely on the white poor. In part this reflects the smaller size and less complex nature of Providence's population. With a less developed shipping industry and therefore a less complex labor force, and with relatively few slaves, Providence did not confront the same kinds of social problems that Newport faced. But Providence officials, in their increasingly obsessive concern with poverty, both in ordering out transients and in taking a harder line on poor relief, seemed to be trying to prevent the more serious kinds of problems present in Newport. It seemed as if the town fathers wished to halt urbanization by refusing to accept its consequences.

As for the poor themselves, their thoughts were not recorded. Slaves often tried to run away, while the transient poor, both black and white, tried to return when they were forced out of the towns. Neither they, nor the nameless hundreds of people living on the edge of poverty, had the economic security, or political voice, that might have allowed them to change their position at the bottom of society.

5

The Revolution in Rhode Island: Economic Collapse and Recovery

By THE EARLY 1770's, although Providence was still less than half the size of Newport, it was clearly on the way to achieving economic and political dominance. Rivalry among the two cities' merchants, the contest over the governorship, and the controversy over the location of Rhode Island College, all indicated that Providence was increasing its competitive edge over its rival, both in trade and in politics.

The Revolution accelerated this trend. The war devastated Newport's trade and forced a substantial part of its population to flee the city. Providence suffered too, but not nearly so seriously; unlike Newport, it was not occupied by British troops, did not lose population during the war, and kept its social and political leadership largely intact. Providence merchants were not only able to maintain a considerable trade, but also managed to capitalize on Newport's distress by moving into new markets more readily than their competitors could. While Newport merchants were forced either to leave town and try to set up shop elsewhere or, if they stayed, to sharply curtail their business, their Providence counterparts continued to function as normally as conditions of war would allow. Some even managed to develop new markets. As a result, Providence made a much faster and more complete economic recovery than Newport. In short, the war did what all the efforts of Providence merchants before the war had not been able to do: it made Providence the dominant city in Rhode Island.

Obviously, the Revolution was not solely responsible for Newoprt's decline and Providence's rise to pre-eminence. But the war did help push forward a set of changes that were already in progress—acting, in effect, as a catalyst for change. Newport, as a major port and capital city, was a primary target for British troops, and its exposed location made it highly vulnerable to attack. Its residents, fearing the worst, began to flee even before British soldiers occupied the town in late 1776. With the arrival of troops, most of the remaining residents left; and many of them never returned. The war crippled Newport's commerce, even though some merchants managed to continue some trading through other New England ports. The combination of population loss and decline in trade made it extremely difficult for Newport to recover economically when the war ended.

Providence, on the other hand, was not only a less critical target but also, by virtue of its location, more immune to attack. Ships launching an attack on Providence would have had to get past Newport harbor and then travel some distance up a narrow strait, where they would have been easy targets for counterattack. There was never any serious danger of invasion in Providence; and, although its trade suffered from the British blockade of Narragansett Bay, the city suffered neither physical damage nor serious depopulation. Having at least their homes, shops, and wharves intact, Providence merchants were able to pursue alternate routes more easily than Newport merchants in exile. Providence's major wartime problems were coping with refugees, many from Newport, supporting its own poor, and finding alternate trading routes. After the war, it was easy to slip back into the old routines, particularly since the town's population was largely intact and its economy in reasonably good condition.

Providence, in fact, in many ways profited from Newport's problems during the war—and so gained an extra advantage over its rival. Merchants were more successful in continuing their trade during the fighting, despite the British blockade; they made inroads on Newport's commerce, which they managed to maintain and expand after the war. Wartime profits also put these merchants in a better position to invest in risky commercial and manufacturing ventures when the Revolution ended. Providence leaders' willingness to profit at their neighboring city's expense was not lost on Newport residents; the Rhode Island general, Nathanael Greene, commented that "some of the inhabitants of Newport are very jealous of the views of the town of Providence, fearing that the latter has in view the destruction of Newport, for their own private advantage."[1]

The tension that Greene observed between Providence and Newport residents was not simply a result of economic competition. Providence residents were, on the whole, much more enthusiastic in their support of the Revolution than their Newport counterparts. Providence men resented the Toryism rampant in Newport, while many Newporters thought Providence patriotism was tinged with desire for economic gain. These differences in attitudes about resistance to the British, coupled with Newport's more endangered position during the war, only heightened the existing rivalries and resentments between the towns.

The greater incidence of Toryism among Newport's elite can be attributed, in part, to the presence of more men with direct ties to England —either by birth or by patronage—and the greater influence of the Church of England there. In addition, many residents must have felt that they had more to lose from war with Britain than they might gain from independence. The exposed position of their city, the expectation of British attack in the event of war, the fear that wartime disruption of commerce would mean economic ruin—all made Newporters reluctant to embrace the cause of independence.

Perhaps more important than explaining the high degree of Toryism in Newport, however, is explaining the intense patriotism of Providence. On this score the political views of the town's elite were extremely important. Stephen Hopkins and the Browns were outspoken in their support of resistance to Britain; they wielded so much influence in the town that their political opinions carried a great deal of weight.[2] They were supported by the majority of Providence's freemen, who were generally more radical on these issues than the merchants.

This mutual suspicion was first apparent in the nonimportation movement of 1769–70. Few merchants anywhere were enthusiastic about nonimportation, but those in Rhode Island, and especially Newport, were even less enthusiastic than most. When the merchants of Boston, New York, and Philadelphia made agreements not to import British goods in the wake of the Townshend Acts (passed in 1767), Rhode Island merchants did not immediately follow suit. They were finally pressured to do so in 1769 when New York cut off trade with the colony and other cities threatened to do the same. Providence drew up agreements first, under the leadership of John Brown and a few other merchants. Finally Newport fell in line, although merchants there tried at first to get away with only a limited boycott.[3]

The agreements were not very well observed, in Rhode Island as elsewhere, and when the Townshend duties were repealed in 1770, with the tax on tea as the only exception, most merchants rushed to abandon them. The Providence town meeting, however, voted to continue nonimportation, even after the merchants had decided to resume importing. The meeting appointed a committee to convince the three major mercantile firms to reconsider their decision. This committee was composed entirely of merchants—including Stephen Hopkins, Nicholas Brown, and John Jenckes—a tactic that helped ensure the success of the effort to continue nonimportation. At the same time, the meeting took steps to try to put pressure on Boston and Newport merchants who continued importing, by prohibiting Providence residents from purchasing goods imported by merchants in those towns. Anyone who violated this order was to have his name published in the newspaper, "that they may thereby Receive the Displeasur and discouragement of their Injured Neighbors and Country."[4]

A month later, the committee reported that the merchants had agreed to continue nonimportation in principle, but wanted a longer list of exceptions to the agreement than the meeting was willing to grant.[5] The more serious problem, however, was the refusal of Newport merchants to continue nonimportation. Their intransigence led the other major ports to stop all trade with Rhode Island. Providence merchants understandably resented being tarred with Newport's brush. Moses Brown, corresponding with his family's long-time friend and political ally in Newport, Joseph Wanton, Jr., tried to get Newport merchants to comply with the agreements, and noted that many people in Providence blamed Newport for their troubles.[6] By this time, however (summer 1770), the nonimportation movement was disintegrating throughout the colonies, and it was soon abandoned.

The Tea Act of 1773 sparked a renewal of the nonimportation effort, and this time there was more general agreement among Newport and Providence merchants. Christopher Champlin, not noted for his revolutionary sentiments, wrote to his London correspondent George Hayley in 1774:

> We find a very different nonimportation from the former one will take place, no one that regards Peace or Property will dare infringe upon it, the temper of the times runs very warm, its now become very generally the Sentiments of most orders of men, that from the late manovres of the ministry, they have a fixed plan of enslaving the Colonies by arbitrary taxation at will—if so, of little value will the Trade of this Country be to its Mother Country as nothing but Chaos & Confusion must ensue. . . .[7]

William Vernon also warned Hayley that the agreement would be "religiously observed."[8] But some merchants, again in Newport, still dragged their feet. Blame fell primarily on the Jewish merchants, apparently because Aaron Lopez was openly uncooperative with the nonimportation effort.[9] Most merchants, however, in Newport as well as Providence, supported the 1774 agreements. The Newport Town meeting tried to ensure compliance by appointing a committee of inspection that included eighteen merchants among its thirty-five members.[10]

Merchants were not above trying to get around the agreements legally. William Vernon noted, just before the agreements went into effect, that everyone in Newport was rushing to get his ships out before the deadline. And in 1776, Vernon himself petitioned the Continental Congress, which had prohibited the sale of imported tea, to make an exception for him, since he had imported a large quantity just before the law was passed. He pointed out that he had consistently adhered to the patriots' cause, but was losing money because of his principled position.[11]

Newport and Providence residents also had different perspectives on the impending crisis with Britain because of the differences in the potential dangers to which they were exposed. As early as the spring of 1775, increasing numbers of British ships collected in Newport's harbor, threatening both its commerce and the safety of its inhabitants. For over a year, the Newporters lived in fear of invasion and negotiated truces with the captain of the British fleet—truces that sometimes caused the less-endangered Providence residents to question Newport's loyalty.

By early 1776, British ships in Newport's harbor, according to one resident, "have put almost a total end to commerce; have committed repeated depredations in different parts of the colony; have kept our coasts constantly alarmed, and obliged the inhabitants to keep almost continually under arms." The severe decline in Newport's commerce occasioned by harrassment from these British ships reduced the revenues the colony had expected to help defray military expenses, forced many residents to leave, and left the colony government with most of the burden of caring for Newort's poor. Residents of other island and coastal towns also sought safer quarters in these months.[12] Former governor Samuel Ward, a delegate to the Continental Congress, urged island residents to take themselves and as much property as possible to places of greater safety; the General Assembly gave its official sanction to this evacuation with a resolution, in January 1776, encouraging Newport residents to leave.[13]

The presence of British ships in their harbor posed a serious dilemma for Newport. James Wallace, captain of the British fleet, demanded provisions from local residents and also demanded that troops raised for the island's defense be removed. Needless to say, residents were not interested in helping Wallace; but they also lived with the constant fear that he would attack Newport. Even if he restrained from such an attack, he was capable of causing serious shortages of supplies by preying on local shipping. Finally a truce was worked out under which Wallace was supplied with provisions and, in return, agreed not to molest ferry and market boats or fire on the island without adequate warning.[14] Rhode Islanders not faced with the immediate threat posed by Wallace and his men, however, took a rather dim view of this truce. The colony's Committee of Safety, based at Providence, tried to prevent the provision of supplies to Wallace, a move that generated protests from the Newport Town Meeting and eventually resulted in an appeal from Newport to the Continental Congress, which agreed that the truce could continue.[15]

Wallace's second demand—removing troops from Newport—generated more controversy. Many residents wanted to go along with his demands and quarter the troops some distance from Newport to avoid provoking attack; some wanted troops removed from the island altogether. In the fall of 1775, the Continental Congress agreed that troops should be removed from Newport, but should remain on the island.[16] Others, however, objected to such a move. William Ellery, an avid patriot and prominent Newport lawyer, was convinced that pressure to move the troops away from Newport was the work of people sympathetic to Britain, who would do anything necessary, including virtually taking over a town meeting, to accomplish their objectives. Ellery's opponents professed to believe that the town was in greater danger of attack if the troops remained. The confusion surrounding this issue was apparent in a letter of merchant Samuel Fowler, writing after the General Assembly had ordered all men remaining in Newport to help defend the city against British attack. He believed that if the men of Newport agreed to this order, the British navy would immediately destroy the city, but if they remained loyal to the King, all communication with other colonies would end. "Our destruction seems unavodble [sic] and that I fear very soon," he concluded.[17]

The uncertainty of Newport's position ended on December 7, 1776, when 8,000 British troops took possession of the city, with no resistance.[18] By this time, most residents were gone; many of those who remained were loyalists. Ezra Stiles made a list of people remaining in the city; of the 309 who chose to stay, according to his calculations, 76 were loyalists. Others who stayed were Quaker pacifists; widows, who presumably had no place to go; and people who were too poor to leave.[19] As early as the fall of 1775, the General Assembly took up the question of helping the poor leave Newport; but it proved impossible for all of them to leave, and the problem of supporting the poor continued throughout the war. The colony government continued to concern itself largely with the problems of the people who had fled Newport and the other island towns, those who had been "thrust out from their late comfortable and peaceable dwellings," and were "destitute of the means of support and subsistence." The legislature ordered an enumeration of those who had left these areas, noting the towns where the refugees settled. They then solicited donations from other towns and individuals; this money, along with funds allocated from the colony treasury, was distributed to towns which had taken in the former island residents.[20] A substantial number of them went to Providence. In March 1775, residents of Providence County agreed to take in 400 impoverished refugees from Newport, and the Newport Town Council organized the evacuation of those willing to move.

By 1778, between 200 and 300 Newport residents were living in Providence, receiving relief money allocated by the General Assembly.[21]

The burden of caring for the poor in Newport itself, however, fell heavily on the Quakers, who established special committees to look after the poor in critical areas throughout the colonies. Moses Brown, one of the most prominent leaders among Rhode Island Quakers, took much of the responsibility for raising money and distributing charity to destitute Rhode Islanders. A Newport woman, writing to Brown to solicit his aid for the poor of that city, discussed the legislature's efforts to solve the poverty problem by moving the poor out of Newport, but pointed out that there was really no place for them to go.

> Where can they go," she asked, "to find imploiment at this season of the year. Who will fead, clothe or receive them into their houses, and many hundreds if not thousands are not able to provide for themselves. I have reason to think many for want to imploy are already reduc'd to live many days together on bran and water boiled together and a bit of bread, and some have hardly that, to eat at a time."[22]

Brown, who was chairman of the Quakers' Committee for Sufferings, responded favorably to the appeal from Newport; a combination of money from the committee, contributions from neighboring towns, and a loan from Brown himself was dispatched to Newport for poor relief.[23] Meanwhile, Providence had its own poor relief problems. A committee appointed by the Town Council reported in 1779 that 275 families were "wholly destitute," 117 of them with less than a bushel of corn per family. James Manning, president of Rhode Island College, argued that families with more than enough meal to supply themselves should turn over their surplus to the town, to be repaid later.[24]

Still, Providence's problems were much smaller compared to those of Newport and the other island towns, despite a small drop in population and fears that Providence, too, would be invaded.[25] When the town petitioned the General Assembly for a reduction in their tax rate in 1778, they painted a grim picture of the ravages of war in Providence:

> Our stores and shops almost empty, our navigation demolished, our shipbuilding at an end, our houses . . . many of them standing empty and going to decay by degrees, or more suddenly by barracking troops in them. Many foreigners residing among us as well as others of our most wealthy Inhabitants . . . have packed up their fortunes and removed to places of greater security. The common sort of people who are left behind are mostly out of employment and the poor are all yet among us to be supported by the remaining persons of property.

Providence, they argued, suffered more than country towns because its residents' principal means of livelihood was vastly diminished, but they still had to buy food at inflated prices.[26] The issue of wartime damage was a relative one, however; certainly Providence, along with any other place dependent on trade and having a substantial lower-class population, suffered during the war. But problems there were far less serious than in Newport and other ports invaded by the enemy. As one Providence resident noted at the end of the war, "This Town has been remarkably shielded from the ravages & desolations which others have experienced, and public matters proceed in a regular line."[27]

Although limited commercial trade continued during the war in both cities, Providence's more protected position made it easier for the smaller city's merchants to continue their trade. They faced serious obstacles: all trade with Britain was cut off; Narragansett Bay was blockaded, forcing them to use slow and expensive overland routes to other ports much of the time; and American ships, regardless of destination, were subject to capture by the British. But Providence merchants, at least, could work from their familiar wharves and countinghouses, and sell to their usual customers; most of the Newport merchants who managed to continue trading were forced to move to other towns and get used to new surroundings. William Vernon, for example, conducted his business from Boston, with one son in Newport overseeing family affairs and another in France developing new business contacts.[28] Christopher Champlin continued his trade from a family estate in southern Rhode Island.[29] And Aaron Lopez moved several times during the war, first to Portsmouth, then to Providence, and finally to Leicester, Massachusetts, where he continued to maintain some trade by shipping goods overland to Boston.[30]

The combination of their dislocation and the risks of wartime trade worked considerable hardship on these men. The West Indian trade, always the mainstay of Rhode Island commerce, was particularly risky; Champlin had shares in at least twenty West Indian voyages between 1777 and 1781, but about half of these ships were captured by the British.[31] George Gibbs also lost heavily on a series of West Indian voyages in the 1770s.[32]

Providence merchants, on the other hand, managed to turn some of the liabilities of wartime trade into advantages. Welcome Arnold, forced to ship goods overland to port, began to develop new markets in the rural parts of Rhode Island, southern Massachusetts, and eastern Connecticut. Rather than trade entirely through Boston, he also explored overland routes to New York, New Jersey, and Pennsylvania. And he, along with a number of other Providence merchants, capitalized on the one significant advantage of wartime commerce: the end to British restrictions on American trade with other countries in Europe. Arnold, who had never ventured into European trade before the war, now opened trade with several Baltic ports, in partnership with several other Providence merchants: John Brown, Joseph and William Russell, Nicholas Tillinghast, and Robert Stevens.[33] By 1780, he had expanded his trade to include Spanish, French, and Dutch ports as well.

The Browns continued their European commerce during the war, opening trade with France in late 1776, and with Sweden in 1780. Trade with France required some changes in strategy, because whale oil, which had been the staple export to England, did not do well in the French market. Instead, they began shipping rice and indigo from ports in the southern states to France. The value of these products, combined with the difficulty of continuing the West Indian trade, encouraged the Browns to increase their trade with the South as a source of export commodities.[34] Newport merchants, notably Christopher Champlin, also opened trade with Baltic ports, but it was but a poor substitute for their flourishing prewar London commerce.

Wartime trade laid the groundwork for the resumption of commerce after the war. Providence merchants managed to minimize the risks of wartime trade and use the new freedom from British restrictions to expand the scope of their activities; the temporary decline in competition from Newport also worked to their advantage. Newport's trade, on the other hand, was brought to a standstill; the city's merchants continued to trade, but in scattered locations, and many of them suffered heavy financial losses. All these conditions set the stage for Providence's economic expansion after the war.

The British evacuated Newport in December 1779; the following spring, several thousand French troops took up residence with the intention of using Newport as a base for further actions against the British and, incidentally, to protect what was left of Newport from further attack. Many of the people who had left in 1778 trickled back into Newport, but many others never returned; by 1782 the city's population was still only 5,530, slightly more than half of the 1774 population of 9,208. Newport continued to grow slowly after the war ended, but even as late as 1800, the city's population was still only 6,999 people, less than the pre-Revolutionary total[35] (table 6).

Among those who failed to return were a significant number of merchants and city leaders. Christopher Champlin returned, as did the Vernon family; so did some of the younger merchants, including George Gibbs and Samuel Fowler. Aaron Lopez intended to return, but he died suddenly on his way back to Newport in 1782. Others, however, had either established themselves comfortably elsewhere and saw no point in returning to Newport, or, because of loyalist sympathies, felt themselves unwelcome there. Newport had a disproportionate share of Rhode Island's loyalists—and they tended to

TABLE 6
PRE- AND POST-WAR POPULATION STATISTICS
FOR NEWPORT AND PROVIDENCE

YEAR	NEWPORT	PROVIDENCE
1774	9,208	4,321
1782	5,530	4,310
1790	6,725	6,380
1800	6,999	7,614

SOURCE: Appendix A, table A-2.

be among the city's leading citizens—so punitive action taken by the State deprived Newport of leadership. In 1778, Rhode Island's General Assembly banished thirty-seven men who had "joined the enemy"; all but five were from Newport, and most of them were merchants. After the war, all men suspected of being loyalists were disenfranchised.[36] Some were permitted to return—in 1783, for example, a group of Newport citizens petitioned the General Assembly to permit merchants Stephen DeBlois and John Maudsley to return on the grounds of their "irreproachable" characters—but most loyalists never returned.[37]

The combination of physical destruction, loss of trade, general depopulation, and loss of leadership severely impeded Newport's recovery after the war. Providence, by contrast, fared much better. Not only did the smaller city suffer no significant population loss during the war, but it also continued to grow during the postwar years at a rate much faster than Newport. By 1800, with 7,614 people, Providence had passed Newport to become Rhode Island's largest city.

Providence also enjoyed a high continuity of leadership during and after the war. Among the wealthiest 10 percent of Providence's population, there was remarkable continuity from 1775 to 1790; 84 percent of the 1775 group still lived in Providence at the later date, and most of them maintained their position at the top of the economic scale. In Newport, however, only 40 percent of the 1775 group remained. At least one-fourth of them were dead by 1789, and the rest had left town (table 7). This loss of leadership paralleled Newport's general demographic problems; in the population as a whole, only 27 percent of household heads remained in Newport from 1775 to 1790.[38]

The high continuity in wealth in Providence did not necessarily mean that the elite group was totally closed to newcomers, however. Providence's population was expanding in this period, and opportunities were created for men to move up from the lower ranks; population shrinkage in Newport produced the opposite result. Even in Providence, however, few upwardly mobile men made it all the way to the top. With a few exceptions, the extremely rich in 1790 included the same faces as in 1775. Of the men in the top 5 percent in 1790, 91 percent had been living in Providence in 1775, and 64 percent ranked at least in the top 10 percent in that year. Over half the men in the second 5 percent, however, had moved up from lower positions in 1775.[39] Heading the list of the wealthy, in 1790 as in 1775, were three of the Brown brothers. Nicholas, Moses, and John had ranked first, second, and third in 1775; they were first, fifth, and second, respectively, in 1790. Joseph and William Russell and Nathan Angell also were among the handful of richest men in both years.[40] Thus Providence after the Revolution continued its earlier pattern of a strong and unified elite, dominated by the Browns, combined with enough flexibility to permit the entry of new faces into the ranks of the rich.

In Newport, a high percentage of the very wealthy men in 1790 had been similarly well off before the war, despite the general pattern of population loss at all wealth levels. Although a substantial number of the town's wealthy men either died or left after the war, those who remained tended to maintain their elite status, and Newport did not experience a wholesale turnover of leadership. Here, however, the percentages were not as high—72 percent of the top 5 percent in 1789 had been present in 1775.[41] And, more important, there was no core of leaders comparable to the Browns and the Russells who helped shape the town's economy both before and after the war. The three wealthiest men in Providence in 1775 had been the Browns; their counterparts in Newport were Aaron Lopez, George Rome, and Joseph Wanton. Lopez left Newport during the war and died in 1782; Rome was an Englishman, an agent for London merchants, and an obvious loyalist; Wan-

TABLE 7
CHANGES IN ELITE GROUPS, 1775–90

I. TOP 10 PERCENT IN 1775

	Newport	Providence
Number present in 1789/90	38 (40%)	63 (84%)
Number remaining in top 10%	23 (24%)	47 (63%)
Number present, in lower position	15 (16%)	16 (21%)
Number dead (minimum)	23 (24%)	?
Number not present, unaccounted for	35 (36%)	12 (16%)
N	96	75

II. TOP 10 PERCENT IN 1789/90

	Newport	Providence
Number present in 1775	37 (63%)	90 (85%)
Number in top 10% in 1775	23 (39%)	48 (45%)
Number present in lower position	14 (24%)	42 (39%)
N	59	106

SOURCES: Providence: 1775 and 1790 tax lists, Rhode Island Historical Society. Newport: 1775 and 1789 tax lists, Newport Historical Society. No data on dates of death for Providence men.

ton, a former governor, also became a loyalist. Neither of these men was living in Newport after the war. Nor were most of the other of Newport's wealthiest men of the 1770's: Peleg Anthony, Elisha Sheffield, Jacob Rivera, Simon Pease, Evan and Francis Malbone—all important merchants before the war—were all either dead or had left town by 1789. Among this handful of the extremely wealthy, only Samuel and William Vernon remained, and they were considerably less active in trade than they had been before the war.

The men who took their places as the wealthiest dozen or so residents were almost all men who had lived in Newport before the war, and had ranked within the top 10 percent in 1775; but at that date they were not yet at the peak of either their careers or their wealth. Charles Handy, George Gibbs, Christopher Champlin, and Samuel Fowler were the richest four men in 1789; they were all relative newcomers to the commercial scene in 1775, and did not become major figures until after the war. Only Stephen Ayrault, Jr., who ranked fifth, came from an old, elite Newport family. In short, Newport lost the experienced hands who might have aided its recovery, and also the very wealthy merchants, the men with substantial amounts of accumulated capital, who might have been in a position to launch more experimental economic ventures.

The physical destruction of war, loss of population, and, particularly, loss of leadership seriously hampered Newport's recovery. "The Inhabitants of the Town are greatly diminished both in numbers and Circumstances, Commerce at a low Ebb—our Society small—our Taxes high," Christopher Champlin complained to a friend in 1782.[42] Providence, having suffered none of these problems to any serious degree, was in a much better position to recover and expand its economy—a fact that is apparent in the postwar shipping statistics for the two cities. In 1785 (the first postwar year for which complete statistics exist), Rhode Island's trade was still only about half of what it had been in the early 1770's, but most of the loss was sustained by Newport, not Providence. Whereas before the war Providence's trade had been about one-fourth to one-third of the total for the two cities, by 1785 it equalled Newport in shipping volume. And while both cities' shipping increased in the next fifteen years, Providence's increased faster; by 1790, its shipping exceeded Newport's for the first time, and by 1820, it was about double that of Newport[43] (table 8).

Nevertheless, despite Newport's problems in recovering from the war and the increasingly stiff competition from Providence, Newport did recover —at least up to a point. By 1800, both Newport's population and trade came very close to their prewar levels, and they continued to grow slowly in the early years of the nineteenth century. But the significant development of

TABLE 8
NEWPORT AND PROVIDENCE SHIPPING
BEFORE AND AFTER THE REVOLUTION

YEAR	NEWPORT	PROVIDENCE
	I. *Total Number of Vessels Entering and Clearing*	
1774*	1,163	498
1785	361	371
1793	628	770
1795	605	707
	II. *Total Tonnage Registered, Enrolled, and Licensed*	
1790	6,600	10,590
1800	9,000	9,789
1810	12,517	15,864
1820	10,072	20,576

SOURCES: Part I: Appendix B, table 1; Part II: Peter Coleman, *The Transformation of Rhode Island, 1790–1860* (Providence, 1963), p. 65.
*Estimates; pre-Revolutionary statistics did not specify town of origin of ships.

these years is the extraordinary growth of Providence and the fact that it finally eclipsed Newport as southern New England's largest city. The damage done by the war can perhaps explain Newport's slow recovery in the years following, and the differential impact of the war on the two cities certainly contributed to Providence's competitive edge over its rival. But the war only hastened a process that was already well under way. Had the war never happened, Newport would probably have maintained its hegemony a few years longer—but its rate of demographic and economic growth would eventually have slowed, and Providence would have dominated in the long run. Understanding the long-term, significant reasons for Providence's growth and Newport's decline requires a closer look at both the economic and social changes of the years just after the Revolution.

6

Economy and Society in
the Post-War Years

THE CHANGING FORTUNES of Newport and Providence, like those of any other cities, depended in part on national changes over which their residents had little control, and in part on local and regional peculiarities. Looked at another way, changes in the national economy stacked the odds against Newport and in favor of Providence, but individuals in both places made decisions that contributed to their cities' growth or decline.

The major postwar economic changes that so profoundly affected Newport and Providence were of two types—the increasing centralization of commerce and the beginnings of manufacturing as a mainstay of the American economy, particularly in New England. The centralization of commerce made both Newport and Providence increasingly dependent on a few key ports, especially New York, and made it nearly impossible for either city to continue as a center of international trade. Instead, their merchants were forced to concentrate more heavily on regional trade, and there Providence's advantages and more aggresive leadership worked to its benefit. Even more significant, as commerce declined in importance in this part of New England, Providence became one of the first manufacturing centers. Thus, on both economic fronts—commerce and manufacturing—Providence emerged the leader at the expense of Newport.

At the time the Revolution ended, the advent of manufacturing as a significant economic enterprise was still some years in the future, and merchants in both Newport and Providence first turned their attention to renewing and expanding commerce. Independence from Britain had brought both positive and negative effects; all European markets and, potentially, even those of Asia, were now open to American merchants, but America's favored status in trade with Britain and its possessions ended. American trade with the

British West Indies, long a mainstay of New England's commerce, was prohibited; and American exports to Britain were now taxed, some of them at rates so high they were no longer profitable commodities for trade.[1]

American merchants had gained some experience with the new conditions during the war, of course, but the risks of wartime trade had limited their activity. Now, although the potential benefits of expanded international trade were substantial, it required well-established merchants with significant amounts of capital to succeed. The Asian trade, in particular, required enormous outlays of money. In part as a result of these capital requirements, American commerce gradually became more centralized in a few ports— notably New York, Philadelphia, and Baltimore. These ports had a competitive advantage, in part because they had well-established wealthy merchants capable of investing the sums required, but also because of their proximity to expanding agricultural regions that produced marketable surpluses of grain and flour. Baltimore, in particular, built its commercial economy by exploiting and expanding its hinterland. Smaller than Newport before the Revolution, it became the nation's third largest city by 1815, proving that pre-Revolutionary commercial advantages were not necessarily the key to post-Revolutionary growth.[2]

After the turn of the century, new developments in technology and marketing helped consolidate the position of the handful of major seaports. New York, in particular, achieved its commercial dominance after 1815 in part by such practices as instituting regularly scheduled transatlantic packet ships and a system of commodity auctions that undercut the prices of competitors in other cities.[3] Improvements in transportation, which permitted a single city to draw upon an ever larger area for export commodities, further contributed to the growth of key cities. These changes all combined to bring about a major realignment of American seaports in the late eighteenth and early nineteenth centuries. The pre-Revolutionary system had been one in which many ports, spaced quite closely together, could prosper as centers of international trade, although none became very large. (Philadelphia, America's largest city before the Revolution, had about 40,000 inhabitants in 1775; New York had about 25,000.[4]) In later years, as the economy became more centralized, capital requirements increased, and transportation systems improved, only a few cities—substantially larger and regionally separate—could continue to grow as major commercial centers.[5]

These major national changes ultimately made it impossible for Newport and Providence to expand as trading centers. Their effects were not immediately apparent, however, and most Newport and Providence merchants attempted to continue their businesses much as they had before and during the war. Nevertheless, certain kinds of changes did have immediate effects, and required that merchants make some adjustments in their ways of doing business. The British prohibition on trade with its colonies in the West Indies hit Rhode Island particularly hard, since the West Indian trade had been a major source of exports. Heavy British import duties—particularly on whale oil, which had been Rhode Island's largest single export to Britain before the war—made some commodities so expensive on the London market that it was no longer profitable to import them.[6] Both developments forced Rhode Island merchants to find new sources of exports; and, unlike the mid-Atlantic ports, they could not look to regionally produced grain as a primary commodity.

Rhode Island merchants, who had long made a specialty of illegal and shady branches of commerce, found that the United States' status as an independent nation also required some change. Rhode Island outlawed the slave trade in 1787, and, although the trade continued in defiance of the ban, it became even riskier than it had been earlier. The federal ban in 1804 was also ignored at first, but the trade was virtually dead in Rhode Island by 1807.[7] And the establishment of a United States Customs Office helped put an end to the smuggling and tax evasion that had contributed to Rhode Island merchants' profits in colonial days. It was more difficult, and less acceptable, to evade taxes levied by a legitimately constituted government. All of these changes required modifications in Rhode Island merchants' trading methods, but for many of them, old ways of doing business died hard. On the whole, Providence merchants were more successful in adapting their methods to changing conditions.

Both Newport and Providence merchants had taken steps to expand their European trade to new ports during the Revolution, and after the war they continued to trade with these ports. Their immediate concern, however, was to reopen trade with England. Revolution or no, Americans still seemed to prefer English goods. The usual ways of making remittances, however, were no longer suitable, since new British restrictions on American trade had eliminated some of their most profitable export commodities. English merchants, who were just as eager to reopen trade with the United States, tried to compensate for these new restrictions by extending extremely generous credit terms to American merchants, but their plan backfired. English goods flooded American markets as a result; prices dropped, and American merchants, unable to sell their imported goods at a profit and still having difficulties finding suitable exports, fell deeper and deeper into debt. This situation was one of the major causes of the depression of the late 1780s.[8]

Newport and Providence merchants were hit especially hard by the depression of the 1780's because success in European trade, for them, depended on a precarious balance of several different lines of trade undertaken to collect exports for Europe. By the late 1780's, London firms that did business with Rhode Island merchants were sending frequent and increasingly strident letters across the Atlantic, dunning their correspondents for payment. The more adaptable merchants, however—notably Christopher Champlin in Newport and the Browns and Welcome Arnold in Providence —managed to continue their international trade through a variety of schemes: expanding trade with the mid-Atlantic and southern states to obtain more marketable exports; shifting much of their European trade from Britain to the Baltic, where American commodities fetched better prices; and entering the risky but potentially very profitable Asian trade.

To compensate for the loss of old sources of exports, Newport and Providence merchants relied more heavily on the products of other states, especially New York, Pennsylvania, Virginia, and South Carolina. In both New York and Charleston, they did business with former Rhode Island merchants who had settled there—Nathaniel Russell, in Charleston, and the firm of Murray, Mumford and Bowen, in New York. Welcome Arnold went a step farther and opened a branch office in Charleston.[9] The Rhode Islanders bought tobacco and rice in Charleston, and principally wheat and flour in the mid-Atlantic ports; they also made use of their New York contacts to receive and reship goods for them. It was one sign of the growing influence of New York that Rhode Island merchants found it increasingly convenient to have their European goods shipped to New York and then re-shipped to Newport in one of the growing number of packet boats that regularly plied the routes from Newport or Providence to New York. Champlin, for example, instructed his London correspondents to ship cargoes to New York, "with liberty to reship by way of our coasters for Newport—by no means send them by Boston as they may lay there many weeks before they come to hand."[10] Because of the increasing frequency of ships between London and New York, Rhode Island merchants could actually get their goods faster (and therefore tie up their capital for less time) by having them shipped to New York, instead of waiting until they could afford to accumulate a large enough cargo to send one of their own ships for it. Rhode Island's regular trade with New York developed largely in response to this situation. This increasing reliance on trade with other American ports, particularly New York, is apparent in the postwar shipping statistics for Rhode Island. Trade with other United States ports jumped from slightly over 60 percent of Rhode Island's total in the 1770s to nearly 80 percent in the 1790's; trade with New York increased from about one-fifth to one-third.[11]

In European trade, the most successful merchants were those who reduced their reliance on London and diversified their ports of call. Champlin, for example, maintained some trade with England, but increasingly looked to other countries in expanding his activities. Shortly after the war, he reopened the Irish trade that he had initiated in the 1770s. One of the chief advantages of the Irish trade was the ease of obtaining flaxseed, the principal export to Ireland, which was produced in Rhode Island. Champlin and his frequent partner, Samuel Fowler, imported some Irish linens in return, but remitted most of the proceeds of their cargoes to London merchants in payment for British goods.[12]

By the early 1790's, Champlin was devoting much of his attention to trade with the Baltic.[13] He had taken tentative steps towards trading with ports in northern Europe, in 1780 and 1781, with two Swedish merchants as his principal contacts.[14] These men then provided Champlin with introductions to merchants in other Baltic ports. With this assistance, he began sending ships to Hamburg and Copenhagen in 1785. These voyages were usually joint ventures involving Champlin's brother George; two other Newport men, James Robinson and George Gibbs; and a New York merchant, William Minturn, a former Newport resident.[15] But it was not until 1786, when Champlin began a long-term correspondence with Nicholas Ryberg & Co. of Copenhagen, that the Baltic trade became important enough to supplant his commercial ties with Britain. Champlin set up a regular trade with Ryberg, using his influence to get a reduction in duties on goods sent there and establishing an annual contract for the importation of rum.[16] Through Ryberg he also initiated trade with St. Petersburg.

Exports to the Baltic consisted primarily of tobacco from Virginia and rice from South Carolina; they were exchanged for tea, iron, hemp, and Russia duck. Champlin regularized this trade by following the same basic procedures year after year, using the same ships and captains, and relying on one merchant to make sure that business was transacted smoothly at the European end of the voyage.[17] Champlin was also in a position to do favors for his Copenhagen contacts; he and his brother George wrote to George Washington in 1789 to try to get a member of Ryberg's firm appointed consul general.[18]

Welcome Arnold, who had also begun his post-Revolutionary ventures by renewing trade with Britain, left the English trade entirely and became a specialist in the Baltic trade by 1787. More than other merchants, he relied on the prewar commodities for export, including lime, which had been the mainstay of his business in the earlier years. He also continued the West Indian trade to a considerable extent and cooperated with Brown and Benson in distilling rum for the Baltic trade. Arnold modified old methods to suit new times, however; in addition to establishing a branch house in Charleston, he maintained two or three sloops regularly traveling the route to the West Indies and continued the task, begun during the Revolutionary years, of expanding regional markets.[19]

Champlin and Arnold, along with the Browns and other Rhode Island merchants, also attempted to develop trade with France after the war—a logical move because of the French alliance with America—but these efforts never proved very successful. Champlin, who sent ships to several French ports in the 1780s, including Dunkirk, Bordeaux, and L'Orient, thought it sufficiently promising to send his son, Christopher Grant Champlin, to France in 1790 to learn something about the country's commerce. By the early 1790s, however, Champlin, Arnold, and the Browns had given up the French trade as unprofitable. The prices of French goods—chiefly wine and brandy—were apparently prohibitively expensive for Rhode Island markets. Political problems in France and the failure of many French firms also made trade difficult.[20]

The most innovative change in Rhode Island's international trade was the beginning of trade with Asia. Shut out of this trade in the colonial period, Americans had obtained Asian spices and cloth from England. Now they were free to initiate trade themselves, but the distance involved required larger ships and more capital than European trade did; and the conditions of the trade itself required different business practices. For example, Champlin, the first Rhode Island merchant to undertake trade with Asia, had to obtain special documents from the United States Congress to establish contacts with merchants in Asian ports and to prevent tangling with the European countries having trade agreements in Asia. He also used a supercargo to oversee the actual trading, rather than trusting that task to the ship's captain or to a local merchant. Champlin first entered the Asian trade in the 1780's, sending ships from European ports to India and Canton. (The Newport customs officials did not record any Asian voyages originating locally until 1796.) In later years he also sent ships to Java and Mauritius. By 1797, he was able to purchase a new, 350-ton ship to use specifically for Asian voyages.[21]

Although the Asian trade was a profitable addition to Champlin's business, it remained a rather small part of his total trade. The leaders in Rhode Island's Asian trade were the Browns, and the bulk of the state's trade with Asia centered in Providence. One of the reasons for their success was the large number of merchants involved; together they could amass more capital than could any one or two men. By 1790, when the Browns first sent ships to Asia, the brothers had formed two firms, each involving partners outside the family; Nicholas Brown had formed the firm of Brown & Benson, and John Brown, the firm of Brown & Francis. The two firms joined forces in the Asian trade, along with Clark & Nightingale, with other Providence merchants also taking shares in some of their voyages. By 1800, they had five large ships, all 350 tons or more, regularly employed in the Asian trade.[22] The only prominent merchant notably absent from this trade was

Welcome Arnold. He took a small share in one of the Browns' early voyages, but never became heavily involved; instead, he made an informal agreement with Brown & Benson, Brown & Francis, and Clark & Nightingale to stay out of the Asian trade, in return for their staying out of the Baltic trade.[23]

If Providence dominated the Asian trade, Newport, too, had its exclusive branch of commerce—the slave trade. It is significant that it was an old, well-established trade, rather than one requiring new methods and new risks. The slave trade, which had been highly profitable for many Newport merchants before the war, had many advantages from their point of view: it required relatively small ships, its principal export—rum—was locally produced, and the profits per voyage were potentially substantial. Its major disadvantage was one they may not even have recognized at the time: the slave trade was doomed to end, and soon. The Rhode Island legislature outlawed the slave trade in 1787.[24] Newport merchants, however, ignored the law; by 1800, slaving voyages equalled the volume of the 1770's.[25] And the voyages continued even after the federal government enacted the first antislave trade legislation in 1804. A complete federal prohibition on the slave trade in 1807, however, effectively ended the trade. The merchants who had persisted in the trade, against all signs of its imminent demise, sacrificed long-term commercial stability and potential growth for short-term profits.

Providence merchants were generally more innovative than their Newport counterparts in developing new trade routes and new business practices; but they also excelled in other kinds of innovation—improving their harbor, building roads, and establishing banks and insurance companies. These projects cemented Providence's economic advantages by strengthening ties with other towns in the region, expanding local markets, and freeing merchants from dependence on financial institutions in other cities. In the long run, they had a positive effect not only on the city's trade, but also on its early manufacturing enterprises. The Browns and other prominent merchants were always backers of these projects, and their motives were always the same: to expand the markets for Providence merchants and generally improve the town's business climate. The Brown brothers, for example, were the principal organizers of the River Machine Company, incorporated in 1790 to dredge the Providence River to deepen it and make it easier for large ships to enter. The men involved in this corporation included, in addition to the four Browns, all the town's major merchants, among them Welcome Arnold, John Innes Clark, John Jenckes, and Joseph and William Russell.[26]

Most of the same men were involved in other corporations designed to improve the network of roads around Providence, in order to expand the town's potential markets in outlying areas. They were particularly concerned to divert the trade of eastern Connecticut and portions of Massachusetts away from other centers like Hartford, Worcester, Springfield, and even, to some extent, Boston. The first of these turnpike companies was established in 1794, one to build a road between Providence and Glocester, in northwestern Rhode Island, and the other to improve an existing road between Providence and Norwich, Connecticut. Turnpike building expanded considerably during the early decades of the nineteenth century, most of it occurring in the northern and western sections of the state—the area clearly within Providence's economic orbit.[27]

A much more ambitious project, launched in 1796, was the proposal to build a canal through the Blackstone Valley northwest of Providence into central Massachusetts. Its goal was to divert trade from northern New England and from the Worcester area to Providence, away from Springfield and Boston. Its promoters justified it on the grounds that it would provide cheaper imported goods and easier access to markets for everyone in the area concerned. John Brown, the principal backer of the proposal, offered to subscribe $40,000. But Massachusetts commercial interests intervened, and that state denied a charter for the enterprise.[28]

The same men also attempted to organize Providence's financial resources by establishing banks and insurance companies. Before the Revolution, banking and insurance had been handled informally through partnerships of local men, or through the assistance of merchants in larger ports. Shortly after the Revolution, however, a group of Providence merchants attempted unsuccessfully to establish a bank. They finally did succeed in organizing Rhode Island's first bank, in 1791. Again, the Browns took the lead; a letter from John Brown to his brother Moses informed him that there was talk of a bank being formed, and that the brothers ought to take the initiative. He argued for the bank in a competitive spirit; towns smaller and commercially less important than Providence had already established banks, and Providence was in danger of losing both capital and bright young men to other places if remedial steps were not taken.[29] The Providence Bank was incorporated in 1792, three years before a similar effort took root in Newport. Similarly, Providence was the first to establish an insurance company, in 1794, followed by Newport, in 1799.[30] By 1800, the amount of capital invested in banking in Providence was more than three times that invested in Newport.[31]

In the long run, of course, Rhode Island's commerce in general declined, supplanted by manufacturing as the basis for the state's economy. Here, too, Providence men were the innovators; their success in establishing Providence as a center of textile manufacturing ultimately had far more significance than the city's modest commercial gains over Newport. Moses Brown's experiments in cotton textile manufacturing, beginning in 1789, ushered in the era of industrialization for Rhode Island. Providence's dominance in these early industrial experiments ensured its position as the economic center of the state.

Manufacturing was not entirely new in postwar Rhode Island, however. Distilling rum and manufacturing candles, iron, and lime were only the most important of several small-scale industries in the prewar period. All of them were inspired by the demands of trade, and all began to decline in the years after 1790 as trade gradually became less important.[32] There were in addition a wide variety of other goods produced in home workshops by small numbers of people. A report prepared by the Providence Association of Mechanics and Manufacturers in 1790, in response to Alexander Hamilton's request for information on manufacturing, reported twenty-one different kinds of manufactures, from relatively large-scale cotton, woolen, and paper manufacturing, to the making of hats, boots, nails, clocks, chocolate, silverware, and fire engines.[33]

Cotton textile manufacturing differed from these traditional crafts and industries in the scale of production and the fact that it was not a direct outgrowth of commercial activities. The differences should not be exaggerated, however; throughout the late eighteenth and early nineteenth centuries, much of the work of cotton manufacturing was done by people working at home, and in that sense, early manufacturing efforts simply expanded a well-developed cottage industry.[34] It was also logical that this industry should develop first in Providence, and under the leadership of one of the Brown brothers, since Providence men and the Browns in particular had long been interested in manufacturing. Of the four brothers, Moses and Joseph were the more interested in manufacturing, while Nicholas and John had been, and continued to be, primarily merchants.

Moses Brown began in 1787 to collect all the information available on cotton manufacturing. After an unsuccessful effort to duplicate the British methods of manufacturing cotton yarn, in 1789 he recruited a recent English immigrant, Samuel Slater, to come to Rhode Island from New York to set up a mill. This mill, located at Pawtucket just north of Providence, began operations a year later, the first successful cotton manufacturing establishment in the United States.[35] Brown, in partnership with his son-in-law William Almy, began to show a profit by 1793. Interest in the cotton industry spread to other members of the Brown family, and to other Providence entrepreneurs as well. As early as 1791, there were four cotton manufacturing establishments besides Almy & Brown, although two of them were very limited in output.[36] The extent of mechanization was very limited in these early years, however. Factories were used primarily for spinning, with weaving done mostly on a piece-work basis. This situation resulted partly from the limitations of technology, but also from cotton weavers' resistance to becoming incorporated into a factory system.[37] After about 1810, cotton became more fully mechanized and the scale of the industry expanded rapidly; the number of mills increased from 25 in 1809 to 38 in 1812 and to 100 in 1815. Over half of these mills were in the Providence area. There were none in Newport, and only 6 in Newport-area towns by 1815.[38]

There were several reasons that Providence, rather than Newport, became the manufacturing center of Rhode Island. A good location, strong leadership, a tradition of interest in manufacturing, and widespread popular support for manufacturing all played a part in the development of industry in Providence.[39] The Providence area had a good supply of easily accessible water power, with many sites where dams could be built at reasonable expense, and innovative leaders who capitalized on these geographical advantages. Local residents' propensity to experiment with manufacturing also encouraged innovation in industry. Not only men like the Browns, but many ordinary residents as well, were prepared to encourage manufacturing. The cotton weavers may have resisted mechanization, but the general climate was favorable to industry. The Association of Mechanics and Manufacturers, founded in 1789 by master craftsmen, engaged in concerted efforts to encourage manufacturing in the Providence area. Their report on the state of manufactures in 1791 was dotted with comments on the disadvantages of importing goods and the potential for increasing local manufactures in a variety of areas.[40]

Newport's situation was almost the reverse. Its island location was excellent for trade but poor for manufacturing, because it had no source of water power and access to the mainland was inconvenient. Its economic leaders had never shown much interest in manufacturing and, after the war, were preoccupied with trying to restore trade. In addition, the lack of interest in manufacturing among the city's elite was matched by a similar disinterest among most of its other residents.

On the face of it, location would seem to be the critical factor in Newport's failure to establish itself as a manufacturing center. And yet, a closer examination suggests that location alone was not the critical difference. Providence admittedly had a more advantageous location for manufacturing, but its economic and political leaders had capitalized on its location by dredging the harbor and building roads. They had undertaken those improvements initially to improve their commercial prospects, but the improved roads eventually helped in their meanufacturing enterprises as well. Newport men made no such efforts. Nor did they show any interest in establishing manufacturing operations that did not require water power, or in promoting manufacturing in nearby mainland towns, or even in investing in Providence enterprises. It was a South Kingstown man, Rowland Hazard, who established the first textile factory on the southern Rhode Island mainland, in 1804.[41] A relative of his, Benjamin Hazard, was the sole Newport man to invest in Providence-area mills, and even he had only a small share.[42] In Newport itself, there was little activity.

The prominent Newport lawyer and politician, William Ellery, was one of the few exceptions to the general lack of interest in manufacturing in Newport. He attributed this lack of interest to inertia and to a preference for the certain profits of trade over the riskier benefits of industry. Ellery, who was interested in the possibilities of manufacturing as a means of economic recovery for Newport, sought the advice of Moses Brown on this subject. Brown urged Ellery to suggest the possibility of manufacturing duck cloth to Newport investors. Such an operation required neither water power nor extensive mechanization. The sort of enterprises that Brown proposed to Ellery would have involved farming out both spinning and weaving to people working in their homes. Duck manufacturing would offer at least two advantages to Newport, Brown thought. Flax was easily grown in the area around Newport, and such a manufacturing establishment would provide employment for Newport's poor, who were becoming an increasingly serious problem. Brown also hoped that the establishment of manufacturing enterprises in Newport might shift the city's merchants away from their reliance on the slave trade, which he, as a Quaker and leader of the state's growing antislavery movement, abhorred.

Ellery, however, although he liked Brown's suggestions, did not hold much hope of investment in manufacturing from Newport's prominent men. Newport's "people of property" were well aware of the advantages of duck manufacturing, he told Brown; "They talk about it . . . but they are not possessed of that spirit of enterprise and combination with which your people of property are animated, and which is necessary to the commencement and perfection of any consequential manufacture." He hit upon one of the most important reasons for their reluctance to invest in manufacturing in responding to Brown's comments on the slave trade. Of course manufacturing would provide a much more significant source of employment for the poor than commerce; but, he pointed out, "an Aethiopian could as soon change his skin, as a merchant could be induced to exchange so lucrative a trade as that is for the slow profits of any manufactory." Not until the end of the eighteenth century was any attempt made in Newport to manufacture duck cloth, and even those efforts were unsuccessful.[43]

Ellery's exchange with Brown not only points out the major reason for the lack of interest in manufacturing in Newport—its' leaders' extreme reluctance to divert any money or energy away from trade—but also indirectly suggests a second reason. Most Newport merchants did not have much capital to spare, and they quite logically did not want to risk it on an enterprise that might, at best, take years to yield a profit and, at worst, fail completely. The Browns were exceptionally wealthy men, able both to take greater risks and to wait—years, if necessary—to see the fruits of their investment. No one in Newport came close to equalling them in wealth. The one man who had been equally wealthy before the war, Aaron Lopez, was dead, and he had left no family in Newport to carry on his business. The perspective of time shows the wisdom of the Browns' experiments, but to most of their contemporaries, the time-honored practices of commerce seemed to be a far safer road to economic recovery and prosperity.

Ironically, then, it was the existence of great wealth and the dominance of a single family that initially promoted economic innovation in Providence. The Browns and their business associates formed a tightly knit, elite group that had come through the Revolution with little or no financial hardship, a substantial supply of capital built up through commerce in the prosperous years before the war, and a propensity towards experimentation in both commerce and manufacturing. Newport, by contrast, had a diffuse and weakened elite group, who had been scattered during the war, and faced a struggle simply to get their businesses functioning and their city on its feet again. Added to the facts that their location was poor for anything but trade and that they had neither a history of experimentation in manufacturing nor any single individual with the talent and capital of a Moses Brown, it is hardly suprising that Newport leaders did not embrace the idea of duck cloth manufacturing or any other type of industry.

The early industrialists of Providence had one further advantage. Although they controlled most of the wealth and political power in Providence, they enjoyed substantial support from middle-class artisans who thought of themselves as "manufacturers"—as distinct from farmers, merchants, and shopkeepers—and identified themselves with nascent industrial enterprises around Providence. These men defined "manufacturers" as people who created goods, whether by hand or machine, in a small shop or a factory; their definition is a reminder that early industry was small in scale, just one step removed from the craftsmanship of artisans.

A group of Providence artisans organized the Providence Association of Mechanics and Manufacturers in 1789, following in the footsteps of similar organizations in Boston, New York, and Philadelphia. The Association served both as a mutual aid society and as a pressure group to promote the interests of artisans—which, in their view, included the interests of industrial manufacturers as well. Two characteristics of the Providence organization were significant: the generally high level of prosperity of its members, and their eagerness to support the manufacturing enterprises of Providence's elite. In this respect they differed from similar organizations in other cities, where the members were generally not so well-to-do and the relationship with members of the elite was more one of antagonism than support.[44] It is also significant that a similar association was established in Newport, in 1792, only at the prodding of the Providence Association. Its members were generally poorer than their Providence counterparts, and the organization was not so active or influential.

The membership of the Providence Association was composed largely of master craftsmen; the bylaws restricted membership to men who "depend solely . . .on some mechanic or manufacturing business," although men who engaged in some buying and selling in addition to practicing a trade were not excluded. Admission of journeymen as members was tightly controlled; only men who had served apprenticeships locally, or produced references from three master craftsmen, or proved their character by working as journeymen in Providence for a period of time were admitted.[45]

As a result the membership was limited for the most part to well-established and generally prosperous artisans—precisely the sort of men who were able to foresee the increasing importance of locally produced goods in the future and were concerned about establishing a strong position for themselves in post-war society. About half the members ranked in the top half of all taxpayers, and 22 percent were in the top quarter.[46] (In Newport, on the other hand, only two of the seventy-four original members ranked in the top 20 percent of taxpayers; a little over a third were in the top half.[47])

The greater strength and prominence of the Providence Association may be explained in part by the presence in that town of a few unusually successful artisans who not only were leaders in the organization, but enjoyed prominent standing in the community at large. Charles Keen, for example, a native of Providence, was a prosperous blacksmith who began manufacturing axes and scythes shortly after the war. He was among the wealthiest 10 percent of taxpayers in 1775, and just below that point in 1790; he was active in both town and state politics, having served as a representative to the General Assembly and on the Town Council both before and after the Revolution.

Amos Atwell, another blacksmith who branched out into manufacturing and, in addition, kept a hardware store, was equally prominent. He too served in the General Assembly and on the Town Council, in addition to holding several minor town offices. And he also was among the top 10 percent before the Revolution; by 1790, he was one of the richest men in Providence. Both Keen and Atwell were wealthy men and held positions of political influence; Atwell had become something of a merchant; yet their occupations inclined them to identify more with artisans than with merchants, and they were both among the founders of the Association. Keen served as its first vice president and Atwell as its first treasurer.

Another of the first officers, Bennett Wheeler, was a newcomer to Providence, having arrived in Providence from Nova Scotia in 1776 at the age of 18 as a soldier in the Revolutionary Army. Although not a particularly wealthy man, he became prominent in his own way; he went into the printing business with Solomon Southwick, Providence's long-established printer and newspaper publisher, and then in 1784 established his own newspaper. Barzillai Richmond, the Association's first president, was a hatter who ranked in the top 20 percent of taxpayers both before and after the Revolution and had served on the Town Council in the prewar period.

Robert Newell's multiplicity of interests made him a good example of the blurring of distinctions between artisans or "mechanics" and "manufacturers"; a clothier, he owned a shop for coloring and finishing cloth, a fulling mill, and a chocolate mill. He also owned several buildings in addition to the one where his mills were located, and, in the 1790's, became involved in calico printing and wallpaper printing. His enterprises made him a rich man; a middle-ranking tax-payer in 1775, he rose to the top 10 percent by 1790.[48] There were no men of comparable prominence in the Newport Association; nor were the connections between artisanry and manufacturing as close there as they were in Providence.

Promotion of manufacturing and craft interests was, above all else, the concern of the artisan organizations. They perceived their interests as clearly opposed to those of men involved in trade, and contrasted the "poor Manufacturer" with the "rich Farmer" and the "opulent Merchant." They linked their interests with the general interest, however, by arguing that reliance on commerce was detrimental to the economy in general, and particularly to "the middling and poorer classes of People."[49] In a letter to Newport artisans, the Providence Association suggested that manufacturing was the only way to help Newport regain its "former Lustre," an appeal that fell as flat as did Moses Brown's to the merchants of Newport.[50]

The Providence Association promoted its interests most directly by campaigning for import duties that would discourage importation of foreign products and give a competitive advantage to native manufactures; the members also tackled the problem from within their own ranks by supporting inspection requirements for locally produced articles that were exported, to "place the Manufactures of this Town & its Vicinity upon a more respectable Footing than they have heretofore been."[51] Included in the inspection requirements were hats, carriages, leather work, cabinet work, textiles, shoes, and tools. The Association also directed members within each craft to establish regulations for their own products, and to keep a close watch on their apprentices in order to maintain high standards. Any complaints made about inferior quality products were to be referred to an Association committee for investigation.[52]

This concern about setting high standards of craftsmanship—which was also reflected in the restrictive policy on admission of journeymen to the Association—was part of a program to promote manufacturing interests, but it was also part of the artisans' efforts to enhance their own respectability and improve their place in society. Poor quality work and careless apprentices were bad for business, but they were also bad for the image of upwardly mobile craftsmen. The Providence members acknowledged this concern about respectability in one of their letters encouraging Newport artisans to form an association, stating that one of their major goals was to promote an "honorable Idea of the several mechanical pursuits in which we are engaged—instead of repining, that Providence has not destined us, to move in a higher sphere."[53]

One of the means of reaching this goal, along with ensuring a high standard of craftsmanship, was encouraging unity and a high standard of behavior among the members. The bylaws of the association, in addition to urging each craft to regulate its members' work, recommended that they not get too deeply in debt, proscribed law suits among members, and established a fund for the relief of members in financial difficulties.[54] Public service and education were also part of the artisans' program to enhance their positions. Among the advantages of organization that the Providence mechanics pointed out to their Newport brethren was the process of debate and elections in the Association itself, which helped prepare them to serve in public office. And they were active in petitioning for the establishment of free schools, justifying their action on the grounds that universal education was essential for a republican state.[55] The members' concern for knowledge extended to themselves, as their meetings included lectures "for the promotion of useful knowledge."[56]

The artisans' public goals, however, did not obscure their private goals. They saw their Association not merely as an organization devoted to the public pursuit of their economic interests, but also as a brotherhood for the mutual benefit of each other. The Association monitored the behavior of its members, disciplining them not only for shoddy workmanship but also for disorderly conduct. The motives for such activities were partly those of mutual support, but also involved a concern for the artisans' respectability in the outside world. Artisans as a group were respected, the Association members thought, but individuals sometimes had tarnished reputations; "It is our business," they announced, "to support the depressed, and if possible to reclaim the profligate."[57] The Providence Association summed up all its concerns in a circular letter to mechanics in other cities, which said that they had organized to encourage each other in their work, to try to suppress fraudulent practices that gave all mechanics a bad name, and to try to place native manufacturing on an equal footing with that of European countries.[58]

This emergence of artisans as a vocal group in society was one of the most important social developments of the years after the Revolution in most eastern cities. In Providence, it helped create popular support for those wealthy merchants who were attempting to establish their city as a center of textile manufacturing.

Demography and geography both provided a strong basis for Providence's growth and Newport's decline after the Revolution, but the decisions of individuals in both cities were more important in creating the new balance of economic power. Providence's natural advantages, after all, were not immediately apparent in the years just after the Revolution. Its location was advantageous for manufacturing, but the first factories were still some years in the future; and Newport clearly had the better location for commerce. Newport's loss of population during the war was a serious problem, but there was no reason to think that it wouldn't recover quickly. Many other cities did. But Providence did have ceratin advantages—a stable population base and a tightly knit elite that had managed to increase rather than deplete its capital during the war—and the city's leaders set about making the most of these advantages.

They used their capital to initiate new trade routes, a process that required them to find new exports and establish business contacts in ports up and down the Atlantic seaboard and in several European countries. For expensive voyages, notably those to the Orient, they pooled their capital in larger partnerships. And closer to home, they expanded their regional markets by building new roads and establishing contacts with local shopkeepers in Massachusetts and Connecticut as well as Rhode Island. Somewhat later, they took an even more forward-looking step, to establish the first cotton textile factories in the United States. But for the most part, the battle for dominance between Providence and Newport was a battle of commerce. Before its factories expanded beyond their most primitive phase, Providence had passed Newport in population, in wealth, and in volume of trade. Indeed, the profits of that trade, to a considerable extent, helped finance the development of manufacturing.

There were innovative men in Newport who tried to accomplish the same kinds of things for their city—Christopher Champlin also pioneered new trade routes, and William Ellery wanted merchants to divert some of their capital to manufacturing. But what Newport lacked was the organized, concerted effort of a group of men with new ideas and sufficient capital to put those ideas into effect. Postwar economic ventures—whether commercial voyages, textile factories, banks, or turnpikes—required more capital than any single individual was likely to be able to command. In Providence, the four Browns invariably led the way, but they could count on the support, both moral and financial, of Welcome Arnold, John Innes Clark, Joseph Nightingale, Joseph and William Russell, and others. In Newport, no comparable group existed, and neither a Christopher Champlin, nor a William Ellery, nor even an Aaron Lopez—had he lived—could accomplish the same kinds of tasks alone.

7
Conclusion

IN THE YEARS BEFORE THE REVOLUTION, Newport and Providence, along with other New England seaport towns, had been distinctive for their commercial economies, their specialized occupational structures, their relatively complex institutional and cultural development, and their diverse populations. Sparked by the rapid expansion of trade from the beginning of the eighteenth century to the time of the Revolution, increasingly complex societies developed in both towns—societies characterized by extremes of rich and poor and diversity of national background, race, and religion.

Both Providence and Newport represented a significant contrast from the agricultural villages of rural New England. They were, however, also significantly different from each other, and their differences give some indication of the complexity of eighteenth-century urban society. Newport dominated the colony economically and politically. It had a larger and more varied population, a more complicated elite structure, greater variety of religions, and a more extensive display of affluence and sophistication in the form of elegant homes, fine craftsmanship, and imposing public buildings. Providence, on the other hand, retained much of the quality of an agricultural town and was more insular in both its general population and in its elite. As it expanded economically, Providence took on many of Newport's social characteristics, but it retained its distinctive style of leadership.

Although Providence served as an economic center for its immediate region, on the whole it was dominated by Newport both economically and politically. In the years just before the Revolution, however, Providence went through a period of major economic expansion—partly as a result of the rapid population growth in northern Rhode Island, and partly because of the aggressive commercial efforts of its major merchants. At one time these merchants had accepted the dominance of Newport in Rhode Island's economic affairs, but by the 1770s that dominance was being challenged. The changing relationship between the two towns was symbolized by rancorous debate over gubernatorial elections and by the controversy over the location of Rhode Island College. On the eve of the Revolution, Providence was coming into its own as a commercial center, and the two towns' long-standing relationship of dominance and dependence was changing into an increasingly heated rivalry. The future direction of their development at that point was uncertain.

By the end of the eighteenth century, however, Newport was in decline as a commercial center while Providence was fast on the way to becoming Rhode Island's dominant city and one of New England's major manufacturing centers. The Revolution contributed substantially to this shift in balance between the towns. The British occupation of Newport, its serious depopulation, and especially the loss of leadership all contributed to Newport's decline, while Providence was able to capitalize on its relatively protected position during the war. While Newport failed to recover from wartime depopulation and loss of trade, Providence entered a period of substantial economic and demographic growth. This reversal in the positions of the towns had its origins in the 1770s and was completed in the early nineteenth century by the major economic transformation that made manufacturing, rather than commerce, the basis for Rhode Island's later growth. The Revolutionary years, however, brought destruction from which Newport could not easily recover and significantly hastened this process.

Newport was not alone in suffering from the war, nor was Providence unique in benefiting from it. Many seaports were occupied by the British and experienced severe damage; a few were able to take advantage of their relatively unscathed condition to increase their commercial importance. The post-Revolutionary problems that afflicted the Rhode Island towns were widely shared—the decline of the West Indian trade, new British duties on American goods, the depression of the 1780's, and increased competition from newly developing ports. The experiences of Providence and Newport throughout the Revolutionary era were part of fundamental changes in urbanization that affected the country as a whole.

The major ports—Boston, New York, and Philadelphia—were all occupied by the British at some point during the war, but all recovered more quickly and more completely than Newport. Boston had felt the brunt of Britain's anger towards the colonies in the months before war actually began; when British troops evacuated that city in 1776, its merchants were able to resume a limited trade. Philadelphia, occupied in 1777–78, also recovered fairly quickly. Most of its merchants retreated to the countryside near the city, and carried on their business as much as possible by overland routes. The area's rich hinterland prevented complete collapse, and by 1779 Philadelphia merchants had recovered substantially from the years of the occupation. Only New York City was occupied longer than Newport; the British made it their headquarters from 1776 to 1783. New York, however, was in a unique position; it became a center for loyalists from all parts of the country and continued to trade openly, although under strict British regulations.[1]

The experience of Norfolk, Virginia was closer to Newport's. It too had been heavily dependent on the West Indian trade as a basis for its commerce, was severely damaged by British occupation, and faced increased competition from a fast-growing rival—Baltimore—after the war ended. And if Norfolk resembled Newport, Baltimore provides a close analogy to Providence. A rather insignificant port before the war, it also escaped British occupation and was able to overcome British efforts at blockading the Chesapeake Bay to maintain its trade. Both Providence and Baltimore were aided by the creation of their own customs house districts in 1780; before that time Baltimore came under the jurisdiction of Annapolis, and Providence, of Newport.[2]

After the war, Baltimore merchants, like Providence merchants, began aggressively developing trade in part by expanding the size of the area they served, building an extensive network of roads into the interior regions of Maryland, Virginia, and Pennsylvania.[3] This expansion proceeded at the expense not only of Norfolk's trade, but also that of Annapolis, which had been the dominant Chesapeake port throughout the eighteenth century. Annapolis was not occupied by the British, but it was like Newport and Norfolk in that its merchants had a difficult time recovering from the war and suffered badly from this new source of economic competition.[4] The similarity of the Baltimore-Annapolis rivalry to the Rhode Island situation was not lost on Providence merchants. John Brown hoped to learn something from its growth and dispatched his son to Baltimore in 1782, telling him "that most Flourishing Markantile Town" was experiencing "the Most Rappid Growth that History gives any acct. of under Simmiler Surcumstances."[5]

The Revolution contributed substantially to the changing fortunes of cities throughout the colonies. Large ports like New York and Philadelphia were sufficiently well established that recovery from the war was not a major problem, but smaller towns were much more vulnerable to the effects of such a crisis. Not only did British occupation affect these towns more seriously, but other conditions, such as location, the specific nature of prewar trade, and the existence of competitive ports nearby could make the difference between growth and decline in the postwar period.[6] But the war itself was not the sole reason for the changes in cities that were apparent by the end of the eighteenth century. The growth of manufacturing provided a totally new stimulus for urban development. Basic changes in commercial practices promoted the concentration of trade in a few major ports, making it increasingly difficult for smaller ports to compete.[7] Both of these changes affected the postwar development of Newport and Providence and, in general, helped change the nature of postwar urbanization. A seaport location was no longer a prerequisite for urban development; and much of the trade that had kept small seaports in business was being siphoned off to Boston, New York, and Philadelphia. Newport suffered both ways. Providence enjoyed a brief spurt of commercial growth at Newport's expense, but its trade, too, declined by the early nineteenth century, and only its position as a manufacturing center kept it from going the way of Newport.

As the small cities scattered along the seacoast lost their economic *raison d'être,* they also lost much of their social and cultural distinctiveness. Many of the social characteristics associated with urbanization in the eighteenth century became more widely diffused, as the economic functions of cities became increasingly concentrated in a few major centers. Manufacturing, transportation innovations, and geographical expansion of settlement created new population centers in places that had once been remote and isolated, particularly in the early years of the nineteenth century. Though these towns were generally small in population, their residents strove to make them into "cities" in both the economic and social sense. In Massachusetts, for example, between 1790 and 1820, libraries, post offices, voluntary associations, and other urban trappings proliferated throughout the state, to towns with as few as 300 or 400 people. Settlers in the Northwest Territory, around the turn of the century, seemed as eager to establish towns as to stake out claims to farmland, and they often dignified mere plans on paper with the name of city. And an analysis of Indiana towns in 1820 showed that even small population clusters exhibited social characteristics usually defined as "urban."[8]

Increasing centralization of commerce, a broadening economic base for urbanization, and diffusion of traditionally urban social characteristics created a major change in the nature of American cities around the beginning of the nineteenth century. Providence was an example of a town that successfully made the transition from eighteenth-century seaport to nineteenth-century manufacturing city. For Newport such a transition was impossible; it was saved from obscurity only by its long-standing popularity as a summer resort. The damage inflicted by the Revolution, the difficulty of competing in a new commercial world, and impediments to establishing manufacturing—both geographical and motivational—all contributed to its fate.

Appendix A: Population

RHODE ISLAND TOOK FIVE CENSUSES before the Revolution, beginning in 1708, and another one in 1782, making it easier to determine population growth than in most other colonies. For the seventeenth century, however, only rough estimates are possible. Using estimated figures for the population of Rhode Island in the seventeenth century, it is possible to calculate some approximations of the population of Newport and Providence.[1]

Carl Bridenbaugh has estimated the population of Newport, along with other colonial cities, but his estimates for Newport are clearly inaccurate. His figures indicate a large jump in population between 1660 and 1680, and then virtually no growth from 1680 to 1700. He also estimates Newport's population in 1700 at nearly 600 more people than were counted in the census of 1708. In addition, his figures show Newport constituting 83 percent of Rhode Island's population in 1680, 62 percent in 1690, and 48 percent in 1700 (based on Census Bureau estimates of Rhode Island population), which is clearly impossible.[2] However, by his estimate of Newport's population in 1640, Newport made up 32 percent of Rhode Island's population, compared with 31 percent in 1708. Providence, in 1708, constituted 20 percent of the colony's population. These percentages declined during the 18th century, as settlement in Rhode Island dispersed and new towns were formed. But assuming that populations of the two towns were constant percentages of the population of the whole colony throughout the seventeenth century produces the population estimates given in table A–1. This method may understate the size of the two towns in the early decades of the seventeenth century, since it is quite likely that they constituted larger percentages of the colony's population in those years (and that Bridenbaugh's estimate of Newport's population in 1640 is too low). The population estimates for the

TABLE A–1
ESTIMATED POPULATION FOR NEWPORT, PROVIDENCE,
AND RHODE ISLAND—SEVENTEENTH CENTURY

YEAR	RHODE ISLAND	NEWPORT	PROVIDENCE	%INCREASE/YR.
1640	300	96	60	
1650	785	251	157	16.2
1660	1,539	492	308	9.6
1670	2,155	690	431	4.0
1680	3,017	965	603	4.0
1690	4,224	1,352	845	4.0
1700	5,894	1,886	1,179	4.0
1708*	7,181	2,208	1,446	2.7 (R.I.)
				2.1 (Newport)
				2.8 (Prov.)

SOURCE: U.S. Bureau of the Census, *Historical Statistics of the United States: Colonial Times to 1957* (Washington, D.C., 1960), 756.
*Actual census.

colony assume a constant rate of growth of 40 percent per decade from 1670 to 1700. Since there were few towns in the seventeenth century (four in 1640, nine by 1708), the assumption that Newport and Providence grew at about the same rate as the colony should be reasonably accurate.

Determining growth rates for the cities in the eighteenth century is complicated by several town divisions, which reduced the area and population of the cities themselves. In Newport, only one such division was made, in 1743, when Middletown was set off from Newport. Providence, however, included most of the northern half of the colony until 1731, when this area was divided into four towns. In the 1750s, two more towns were set off from Providence, and in 1765, a third town was established. The adjusted population figures in table A–2 therefore include the population of Providence or Newport plus the town(s) set off since the previous census. The percentage increase in population for each time period was figured by using the adjusted figure for the later date and comparing it with the actual figure for the earlier date. Thus, for example, the rate of increase for Newport between 1730 and 1748 is actually the rate of increase for both Newport and Middletown, since the area that was Middletown in 1748 was part of Newport in 1730. For the next time period—1748–55 or 1748–74, the figures for Newport alone were compared. For Providence, however, this procedure becomes more complicated because of the number of town divisions. The adjusted population figure for 1748 includes the three towns set off in 1730; the 1755 figure does not include these three but does include Cranston, which was set off in 1754. The 1774 figure includes Cranston, Johnston, and North Providence (set off in 1759 and 1765).

TABLE A–2
POPULATION INCREASE IN NEWPORT, PROVIDENCE, AND RHODE ISLAND—EIGHTEENTH CENTURY

I. POPULATION

Year	Rhode Island Population	Newport Population (Actual)	Newport Population (Adjusted)	Providence Population (Actual)	Providence Population (Adjusted)
1708	7,181	2,208	2,208	1,446	1,146
1730	16,950	4,640	4,460	3,916	3,916
1748	32,773	6,508	7,158	3,452	6,336
1755	40,576	6,753	6,753	3,159	4,619
1774	59,706	9,208	9,208	4,321	8,043
1782	51,869	5,530	5,530	4,310	4,310
1790	68,825	6,725	6,725	6,380	6,380
1800	69,122	6,999	6,999	7,614	7,614

II. RATES OF POPULATION INCREASE

Years	Percentage Increase			Percentage Increase/Yr.		
	R.I.	*Newport*	*Prov.*	*R.I.*	*Newport*	*Prov.*
1708–30	136	111	171	6.2	5.0	7.8
1730–48	93	55	62	5.2	3.1	3.4
1748–55	24	24	37	3.4	0.6	5.3
1755–74	47	36	74	2.5	1.9	4.0
1748–74	82	41	133	3.2	1.6	5.1
1730–74	252	117	105*	5.7	2.7	2.4
1774–82	− 13	− 40	− 0.003	− 1.6	− 5.0	—
1782–90	33	22	48	4.1	2.8	6.0
1790–1800	0.4	4	19	0.04	0.4	1.9

SOURCES: Census of 1708, in John Bartlett, ed., *Records of the Colony of Rhode Island and Providence Plantations in New England* (Providence, 1859), vol. 4, p. 59; Census of 1730, in John Callender, *A Historical Discourse on the Civil and Religious Affairs of the Colony of Rhode Island*, vol. 4, *Collections of the Rhode Island Historical Society* (Providence, 1838), p. 94; Census of 1748, in William Douglass, *A Summary, Historical & Political, of the first planting, Progressive improvements, and present state of the British Settlements in North America* (Boston, 1755); Census of 1775, broadside, Rhode Island Historical Society; *Census of the Inhabitants of the Colony of Rhode Island and Providence Plantations in New England, 1774* (Providence, 1858); Census of 1782, reprinted in *New England Historical and Genealogical Register*, 127 (1972), pp. 5–17; 128 (1973), pp. 138–42; *Heads of Families, at the First Census of the United States, taken in the Year 1790* (Washington, D.C., 1908); Census of 1800 (Washington, D.C., 1801).

*This figure is misleading, because it is based on the adjusted population figure for Providence in 1774, which does not include the populations of several towns taken from Providence after 1731. If those towns were included, the figure would be 39%. (See text for discussion of problems of estimating Providence population.)

Appendix B: Trade

THE ONLY CONSISTENTLY AVAILABLE STATISTICS on Rhode Island's shipping are the weekly Customs House lists, printed in the newspapers, which noted all ships entering and clearing the port.[1] There are two major difficulties in using these statistics. Before the Revolution, Rhode Island had only one Customs House, so shipping for Newport, Providence, and the smaller ports cannot be distinguished. Secondly, the newspaper lists are not always complete, particularly for the early years. The second problem can be solved to some extent by estimating yearly totals, based on the lists available. For the period 1720–40, only those years were selected for which at least two-thirds of the weekly lists were available. Total shipping for the weeks for which there is no published list was estimated by averaging the totals for the weeks before and after the week in question. For the period 1740–62, however, lists were so sporadic that no series of statistics could be compiled. From 1763 up to the Revolution, and again from 1784 to 1800, the lists are much more complete; therefore only those years for which complete statistics exist were used in the tables that follow. One exception is the years 1768–72, for which statistics kept by the British Customs Office are available. These statistics include both tonnage and total number of ships entering and clearing. They were used in table B–1 for 1769, 1770, and 1771, years for which the newspaper lists were incomplete.[2] These statistics, however, did not specify destination of ship other than coastal and foreign, so they are not included in the more specific tables below.

For the period 1740–63, only the sketchiest estimates are possible concerning the volume of shipping. Shipping lists appeared in the newspapers sporadically from 1740 to 1744, and then disappeared entirely. The lists for the early 1740s are so incomplete that it is not even possible to estimate to-

TABLE B-1
ACTUAL AND ESTIMATED NUMBERS OF VESSELS
ENTERING AND CLEARING RHODE ISLAND, 1720-1800

YEAR	TOTAL NUMBER OF VESSELS ENTERING AND CLEARING	
	Actual	Estimated
1720	367	620
1721	215	475
1724	291	448
1726	317	526
1728	277	464
1730	310	486
1731	388	510
1732	370	486
1733	293	485
1735	440	526
1737	458	500
1738	464	535
1739	495	640
1763	773	same
1764	1,052	"
1767	636	"
1768	781	"
1769	1,298	"
1770	1,195	"
1771	1,277	"
1772	1,303	"
1773	1,590	"
1774	1,661	"

	Newport (Actual)	Prov. (Actual)	Total
1785	361	371	732
1786	305	*	
1791	*	756	
1792	*	714	
1793	628	770	1,398
1794	*	643	
1795	605	707	1,312
1796	596	648	1,244
1797	572	*	
1798	689	*	
1799	707	*	
1800	771	*	

SOURCES: For 1768–72, British Customs Office documents 16:1, photostats in the possession of Lawrence Harper, University of California, Berkeley (original documents in Public Record Office, London); for 1720–39, Customs House lists in *Boston Gazette*; for 1763–67, 1773–74, and Newport 1785–1800, Customs House lists in *Newport Mercury*; for Providence, Customs House lists in *Providence Gazette*, 1784–1800.

*Figures incomplete for these years.

tals for those years. To get some idea of the magnitude of shipping during these years, however, the average number of ships entering for all weeks reported from April to September was compared with the comparable figures for the years 1735–39. (April–September were the months during which lists were most frequently published in the years 1740–44.) These average figures, listed below, changed very little during the ten-year period, averaging roughly 3.5 to 4.5 ships per week:

1735: 4.55
1737: 3.88
1738: 3.48
1739: 4.45
1740: 9.50
1741: 4.53
1744: 4.58

It is more difficult to determine Newport's and Providence's relative shares of shipping than to estimate the total volume of shipping for the colony. Estimates can be made, however, for three points during the period: 1744–45, 1768, and 1774. These estimates indicate that Providence's shipping accounted for only about 20 percent of the two cities' total in 1744–45, but rose to about 30 percent in 1768 and 1774. For purposes of simplicity, the smaller ports in Rhode Island were left out of the calculation, because their share of total shipping was small.

The most reliable of these figures is that for 1768, when the collector of Rhode Island's Customs House wrote to the Board of Trade, giving a breakdown of Rhode Island's shipping. According to his figures, Providence accounted for 26 percent of all shipping, and Newport accounted for 56 percent, with the remaining 18 percent attributed to five minor port towns.[3] Eliminating the minor towns, Providence accounted for 31 percent, and Newport for the remainder. From March to September, 1774, the *Providence Gazette* published a separate listing of ships entering and clearing the port of Providence. Assuming that the percentage of shipping from the minor ports remained constant from 1768 to 1774, and eliminating them from the comparison, Providence's shipping in 1774 represented 34 percent of the two cities' total.[4]

Estimating the relative shares in 1744–45 is more difficult. A list of vessels paying port taxes from June 1744 to May 1745 lists names of individual ships and masters.[5] By comparing the names of masters with tax lists, it is possible to determine the city of residence of many of these ship captains. A substantial proportion were not Rhode Island residents, but were captains of ships traveling to Rhode Island from other ports. It is likely, however, that a few of the captains who were not identified were actually Newport or Providence residents, but could not be found on any lists. This is particularly true for Newport, where no tax lists survive for the period before 1760. For these reasons, the estimates for 1744–45 are approximate.

Recorded on the list of vessels paying port taxes from June 1744 to May 1745 were 193 ships. Of these, at least 29 to 45 belonged to Newport, and 10 to 13 belonged to Providence. Thus between 15 and 31 percent of the two cities' ships belonged to Providence. The most plausible estimate, however, is at the lower end of this range. Because the earliest available list of Newport residents dates from 1760, it is probable that several of the unidentified, or only tentatively identified, ship captains were actually from Newport. On the other hand, a 1745 tax list ensures a much higher probability of identifying nearly all the Providence ship captains. Assuming, therefore, that the high estimate for Newport (45 captains identified) is closer to the truth, then Providence's proportion of the total number of ships would be at the lower end of the range. Assuming that the high estimates for both Providence and Newport are correct (13 captains identified for Providence, 45 for Newport), then Providence ships represented 22 percent of the total. In 1784, a separate Customs House was established in Providence, and an accurate comparison can therefore be made between the two towns.

Table B–1 and figure 1 (p. 21) summarize these shipping statistics. Table B–2 breaks down the total shipping statistics into the three major branches

TABLE B–2
PERCENTAGE OF RHODE ISLAND SHIPPING TO MAJOR DESTINATIONS

ALL RHODE ISLAND, 1720–39 AND 1763–74

Year	Coastal	West Indies	Foreign	Total No. Ships
1720	48.5	51.5	0	367
1721	46.5	51.6	1.9	215
1724	29.6	66.3	4.1	291
1726	28.7	66.4	4.7	317
1728	13.7	75.8	10.5	277
1730	22.9	73.9	3.2	310
1731	32.2	63.9	3.9	388
1732	34.4	58.6	7.0	370
1733	33.1	62.8	4.1	293
1735	22.7	71.1	6.1	440
1737	21.0	72.9	6.1	458
1738	16.8	75.2	8.0	464
1739	31.7	60.4	7.9	495
1763	70.2	24.1	5.7	773
1764	67.1	26.5	6.4	1,052
1767	31.3	66.1	6.9	636
1768	49.2	45.1	5.8	781

TABLE B-2 (continued)
PERCENTAGE OF RHODE ISLAND SHIPPING TO MAJOR DESTINATIONS

ALL RHODE ISLAND, 1720-39 AND 1763-74

Year	Coastal	West Indies	Foreign	Total No. Ships
1769	71.2	25.8	3.0	1,298
1770	63.7	32.6	3.8	1,195
1771	63.0	33.8	3.1	1,277
1772	64.8	31.5	3.7	1,303
1773	63.5	31.7	4.8	1,590
1774	64.8	31.5	3.7	1,661

NEWPORT AND PROVIDENCE, 1785-1800

	Newport				Providence			
	Coastal	W.I.	For.	Total	Coastal	W.I.	For.	Total
1785	74.0	21.1	5.0	361	66.0	29.1	4.9	371
1786	67.2	27.9	4.9	305				
1791					83.9	10.1	6.1	756
1792					79.8	12.0	8.1	714
1793	77.5	19.6	2.9	628	81.4	11.7	6.9	770
1794					73.7	18.7	7.6	643
1795	78.8	17.2	4.0	605	73.4	16.5	10.0	707
1796	76.0	18.5	5.5	596	71.6	18.7	9.7	648
1797	78.1	16.1	5.8	572				
1798	74.9	21.0	4.1	689				
1799	72.1	20.8	7.1	707				
1800	76.4	18.9	4.8	771				

SOURCES: Same as table B-1.

of trade—coastal (continental colonies), West Indian, and foreign. Tables B-3 and B-4 list the value of Rhode Island's exports for the years 1768-72, the only years for which such information is available. Table B-5 compares the composition of Rhode Island's trade with that of the other major ports.

TABLE B-3
VALUE OF RHODE ISLAND EXPORTS, 1768-72

DESTINATION OF EXPORTS	VALUE BY YEAR (IN POUNDS STERLING)				
	1768	1769	1770	1771	1772
Gr. Britain	5,173	6,461	12,846	14,541	11,495
Ireland	0	0	0	63	388
S. Eur./Wine Is.	2,539	1,145	203	150	1,042
West Indies	38,747	46,841	56,606	57,569	53,961
Africa	9,991	11,669	10,971	9,734	14,288

SOURCE: James F. Shepherd, "Commodity Exports from the British North American Colonies to Overseas Areas, 1768-1772: Magnitudes and Patterns of Trade," *Explorations in Economic History*, vol. 8 (1970), pp. 5-76. His figures come from British Customs Office papers in the Public Record Office, London.

TABLE B-4
VALUE OF COMMODITIES SHIPPED FROM RHODE ISLAND
TO VARIOUS LOCATIONS, 1768–72
(IN POUNDS STERLING)

COMMODITIES	DESTINATION				
	Eng./Ireland	S.Eur./Wine Is.	W. Indies	Africa	Totals
Whale oil	29,646	4	3,225		32,875
Potash	11,546				11,546
Iron	3,687		164		3,851
Naval stores	1,804				1,804
Lumber	1,414	1,063	25,549		28,026
Cotton	1,220				1,220
Flaxseed	699				699
W.I. rum	435	28		22	485
Amer. rum	242			54,883	55,125
Rice	177		1,728		1,905
Beeswax	82	285			367
Beef/pork	15	697	14,854		15,566
Spermaceti candles		719	63,860	1,748	66,327
Bread/flour		1,106	47,220		48,326
Fish		772	42,947		43,719
Livestock			38,138		38,138
Hoops			14,088		14,088
Indian corn		405	1,709		2,114
Wine			238		238
Wheat			4		4
Totals	50,967	5,079	253,724	56,653	366,423

SOURCE: Same as table B–3.

TABLE B-5
TRADE PATTERNS FOR MAJOR NORTH AMERICAN PORTS, 1768–72

DESTINATION	RHODE ISLAND		NEW YORK		BOSTON		PHILADELPHIA		SOUTH CAROLINA	
	Tonnage	%	Tonnage	%	Tonnage	%	Tonnage	%	Tonnage	%
Coastal	102,695	(56.3)	91,147	(35.1)	194,790	(50.9)	124,819	(29.6)	59,264	(19.2)
Europe	8,152	(4.5)	90,970	(35.1)	78,421	(20.5)	163,370	(38.7)	165,840	(53.7)
Africa	3,404	(1.9)	1,103	(.4)	1,599	(.4)	366	(.1)	5,699	(1.9)*
W. Indies	68,062	(37.3)	76,339	(29.4)	106,278	(27.7)	133,314	(31.6)	77,224	(25.1)
Total	182,313	100	259,559	100	383,088	99.5	421,869	100	308,027	99.9

SOURCES: Virginia D. Harrington, *The New York Merchants on the Eve of the Revolution* (New York, 1935), pp. 359–68. Rhode Island figures are from copies of British Customs Office documents 16:1, in the possession of Professor Lawrence Harper of the University of California, Berkeley. (Original ms. in Public Record Office, London.)
*This figure represents almost entirely imports from Africa, most likely in the ships of other colonies.

Appendix C: Social Structure, 1760–75

THIS ANALYSIS OF THE STRUCTURE of society in Newport and Providence is confined to the period 1760–75 largely because sources for such an analysis do not exist for the period before 1760, with the exception of some tax lists for Providence. But more substantively, it was during this period that Newport and Providence reached their fullest development as preindustrial seaports, and it therefore seems appropriate to examine in some detail the nature of society during that period.

The people examined here are taxpayers listed on the 1760 and 1775 tax lists.[1] They are all white, and mostly male (96 percent in Newport, 97 percent in Providence). Most of them are heads of households, although some, especially in Providence, are absentee property owners. About one-third of these individuals in each city appeared on both lists. Additional information was collected on their household size and structure, occupation, political offices and, for Newport, religion. This group represents the established, settled residents of Newport and Providence with enough assets to pay at least a minimal tax. However, they do not by any means represent all the residents of these towns. As table C–1 shows, 45 percent of Newport residents and 30 percent of Providence residents listed on the 1774 census were not listed on the 1775 tax lists. Of course, some of these people had left town by 1775, and others were undoubtedly missed by the tax collectors, but the inescapable conclusion is that substantial numbers of residents were too poor to pay even a minimal tax. The larger percentage of such people in Newport is partly explained by the higher percentage of female household heads in Newport (20 percent, compared with 8 percent in Providence). Most of these women were not taxpayers. Of these people practically nothing is known; with rare exceptions, it is impossible to identify their occupations,

TABLE C–1
NUMBER OF PEOPLE LISTED ON TAX LISTS AND CENSUSES

	NO. ON 1760 TAX	NO. ON 1775 TAX	NO. ON BOTH	TOTAL INDIVIDUALS ON BOTH LISTS
Newport	931	955	372	1,514
Providence	573	722	219	1,076

	NO. TAXPAYERS ON 1774 CENSUS	TOTAL NAMES ON 1774 CENSUS	NO. RESIDENTS ON CENSUS, BUT NOT TAX LISTS
Newport	875	1,583	708 (44.7%)
Providence	462	655	193 (29.5%)

SOURCES: Tax lists, Providence, 1760 and 1775, Rhode Island Historical Society; Newport, 1760, State Archives; 1775, Newport Historical Society; John R. Bartlett, ed., *A Census of the Inhabitants of the Colony of Rhode Island and Providence Plantations in New England, 1774* (Providence, Knowles, Anthony & Co. 1858).

their religious affiliations, if any, or any social characteristics. Of the poorest class of people, only two groups can be described, and those only partially: transients ordered to leave town, and slaves. Detailed information is available for Providence transients, and is presented in chapter 4 and appendix D. Information about slaves, beyond their numbers and the households in which they lived, is available only for those slaves who tried to run away and who were advertised in the newspapers; they are also discussed in chapter 4.

Some estimates can be made of the relative size of different social groups: taxpayers, heads of household who were not taxpayers, servants, and slaves. Table C–2 shows the breakdown of the estimated size of these groups for men and women. The taxpayers and nontaxpaying heads of household discussed above constituted 72 percent of adult males in each town. (In the figures given in section I of table C–2, women taxpayers and heads of household have been subtracted from the totals.) The estimated figure for white servants is one-half of all males over 21 who were not heads of household. Males over 21 were assumed to be 75 percent of all males over 16, (whose numbers were listed in the 1774 census). The same procedure was used for estimating female servants. Of the possible ways of estimating the population over 21, this procedure provides the middle-range estimate. David Lovejoy estimated adult males at 17 percent of the total population; he got approximately the same figures using 75 percent of males over 16 (a procedure Thomas Jefferson used for Virginia). In Newport and Providence, however, the 17 percent method produces a much lower estimate because of the higher than average proportion of adults in these towns. The presence of a substantial Black population complicates the issue as well. On the other hand, working backwards from the 1782 census, which did distinguish 16–21-year-olds from adults, produces a much higher estimate of adults. In

TABLE C–2
BREAKDOWN OF BROAD SOCIAL GROUPS

I. MEN

	NEWPORT	PROVIDENCE
Heads of household: taxpayers	840 (48%)	448 (54%)
Heads of household: nontaxpayers	425 (24%)	153 (18%)
White servants over 21*	155 (9%)	157 (19%)
Blacks over 21 (excluding heads of household)*	316 (18%)	76 (9%)
Total	1,736	834

II. WOMEN

Heads of household: taxpayers	35 (2%)	14 (2%)
Heads of household: nontaxpayers	283 (13%)	40 (5%)
Wives of male heads of household**	1,272 (60%)	601 (75%)
White servants over 21*	189 (9%)	66 (8%)
Blacks over 21*	326 (15%)	84 (10%)
Total	2,105	805

SOURCES: Same as table C–1. See text for explanation of estimates.
*Estimates
**Based on assumption that all male heads of household were married.

Newport in 1782, males aged 16 to 21 were only 16 percent of white males over 16; in Providence they were 21 percent. (The comparable figures for women were 20 percent in Newport, 24 percent in Providence.) Projecting these percentages back to 1774 would obviously produce a higher estimate of men (and women) over 21. Major population shifts during the Revolution, however, make one hesitant to apply figures from 1782 to 1774. Assuming that men and women aged 16–21 were 25 percent of all men and women over 16 produces a compromise figure.[2] Servants were assumed to comprise one-half of adults not heads of household because the relatively late age at marriage in the eighteenth century kept many young adults in their parents' homes past the age of 21. There is no way to check the accuracy of this assumption, but it should produce a conservative estimate of the number of servants.

Occupational Structure

Table C–3 shows the breakdown of occupational structure. Occupations could be identified for about two-thirds of Newport taxpayers, and about one-third of Providence taxpayers; but the close correspondence between the percentages for the two cities indicates that the limited information available for Providence did not badly skew the distribution of occupations.[3] One caution in studying the occupational distribution of both towns, however, is the fact that some occupations are more readily identified than others and

TABLE C–3
OCCUPATIONAL STRUCTURE

OCCUPATION	PERCENTAGE OF TAXPAYERS			
	Newport	Providence	Boston (1790)	Philadelphia (1774)
Retail	41.2	36.5	20.3	15.0
Merchants	21.6	16.9	8.0	7.4
Shopkeepers	19.6	19.6	5.1	7.6
Artisans	37.7	42.1	49.3	48.6
Shipbuilding	4.0	3.6	8.5	4.2
Food	3.5	2.2	6.8	5.8
Clothing	9.1	6.1	11.2	12.0
Building	13.0	12.8	9.5	12.7
Metal	2.0	6.1	5.1	5.1
Leather	1.3	2.9	—	4.2
Other	3.9	5.6	8.2	4.6
Mariners (incl. ship captains)	17.3	7.3	9.9	8.2
Professionals	2.9	4.8	4.1	2.9
Manufacturing	.4	3.4	—	.3
Innholders, etc.*	5.4	3.9	—	4.9
Farmers	2.5**	.5	—	3.2
Laborers	.2	—	7.3	15.3
Others	—	—	—	2.6
Number of occupations	908	413		
Number of individuals	849	358		5,777
Number not identified	665 (44%)	718 (67%)		1,287 (22%)

SOURCES: Occupations determined from tax lists, censuses, court records, advertisements in *Newport Mercury* and *Providence Gazette*, Richardson's "Newport Occupations," photostat of notebook, in Rhode Island Historical Society; Franklin S. Coyle, "The Survival of Providence Business Enterprise after the Revolution," (M.A. thesis, Brown University, 1960). Boston figures from Allan Kulikoff, "The Progress of Inequality in Revolutionary Boston," *William and Mary Quarterly* 28 (1971), pp. 411–12; Philadelphia figures from Jacob Price, "Economic Function and the Growth of the American Port Towns in the Eighteenth Century," *Perspectives in American History* 8 (1974), pp. 123–86.
NOTE: Figures are based on number of occupations rather than number of individuals; a few people had more than one occupation.
*Includes distillers, brewers, tavernkeepers.
**Mostly gentlemen farmers.

therefore can be expected to be overrepresented in this distribution. Merchants and shopkeepers, for example, are easy to identify because they advertised in the newspapers. Laborers are almost impossible to identify. A comparison of Newport's and Providence's occupational distributions with those of Boston and Philadelphia illustrates this problem (table C–3). The Boston and Philadelphia distributions are based on more complete lists of occupations; the principal difference between these cities and the Rhode Island towns is the much smaller percentage of people engaged in retail occupations and larger percentage of laborers. However, because all of these occupational distributions are based on taxpayers, they undoubtedly under-estimate the numbers of common laborers and seamen. Another major occupational group that does not appear in this distribution is domestic servants. Because they lived as members of another person's household, they are almost impossible to identify.

Relationship of Wealth and Other Social Characteristics

As might be expected, there was a close association between occupation and wealth, although the relationship was by no means a rigid one. Table C–4 shows the median wealth for each of the major occupational groups. For this purpose, tax lists were divided into 10 approximately equal groups, with 1 the poorest and 10 the richest. Groups are not exactly equal because many people paid the same tax, and they were kept in the same groups.

Wealth and occupational status were also reflected in other social characteristics. Most notably, Newport's churches had fairly well-defined social characteristics.[4] Tables C–5 and C–6 compare religious denomination with occupation and wealth for Newport. The figures are based on lists of church members made by Ezra Stiles in 1763. Stiles counted 707 families as members of some church. Eliminating the people on Stiles's list who cannot be identified (mostly women and young men) reduces the total number of church members to 465, or 31 percent of the total group being considered

TABLE C–4
MEDIAN WEALTH OF OCCUPATIONAL GROUPS

OCCUPATION	NEWPORT		PROVIDENCE	
	1760	1775	1760	1775
Merchants	9	9	9	10
Shopkeepers	7	7	6	8
Artisans	4	5	6	4
Shipbuilding	4	3	*	6
Food	6	6	*	*
Clothing	5	5	*	5
Building	3	4	*	4
Metal	4	4	*	6
Leather	6	6	*	5
Other	5	6	*	5
Professionals	6	5	*	6
Inkeepers,etc.	7	7	*	8
Mariners	6	7	*	6
Farmers	9	10	*	*

SOURCES: Same as table C–3.
*Sample size too small for meaningful figures.

here. The distribution of people belonging to the different churches is shown at the bottom of table C–5. This distribution is somewhat misleading, since Stiles listed only church members; presumably substantial numbers of people attended churches without being members. This would have been particularly true of the Congregational and Baptist churches, which had restrictive standards for membership, and less true of the Anglican church, which did not. It seems likely, therefore, that the proportion of residents belonging to the Anglican church is overstated in comparison with the others.[5]

Comparing tables C–5 and C–6 shows that the relationship between religion and occupation was somewhat stronger than the relationship between religion and wealth. Nevertheless, the two variables, occupation and wealth,

TABLE C–5
COMPARISON OF OCCUPATION AND RELIGION
(Newport only)

OCCUPATION	CONGREGATIONAL	BAPTIST	QUAKER	ANGLICAN	JEWISH	TOTAL
Merchants	29 (19%)	13 (7%)	16 (11%)	74 (49%)	20 (13%)	152
Retailers	9 (32%)	8 (32%)	3 (12%)	4 (16%)	2 (8%)	25
Artisans	48 (43%)	33 (30%)	24 (21%)	7 (6%)	0	112
Mariners	8 (17%)	10 (21%)	6 (13%)	23 (49%)	0	47
Farmers	0	2 (15%)	10 (77%)	1 (8%)	0	13
Misc.	2 (18%)	5 (46%)	3 (27%)	1 (9%)	0	11
Unknown occ.	32 (30%)	28 (27%)	18 (17%)	25 (24%)	2 (2%)	105
Total, all occ.	127 (27%)	99 (21%)	80 (17%)	135 (29%)	24 (5%)	465
All families	228	190	105	169	15*	707

SOURCES: Data on religion from Franklin B. Dexter, ed., *Extracts from the itineraries and Miscellanies of Ezra Stiles* (New Haven, Yale University Press, 1916), pp. 12–17.
*Smaller than the figures above because of immigration of Jews to Newport after Stiles made his list.

TABLE C–6
COMPARISON OF WEALTH AND RELIGION
(Newport only)

TAX GROUP (1760)	CONGREGATIONAL	BAPTIST	QUAKER	ANGLICAN	JEWISH	TOTAL
1–2	21 (53%)	9 (23%)	7 (18%)	1 (3%)	2 (5%)	40
3–4	20 (37%)	18 (33%)	11 (20%)	4 (7%)	1 (2%)	54
5–6	29 (34%)	21 (24%)	11 (13%)	24 (28%)	1 (1%)	86
7–8	22 (23%)	22 (23%)	20 (21%)	28 (30%)	2 (2%)	94
9–10	21 (15%)	18 (13%)	27 (20%)	61 (45%)	9 (7%)	136
Unknown	14 (26%)	11 (20%)	4 (7%)	17 (31%)	9 (16%)	55
Total	127 (27 %)	99 (21%)	80 (17%)	135 (29%)	24 (5%)	465
Median tax group	6	6	7	9	9	

SOURCES: Same as table C–4.
NOTE: Tax groups are listed from lowest to highest.

cannot be separated. Half of all merchants were Anglicans, but within this group, the wealthier merchants were more likely to be Anglicans than the less wealthy ones (table C–7). In all wealth groups, more merchants belonged to the Church of England than to any other church, but the higher the wealth bracket, the higher the percentage of Anglicans as well. The proportions of Quakers also increased, while the proportions of Congregationalists and Baptists declined. There was, on the other hand, no clear relationship between wealth and religion among artisans; they were overwhelmingly Congregationalists and Baptists, regardless of degree of wealth.

Wealth also affected family size. Households (which included servants and slaves as well as family members) were large in Newport and Providence, with a mean size of seven persons (table C–8). The general effect of wealth on household size can be seen immediately by comparing this figure, which includes taxpayers only, with the mean size for all households recorded on the 1774 census: 6.6 in Providence and 5.8 in Newport. The substantial group of nontaxpayers discussed earlier had much smaller households; in Newport, their numbers were far greater than in Providence, thus making a larger difference between mean household size for the entire population and for taxpayers. (Mean household size for nontaxpayers in 1774 was 4.0 in Newport, 5.0 in Providence.) As table C–9 shows, average household size increased as wealth increased. At each wealth level except the highest, Providence households averaged somewhat larger than those in Newport; the smaller size of wealthy households in Providence can be accounted for by the higher level of slave ownership in Newport. Slavery was

TABLE C–7
COMPARISON OF WEALTH AND RELIGION
AMONG MERCHANTS AND ARTISANS (NEWPORT)

TAX GROUP (1760)	CONG.	BAPTIST	QUAKER	ANGLICAN	JEWISH	TOTAL
I. Merchants						
1–2	0	0	0	0	2	2
3–4	0	0	0	0	1	1
5–6	4	1	0	5	1	11
7–8	9 (32%)	4 (14%)	2 (7%)	12 (43%)	1 (4%)	28
9	7 (23%)	2 (7%)	3 (10%)	17 (57%)	1 (3%)	30
10	2 (4%)	3 (6%)	10 (20%)	28 (56%)	7 (14%)	50
II. Artisans						
1–2	11	6	4	0	0	21
3–4	8	9	3	0	0	20
5–6	14	10	7	3	0	34
7–8	9	3	6	2	0	20
9–10	2	4	3	1	0	10

SOURCES: Same as table C–4.

TABLE C–8
HOUSEHOLD SIZE

SIZE OF HOUSEHOLD	PERCENTAGE OF HOUSEHOLDS	
	Newport	*Providence*
1–2	5.4	4.3
3–4	21.3	21.5
5–6	23.6	24.3
7–8	20.0	19.9
9–10	15.2	13.5
11–15	12.5	15.3
Over 15	1.9	1.2
N	875	462
Mean household size	7.0	7.1
Mean size for all households on 1774 census	5.8	6.6
Mean size for nontaxpayers on 1774 census	4.0	5.0

SOURCES: Same as table C–1.

TABLE C–9
EFFECT OF WEALTH AND OCCUPATION ON HOUSEHOLD SIZE

	NEWPORT	PROVIDENCE
Wealth Group	Mean HH Size	Mean HH Size
1–2	5.0	5.3
3–4	5.8	6.2
5–6	6.5	6.7
7–8	7.3	7.4
9–10	10.2	9.2
N	775	442

SOURCE: Same as table C–1.

much more common in Newport than in Providence (see population figures in Appendix A); 42 percent of Newport taxpayers owned at least one slave, compared with only 25 percent in Providence (table C–10). Slaveholding also helps to explain the sizable gap in average household size between the richest group and all others, since the wealthiest individuals owned the majority of slaves (table C–11).

Social Characteristics of Political Officials

Tables C–12 and C–13 outline the wealth and occupations of the towns' political officials. Political offices were divided into three categories: major town offices, including town councilmen, clerks, and treasurers; minor town offices, including all other elected positions, plus justices of the county Inferior Courts; and colony offices.[6] Comparing wealth and the holding of office reveals a hierarchy of political positions; colony officials were the wealthiest, on the average, followed by major town officials. Minor town

TABLE C–10
DISTRIBUTION OF SLAVE OWNERSHIP

NO. OF SLAVES OWNED	PERCENTAGE OF HOUSEHOLDS	
	Newport	Providence
None	58.1	74.8
One	19.2	10.7
2–3	13.4	10.4
4–5	5.6	2.4
6–10	3.1	1.7
Over 10	0.4	—
N	875	462

SOURCES: Same as table C–1.

TABLE C–11
EFFECT OF WEALTH AND OCCUPATION ON SLAVE OWNERSHIP

	NEWPORT	PROVIDENCE
Wealth Group	Mean No. Slaves Owned	Mean No. Slaves Owned
1–2	0.2	0.3
3–4	0.1	0.2
5–6	0.4	0.4
7–8	1.4	0.8
9–10	3.5	1.6
N	875	462

SOURCE: Same as table C–1.

TABLE C–12
WEALTH OF POLITICAL OFFICIALS

AVERAGE WEALTH	MAJOR TOWN	COLONY	MINOR TOWN
I. Newport			
1–2	2 (6%)	1	26 (15%)
3–4	3 (8%)	0	26 (15%)
5–6	5 (14%)	1	38 (23%)
7–8	11 (31%)	8 (33%)	41 (24%)
9–10	15 (42%)	15 (63%)	37 (22%)
Total	36	24	168
II. Providence			
1–2	3 (11%)	0	29 (15%)
3–4	1	1	16 (8%)
5–6	0	6 (16%)	38 (20%)
7–8	4 (14%)	1	29 (15%)
9–10	20 (71%)	30 (79%)	78 (41%)
Total	28	38	190

SOURCE: Newport Town Meeting Records, Newport Historical Society; Providence Town Meeting Records, Providence City Hall.

officials were relatively evenly distributed among the different wealth groups. Providence officials in all categories, however, were wealthier than their counterparts in Newport (table C–13). Merchants predominated among colony and major town officials. Minor officials were drawn heavily from the ranks of artisans, although merchants were also frequently elected to these positions. Again, in Providence, minor officials tended to be men of higher status than in Newport.

TABLE C–13
OCCUPATIONS OF POLITICAL OFFICIALS

OCCUPATION	MAJOR TOWN	COLONY	MINOR TOWN
I. Newport			
Merchant*	11 (44%)	16 (80%)	31 (28%)
Shopkeepers	4	2	8
Mariners	1	0	8
Distillers	1	0	7
Artisans	6	2	53 (47%)
Schoolmaster	1	0	0
Farmers	1	0	5
Unknown	11	4	56
Total	36	24	168
II. Providence			
Merchant*	9 (47%)	19 (63%)	34 (29%)
Shopkeepers	4	3	19 (16%)
Mariners	0	1	5
Distillers	1	0	5
Artisans	5	7	43 (36%)
Farmers	0	0	2
Others	0	0	2
Unknown	9	8	80
Total	28	38	190

SOURCES: Same as table C–12.
*Includes some manufacturers and professionals.

Appendix D: Poor Relief

THE TOWN COUNCILS OF NEWPORT AND PROVIDENCE, among their other functions, regulated and provided for the towns' poor. By the eighteenth century, the towns were electing overseers of the poor, but they were frequently the same men as the Town councilmen and, in any case, their task was to carry out the orders of the Town Council rather than set policies themselves. The Councils dealt with both the resident poor and the transient poor. For the former, the records generally include only brief notations concerning the individuals—their names, the means of supporting them, and where applicable, the person providing for them. Occasionally descriptive words give a clue to the person's situation, indicating, for example, a widow, or a sick, elderly, or handicapped person. Tables D–1 through D–3

TABLE D–1
NEWPORT POOR RELIEF: METHODS OF SUPPORT

Years	Direct payment	Board in family	Provide necessities*	Relatives to support	Alms house	Apprenticeship (children)
1706–21	1	19	3			3
1721–30	2	15	6		7	15
1731–40	0	10	2		2	2
1741–50	3	69	28		1	37
1751–60	0	118	19	13	0	28
1761–70	1	43	6	19	0	18
1771–80	0	1			10	7
1781–90	32	41	14			1
1791–1800	31	4	3			
Total	70	320	81	32	20	111

SOURCES: Newport Town Council Records, Newport Historical Society.
*Includes providing firewood, clothing, paying rent, etc.

133

TABLE D–2
PROVIDENCE POOR RELIEF: METHODS OF SUPPORT

Years	Sell property	Direct payment	Board in family	Provide necessities	Bind out as servant	Work house	Apprenticeship
1716–20			10	1			
1721–30	1		12	1			7
1731–40			16	2	1		2
1741–50			22				10
1751–60		1	3				29
1761–70	2		1		1	4	11
1771–80			3			2	19
1781–90			3			3	14
1791–1800			2		1	18	23

SOURCES: Providence Town Council Records, Providence City Hall.

TABLE D–3
CHARACTERISTICS OF THE RESIDENT POOR, 1700–1780

TYPE OF PERSON	NEWPORT	PROVIDENCE
Woman	94	13
Widow	13	5
Woman with child	8	4
Man	52	9
Child	165	84
Black/Indian	8	6
Old	11	0
Sick or handicapped	18	4
Total males	52	9
Total females	115	22
Total children	165	84
Total no. individuals*	391	133

SOURCES: Same as tables D–1 and D–2.
*Some individuals were counted twice in the breakdowns; e.g., a black woman or an old man.

include information on the methods of supporting the resident poor and the characteristics of individuals receiving support.

The transient poor were generally simply ordered to leave town, although sometimes they were permitted to stay if they, or someone else, posted bond to indemnify the town from charges for their support in the future. In order to send transients away, however, it was necessary to determine their legal residence; to do this, individuals suspected of being nonresidents were questioned by the Town Council. Detailed records of these examinations exist for Providence (but not for Newport), making it possible to compile detailed statistics on that city's transient poor. Information on the sex, race, age, marital status, and birthplace of these individuals is given in tables D–4 through D–8. In Newport's records however, only the sex of the transients is given; this is included in table D–4.

TABLE D-4
SEX OF TRANSIENT POOR, NEWPORT AND PROVIDENCE

Years	NEWPORT		PROVIDENCE	
	Male	Female	Male	Female
1681–90			6	5
1691–1700			9	9
1701–10			0	0
1711–20	29	6	2	4
1721–30	62	16	5	5
1731–40	13	2	54	10
1741–50	49	27	41	16
1751–60	32	25	30	29
1761–70	15	14	34	28
1771–80	3	0	62	46
1781–90	89	36	101	96
1791–1800	34	17	100	133
Total	203	90	444	381

SOURCES: Same as tables D–1, D–2.

TABLE D-5
RACE OF TRANSIENTS, PROVIDENCE

Years*	White	Black
1731–40	63	1
1741–50	55	3
1751–60	57	2
1761–70	53	10
1771–80	93	15
1781–90	154	43
1791–1800	164	69

SOURCES: Same as table D-2.
*All transients examined before 1731 were white.

TABLE D-6
MARITAL STATUS OF TRANSIENTS
(N = 696)

YEARS	SINGLE		MARRIED		SEPARATED/ WIDOWED		SINGLE W/CH/ COHABITING	
	N	%	N	%	N	%	N	%
1680–1720	12	41	4	14	1	3	12	41
1721–30	4	44	4	44	0		1	11
1731–40	24	55	17	39	2	5	1	2
1741–50	24	47	23	45	3	6	1	2
1751–60	16	36	21	48	4	9	3	7
1761–70	19	46	14	34	5	12	3	7
1771–80	32	33	44	45	11	11	10	10
1781–90	57	30	99	53	20	11	12	6
1791–1800	70	35	93	47	15	8	20	10

TABLE D–6 (*continued*)
MARITAL STATUS OF TRANSIENTS
(N = 696)

YEARS	SINGLE		MARRIED		SEPARATED/ WIDOWED		SINGLE W/CH/ COHABITING	
	N	%	N	%	N	%	N	%
Total: men	111	30	235	64	8	2	10	3
Total: women	142	43	84	25	53	16	53	16
Grand total	253	37	319	46	61	9	63	9

SOURCE: Same as table D–2.

TABLE D–7
AGE DISTRIBUTION OF TRANSIENTS
(TOTAL N = 206)

AGE GROUP	AGE AT TIME OF EXAM						AGE AT FIRST MOVE					
	Men		Women		Total		Men		Women		Total	
	N	%	N	%	N	%	N	%	N	%	N	%
0–9	2	3	4	3	6	3	32	20	51	35	83	27
10–19	2	3	22	18	24	12	54	34	52	36	106	35
20–29	23	29	73	58	96	47	50	32	27	19	77	25
30–39	29	36	16	13	45	23	21	13	13	9	34	11
40–49	12	15	4	3	16	8	1	1	1	1	2	1
50–59	5	6	3	2	8	4	0		0		0	
60+	7	9	4	3	11	5	0		0		0	

SOURCE: Same as table D–2.

TABLE D–8
BIRTHPLACE AND LAST RESIDENCE OF PROVIDENCE TRANSIENTS

	BIRTHPLACE		LAST RESIDENCE	
	N	%	N	%
Contiguous towns	74	11.6	63	14.3
10-mi radius	99	15.5	67	15.2
20-mi radius	97	15.2	49	11.1
30-mi radius	122	19.2	89	20.2
40-mi radius	27	4.3	11	2.5
50-mi radius	18	2.9	12	2.7
Boston	39	6.1	53	12.0
Other N. Eng.	39	6.1	21	4.7
Other colonies*	33	5.2	25	5.7
Foreign**	87	13.7	1	.2
At sea	1	.2	14	3.2
In army			24	5.4
"Wandering around"			12	2.7
TOTAL	636	100.0	44	99.9

SOURCE: Same as table D–2.
*Includes Canada and West Indies.
**Includes Africa.

Notes

Chapter 1

1. The best summary of early Rhode Island settlement is in Sydney V. James, *Colonial Rhode Island: A History* (New York: Scribners, 1975), chaps. 2–4.

2. Carl Bridenbaugh makes this argument in *Fat Mutton and Liberty of Conscience* (Providence: Brown University Press, 1974); James also discusses the commercial aspirations of the first Portsmouth and Newport residents, *Colonial Rhode Island*, pp. 25–26.

3. Roger Williams to John Winthrop, Dec. 30, 1638, *Letters and Papers of Roger Williams, 1629–1682*, photostat, Massachusetts Historical Society, Boston; *The Letter Book of Peleg Sanford of Newport, Merchant, 1666–1668* (Providence: Rhode Island Historical Society, 1928).

4. See, for example, Kenneth Lockridge, *A New England Town: The First Hundred Years* (New York: Norton, 1970); Philip Greven, *Four Generations: Land, Population, and Family in Colonial Andover, Massachusetts* (Ithaca, N.Y.: Cornell University Press, 1970); John Demos, *A Little Commonwealth: Family Life in Plymouth Colony* (New York: Oxford University Press, 1970); Robert Gross, *The Minutemen and Their World* (New York: Hill and Wang, 1976); Timothy H. Breen, "Persistent Localism: English Social Change and the Shaping of New England Institutions," *William and Mary Quarterly* 32 (1975), pp. 3–28; Breen, "Transfer of Culture: Chance and Design in Shaping Massachusetts Bay, 1630–1660," *New England Historical and Genealogical Society Register* 132 (1978), pp. 3–17; John Waters, "The Traditional World of New England Peasants: A View from Seventh Century Barnstable," *New England Historical and Genealogical Society Register* 130 (1976), pp. 3–21; and James Henretta, "Families and Farms: *Mentalite* in Pre-Industrial America," *William and Mary Quarterly* 35 (1978), pp. 3–32.

5. Bruce C. Daniels, "Emerging Urbanism and Increasing Social Stratification in the Era of the American Revolution," in *The American Revolution: The Home Front*, ed. John Ferling (Carollton, Ga., 1976), p. 17.

6. Gary B. Nash, *The Urban Crucible: Social Change, Political Consciousness, and the Origins of the American Revolution* (Cambridge, Mass.: Harvard University Press, 1979), p. vii.

7. Joseph A. Ernst and H. Roy Merrens note that, in the South, isolated country storekeepers served "urban" functions: "'Camden's Turrets Pierce the Skies!' The Urban Process in the Southern Colonies during the Eighteenth Century," *William and Mary Quarterly* 30 (1973), pp. 549–74.

8. Ibid.; Jacob Price, "Economic Function and the Growth of American Port Towns in the Eighteenth Century," *Perspectives in American History 8,* (1974), pp. 123–86. For a variation on the theory of hierarchical urban development, see Carville Earle and Ronald Hoffman, "Urban Development in the Eighteenth Century South," *Perspectives in American History* 10 (1976), pp. 7–78. They demonstrate that southern urbanization was closely tied to the specific commodities exported in each subregion—e.g., wheat, because of its marketing problems, generated more urbanization than tobacco. Edward M. Cook, Jr., outlines a five-part typology that is not explicitly hierarchical and is based on political rather than economic criteria, but his definitions of the five types include economic function: *Fathers of the Towns: Leadership and Community Structure in Eighteenth Century New England* (Baltimore: Johns Hopkins University Press, 1976), pp. 165–83. Stephanie Wolf uses the anthropological concept of a rural-to-urban continuum rather than discrete types of towns, in *Urban Village: Population, Community, and Family Structure in Germantown, Pennsylvania, 1683–1800* (Princeton: Princeton University Press, 1976), pp. 17–21.

9. Bruce Daniels, *The Connecticut Town: Growth and Development, 1635–1790* (Middletown, Conn.: Wesleyan University Press, 1979), pp. 145–7; James T. Lemon, *The Best Poor Man's Country: A Geographical Study of Early Southeastern Pennsylvania* (Baltimore: Johns Hopkins University Press, 1942), pp. 118–49. Lemon describes five orders of towns, with Philadelphia at the top, and finds that towns of each order were arranged spatially so they would not compete economically with other towns of the same order. The pattern was not perfect, however, because the growth of all towns within 30 miles of Philadelphia was stunted. Philadelphia, in other words, served not only specialized functions for the entire region, but also local functions for its immediate area. The presence of so important a city inhibited the growth of nearby secondary centers. Daniels defines only three orders, rather than five. Connecticut towns fit the theory because there was no single, dominant city (apparently because there was no obvious location for one.) No Connecticut town fulfilled all the functions of a Philadelphia, however; merchants in that colony's seaports relied on Newport and New York. Such "unpredictable" considerations limit the usefulness of central-place theory for historical analysis of urban development. If New England is treated as a single region, the theory fits far less well.

10. This point is discussed more fully in chapter 2.

11. For example, Welcome Arnold launched his mercantile career by developing extensive contact with country storekeepers in northern Rhode Island and southern Massachusetts. See chapter 3.

12. Daniels, "Emerging Urbanism," p. 19.

13. These issues are treated in greater detail in chapter 3.

14. This point is discussed more fully in chapter 4.

15. Cook, *Fathers of the Towns,* pp. 23–62, 173–76. He uses such indicators as average number of years in office and percentage of adult males holding office as criteria for classifying towns. He also shows that men from commercial towns were most likely to dominate colony-level office.

16. John H. Cady, *The Civic and Architectural Development of Providence,*

1636–1950 (Providence: The Book Shop, 1957), p. 19: Antoinette Downing and Vincent Scully, *The Architectural Heritage of Newport, Rhode Island, 1640–1915* (Cambridge, Mass.: Harvard University Press, 1952), pp. 13–14. Newport's early settlement was somewhat more irregular, but clustered around the harbor.

17. Bridenbaugh discusses such urban problems as streets, lighting, fire, and water supply in *Cities in Revolt: Urban Life in America, 1740–1776* (New York: Knopf, 1955), pp. 98–133, 292–331.

18. Act dividing Providence, February 1730/1, *Acts and Laws of His Majesty's Colony of Rhode-Island, and Providence-Plantations, In America* (Newport, 1730), pp. 222–34 (hereafter cited as *Laws 1730*). Act incorporating Cranston, 1754, and Act incorporating Johnston, 1759, *Acts and Laws of the English Colony of Rhode-Island and Providence-Plantations, in New England, in America* (Newport, 1767), pp. 257, 259 (hereafter cited as *Laws 1767*).

19. Providence town meetings, August, Sept. 7, and Nov. 26, 1765, *Town Meeting Records* (Providence: City Hall); Petition of Providence to General Assembly, Sept. 1765, *Providence Town Papers*, vol. 2, Rhode Island Historical Society (hereafter cited as RIHS); Petition to divide Providence, Feb. 25, Petitions, vol. 12, p. 2 (Providence: Rhode Island State Archives), p. 765. Act incorporating North Providence, 1765, *Laws 1767*, p. 260. Petition to divide Newport, June 1742, Petitions, vol. 4; and June 1743, vol. 5. Act incorporating Middletown, 1743, *Laws 1767*, pp. 254–5.

20. Newport had 1,158 persons per square mile in 1774; Providence, approximately 617 (based on an estimate of Providence's area in that year). John H. Cady, *Rhode Island Boundaries, 1636–1936* (Providence: Rhode Island Tercentenary Commission, 1936); John H. Bartlett, *Census of the Inhabitants of the Colony of Rhode Island and Providence Plantations in New England, 1774* (Providence: Knowles, Anthony & Co., 1858).

21. Henry R. Chace, *Maps of Providence, Rhode Island, 1650–1765–1770* (Providence, 1914) and *Owners and Occupants of the Lots, Houses and Shops in the Town of Providence, Rhode Island, in 1798* (Providence, 1914). Moses Brown had a 300-acre farm within the town limits; other merchants and tradesmen who owned farms included Knight Dexter and Amos Atwell.

22. These issues are discussed in detail in chapter 4.

23. This point is discussed more fully in chapter 3.

24. See chapter 3.

Chapter 2

1. Howard M. Chapin, *Documentary History of Rhode Island*, vol. 1 (Providence, 1916), pp. 25–26, 78–80; Sydney V. James, *Colonial Rhode Island: A History* (New York, 1975), pp. 25–26; Bernard Bailyn, *The New England Merchants in the Seventeenth Century* (Cambridge, Mass.: Harvard University Press, 1955), pp. 39–41.

2. Carl Bridenbaugh, *Fat Mutton and Liberty of Conscience: Society in Rhode Island, 1636–1690* (Providence: Brown University Press, 1974), pp. 12–17, 21–22; Jacob Price, "Economic Function and the Growth of American Port Towns in the Eighteenth Century," *Perspectives in American History* 8 (1974), pp. 149–51.

3. Chapin, *Documentary History*, vol. 1, 36–37, 110–13; James, *Colonial Rhode Island*, 54–55; Roger Williams to John Winthrop, n.d. (1636 or 1637), *The Com-*

plete Writings of Roger Williams (New York, Russell & Russell, 1963), vol. 5, pp. 4–6.

4. Chapin, *Documentary History,* vol. 1, 78–80; Henry C. Dorr, "The Proprietors of Providence, and Their Controversies with the Freeholders," Rhode Island Historical Society *Collections,* 9 (1897), pp. 19, 32–33, 85–94; James, *Colonial Rhode Island,* 78–80, 88–91, 102–04; Irving Richman, "Introduction" to "Harris Papers," Rhode Island Historical Society *Collections,* vol. 10 (1902); Roger Williams to Town of Providence, August 1654, *Writings of Roger Williams,* vol. 6, 262–66.

5. See below, pp. 31–32.

6. For detailed population figures and sources, see Appendix A.

7. The surrounding towns were Portsmouth, Jamestown, and Kingstown.

8. The rate of increase in Rhode Island's population was 6.2% per year from 1708 to 1730, dropping to 5.2% per year between 1730 and 1748, and to 3.4% between 1748 and 1755. Newport's rate of growth declined from 5.1% per year between 1708 and 1730, to 3.1% in the period 1730–48, and to 0.6% from 1748 to 1755. Providence's rate declined from 7.8% (1708–30) to 3.4% (1730–48), but then increased to 5.3% between 1748 and 1755.

9. See Appendix B for an explanation of the two towns' relative shares of total shipping. Jay Coughtry argues that Providence had a somewhat lower share of the colony's trade, in *The Notorious Triangle: Rhode Island and the African Slave Trade, 1700–1807* (Philadelphia: Temple University Press, 1981), p. 36.

10. Roger Williams to John Winthrop, Dec. 30, 1638, *Letters and Papers of Roger Williams, 1629–1682,* photostat, Massachusetts Historical Society (hereafter cited as MHS).

11. Answer of Rhode Island to the inquiries of the Board of Trade, May 8, 1680, reprinted in Bruce M. Bigelow, "The Commerce of Rhode Island with the West Indies, Before the American Revolution" (Ph.D. diss., Brown University, 1930), pt. 2, Appendix 1, n.p.

12. Bridenbaugh, *Fat Mutton,* 70–71, 93; Ibid., pt. 1, ch. 3, 3–4; *The Letter Book of Peleg Sanford of Newport, Merchant, 1666–1668* (Providence: Rhode Island Historical Society, 1928); Bruce M. Bigelow, ed., "The Walter Newbury Shipping Book," Rhode Island Historical Society *Collections,* vol. 24 (1931), pp. 73–91.

13. William Coddington to John Winthrop, June 12, 1643; to Winthrop, Jr., April 20, 1647; Sept. 31, 1648; and Oct. 14, 1648, Massachusetts Historical Society *Collections,* ser. 4, vol. 6 (1863), pp. 319–21; vol. 7 (1865), pp. 279–80. Robert Williams to Winthrop, April 18, 1647, ser. 5, vol. 1 (1871), p. 343; John Coggeshall to Winthrop, May 24, 1647, pp. 345–46; Bridenbaugh, *Fat Mutton,* pp. 16–20.

14. Peleg Sanford to William Pate, Dec. 7, 1666; Dec. 3, 1667; and Jan. 10, 1667/8 *Sanford Letter Book,* pp. 14–16, 37–38, 45–46. Sanford voiced his complaints about the London business to Pate in an undated letter, pp. 46–47, and Dec. 22, 1668, pp. 47–48; also in a letter to William Sanford, Dec. 28, 1668, pp. 69–71.

15. Bigelow, ed., "Walter Newbury Shipping Book."

16. Some of them, including Abraham Redwood and William Wanton, were involved with Richardson in occasional European voyages. Richardson to Thomas Bond, May 1, 1713, and June 22, 1716, *Thomas Richardson Letter Books, 1710–15,* and *1715–19,* Newport Historical Society (hereafter cited as NHS).

17. Bigelow, "Commerce of Rhode Island," pt. 1, chap. 5, pp. 13, 17–18, 20–21, 26–27.

18. Samuel Cranston to Board of Trade, Dec. 5, 1708, in John Bartlett, ed., Records of the Colony of Rhode Island and Providence Plantations in New England (Providence, 1859), (hereafter cited as RCRI), vol. 4, pp. 55–60.

19. Customs House lists in *Boston Gazette*. See Appendix B for complete shipping statistics. The first year for which these statistics are available is 1720. The undeveloped state of shipping in Providence and other Rhode Island towns in 1720 makes it safe to assume that the destination of most of these ships was Newport. The lack of statistics on shipping before 1720 makes it impossible to discuss growth of shipping before 1720 precisely, but Sanford and Cranston's reports suggest a much lower volume of shipping in the earlier years. Estimates of two writers suggest that trade at least doubled between 1700 and 1720. Bigelow, "Commerce of RI," pt. 1, chap. 4, p. 4; Sheila Skemp, "A Social and Cultural History of Newport, 1740–1765" (PhD. diss., University of Iowa, Iowa City, 1974), p. 51.

20. Skemp, "History of Newport," pp. 55–65; James B. Hedges, *The Browns of Providence Plantations,* vol. 1 (Cambridge, Mass.: Harvard University Press, 1952), p. 47. For a discussion of the effects of the war on the economies of Boston, New York, and Philadelphia, see Gary B. Nash, *The Urban Crucible: Social Change, Political Consciousness, and the Origins of the American Revolution* (Cambridge, Mass: Harvard University Press, 1979), pp. 55–75. He argues that war contributed to these cities' economic growth, but with the ultimate cost of reducing opportunities for people in the lower strata of society. In Boston, especially, these years marked the beginning of serious wealth stratification, with a few men amassing great fortunes and the large number living perpetually at the poverty level.

21. Coughtry, in *Notorious Triangle,* demonstrates that Rhode Island dominated the American slave trade and that it constituted a major part of Newport's economy; although the slaving voyages were few, compared to Newport's total trade, they were a major source of cash for purchasing European goods. Elaine Crane, in "'The First Wheel of Commerce': Newport, Rhode Island, and the Slave Trade 1760–1776," *Slavery and Abolition,* vol. 1 (1980), makes a similar argument. She and Coughtry counter an earlier argument that the slave trade was not an important part of Rhode Island's trade: Gilman M. Ostrander, in "The Making of the Triangular Trade Myth," *William and Mary Quarterly* 30 (1973), pp. 635–44, and "The Colonial Molasses Trade," *Agricultural History* 30 (1956), pp. 77–84, notes that more Rhode Island rum was shipped to other colonies than to Africa, and that no more than one-half the molasses imported from the West Indies was used for rum. These statistics, however, do not deny that the African trade, limited though it was in comparison with other branches of trade, was important to Rhode Island's overall economy. Virginia Platt argues that slave trading was not a major concern for Aaron Lopez, and that most of his slaving voyages were unprofitable; nevertheless, she points out that these voyages were important sources of immediate cash for remittances to England, and in that sense played a significant role in his total trade. "'And Don't Forget the Guinea Voyage': The Slave Trade of Aaron Lopez of Newport," *William and Mary Quarterly* 32 (1975), pp. 601–18. It should also be noted that Lopez was less involved in the slave trade than some other major Newport merchants.

22. Richardson to William Donne, June 2, and July 1, 1712; James Gilbert, Zebediah Wyatt, and Samuel Arnold, June 4, 1712; Thomas Partridge, Richard Champion, and Moses Austell, July 5, 1712; Moses Austell, Nov. 28, 1712; and several other letters at about the same time discussing his move to Rhode Island; to Thomas Bond, May 1, June 19, and July 13, 1713; Thomas Busby, July 13, 1713; Samuel Arnold, Robert Pike, Moses Austell and Thomas Bond, May 7, 1716;

Webb & Coleman, June 4, 1716; Thomas Richardson Letter Books, 1710–15 and 1715–19, NHS.

23. Richardson to Nathaniel Starbuck, Jr., March 8, 1715/6; Richard Partridge, Oct. 5, 1715, and May 5, 1716, ibid., 1715–19.

24. Richardson to Moses Austell, Jan. 1, 1712/3; Samuel Bayard, July 8, 1713; Richard Partridge and William Wilkinson, Oct. 18, 1716. The letter to Austell, written before Richardson left Boston, also reported that he planned to get into the baking trade and the fishing business, ibid., 1710–15.

25. According to him, Rhode Island ships were as good as any made in New England, but he nevertheless got into trouble with one of his London correspondents for whom he had a ship built. The English merchant complained that the ship was poorly constructed and wormeaten; the latter accusation Richardson flatly refused to believe, saying that this problem had never come up before. Richardson to William Wilkinson, n.d., 1715; to Thomas Bond, Sept. 28, 1715, ibid., 1715–19.

26. One of his London contacts was a Quaker; their correspondence covered religious as well as business affairs. Richardson to Abraham Borden, Jan. 3, 1715/6, July 13 and 28, 1716. Borden's exact relationship to Richardson was unspecified. He handled Richardson's business in Antigua. Another relative, Joseph Borden, was a ship captain working for Richardson. Letter to Samuel Arnold, Oct. 31, 1715. This letter was delivered to Arnold by William Wilkinson, another of Richardson's ship captains, and also a Quaker, ibid.

27. Richardson to John George, Nov. 7, 1715, re collecting diary products at Little Compton, ibid.

28. Richardson to Samuel Arnold, Robert Pike, Moses Austell, and Thomas Bond, May 1, 1716, ibid.

29. Bigelow, "Commerce of Rhode Island," pt. 1, chap. 5, pp. 13, 17–20, 23.

30. It is impossible to say just how much of Newport's West Indian trade after 1720 was conducted with foreign islands, since ships often officially cleared for the English island, but went instead to foreign islands. In general, however, North American trade with foreign islands became extensive enough to cause an outcry in the English islands, where planters pressured Parliament to take legislative action. The result was the Molasses Act of 1733, which levied a duty on foreign molasses, designed to discourage the foreign island trade. In Rhode Island this act simply produced an increase in smuggling. Ibid., pt. 2, chap. 3, pp. 11–12; Skemp, "History of Newport," 68–71. Price attributes much of Newport's growth to its independent government, which made evading duties easier, and to its merchants' penchant for risky, but potentially very profitable, illegal trade. "American Port Towns," 146–50.

31. Bigelow, "Commerce of Rhode Island," pt. 1, chap. 5, 13.

32. Ibid., pt. 2, 37–40; chap. 2, 1–19.

33. Ibid., pt. 2, chap. 2, 9–13. Sugar, molasses, and rum accounted for three-fourths of all products obtained from the West Indies by Rhode Island ships.

34. Ibid., pt. 2, chap. 2, 19–20; Coughtry, *Notorious Triangle,* 23–42; Hedges, *The Browns,* 20, 70–71.

35. James Shepherd and Gary Walton argue that the importance of "triangular" trade routes, and particularly the African trade, has been overstated for the American colonies as a whole, in their *Shipping, Maritime Trade, and the Economic Development of Colonial North America* (Cambridge: Cambridge University Press, 1972), pp. 49–53. Coughtry, however, in *Notorious Triangle,* makes it clear that the Afri-

can trade followed the traditional triangular route and that it figured much more significantly in Rhode Island's trade than was the case for other colonies. See especially pp. 6–7.

36. Jacob Price argues that Newport's growth before the Revolution was based primarily on "pushing the most marginal trades"; in "American Port Towns," 150.

37. *Laws and Acts of Her Majesties Colony of Rhode Island, and Providence Plantations Made from the First Settlement in 1636 to 1705*, (Providence, 1896), pp. 14, 51 (hereafter cited as *Laws 1705*); RCRI, vol. 3, p. 32; *Acts and Laws of His Majesties Colony of Rhode-Island, and Providence-Plantations in America, 1719* (Providence, 1895), p. 34 (hereafter cited as *Laws 1719*).

38. *Laws 1730*, 108, 149–50, 159–60; Newport town meeting, July 31, 1743, *Town Meeting Records*, vol. 1, NHS; *Acts and Laws of the English Colony of Rhode-Island and Providence-Plantations, in New-England, In America* (Newport, 1767) 243–44 (hereafter cited as *Laws 1767*); RCRI, vol. 4, 407–8; petition, June 1731, Petitions to the General Assembly, vol. 2, Rhode Island State Archives (hereafter cited as RISA).

39. Hedges, *The Browns*, 24–26; James, *Colonial Rhode Island*, 168–80.

40. For a detailed discussion of Cranston and his accomplishments, see James, *Colonial Rhode Island*, pp. 119–55.

41. Ibid., pp. 135–53.

42. Even before this major expansion, however, some limited modifications had been made to relieve the burden on the single colony-wide Court of Trials. By 1720, petty thefts, all thefts involving slaves, and debt cases involving less than forty shillings could be tried locally, by justices of the peace. And as early as 1663, provision was made for special courts to be called when necessary to hear cases involving merchants and sailors. The court reorganization of 1730 extended these early efforts, replacing the Court of Trials with two courts for each county, one to hear civil cases and another for criminal cases. A single appellate court heard appeals and had original jurisdiction in capital crimes. *Laws 1730*, p. 113; *Laws 1719*, pp. 101–102; *Laws 1705*, p. 14. See also Lawrence L. Lowther, "Rhode Island Colonial Government, 1732" (Ph.D. diss., University of Washington, Seattle, 1964); Patrick T. Conley, "Rhode Island Constitutional Development, 1636–1775: A Survey," *Rhode Island History* 28 (1968), pp. 49–63; 74–94; and John T. Farrell, "The Early History of Rhode Island's Court System," *Rhode Island History* 9 (1950), pp. 14–25, 65–71, 103–17.

43. In Newport County, the number of cases more than tripled in the decade between 1720 and 1730; after 1730, the case load continued to increase, but at a much slower rate. In Providence County, the number of cases was only about one-half to one-third the number for Newport County throughout the period 1730–70; but before the county courts were established, very few Providence residents bothered to use the court at all. In 1715, for example, only 10 percent of individuals involved in cases were from Providence; in 1720, 15 percent were from Providence and another 2 percent from the surrounding towns. In contrast, 84 percent of plaintiffs and defendants were from Newport and surrounding towns in 1715, and 77 percent in 1720.

44. The proportion of merchants among all litigants increased from 27 percent in 1720 to 35 percent in 1750 to 49 percent in 1770. Artisans were the second largest group, ranging from about one-fifth to one-half of total litigants during the same time period. Other occupational groups were represented in smaller numbers, with little change in their relative share of court business over this period. These figures are

based on an analysis of all cases heard by the Newport County Inferior Court in every tenth year from 1730 to 1770. The record books, located in the Newport County Court House, summarize each case, giving names, town of residence, and occupation of plaintiffs and defendants, type of action, plea, and disposition of the case. Estimates of involvement were made by comparing the number of individuals who appeared in court with population figures. The estimates are crude because of the sporadic nature of the censuses, and because not all censuses broke down population into specific age categories.

45. Interestingly, the Providence County Courts during these years involved a much more mixed group of litigants; the percentage of artisans appearing in court closely paralleled the percentage in Newport, but merchants made up only about one-fourth of litigants from 1740 to 1760, years when Newport merchants constituted one-third to one-half of all plaintiffs and defendants. By 1770, however, the proportion of merchants appearing in court jumped to almost one-half in Providence as well. The major difference between Providence and Newport was the relatively high representation of farmers in Providence courts, ranging from a high of 38 percent in 1732 to 22 percent in 1760 and 1770. The increasing commercialization of Providence was apparent in changes in the types of people who appeared in courts, as the number of farmers declined and the number of merchants rose dramatically. But throughout the period before the Revolution, the types of people who appeared in court in the two towns indicate the extent to which Providence retained the characteristics of a country town, qualities that had disappeared from Newport by the early years of the eighteenth century. This information is based on file papers of the Providence County Inferior Court, located in the basement of the Veterans Memorial Auditorium in Providence. For each of five sample years, I looked at all cases in one file, and noted the number of cases that involved Providence people and the number that did not. I also made an effort to estimate the total number of cases by quickly surveying the other boxes for each sample year. The minute books and docket books for Providence County are in the Judicial Records Center in the Providence County Court House. They have been microfilmed — badly — and as a result researchers are no longer allowed to consult the original books. These books, however, do not identify the residences of individuals appearing in court and cannot therefore be used to determine the total number of Providence cases.

46. David Lovejoy, *Rhode Island Politics and the American Revolution, 1760–1776* (Providence, 1958), p. 52.

47. There are no detailed trade statistics extant for the 1740's and 1750's. For statistics from the 1730's and a discussion of estimating trade levels in the 1740's and 50's, see Appendix B.

48. Bigelow, "Commerce of Rhode Island," pt. 1, chap. 5, pp. 23–24, 28–35, 60–62; Skemp, "History of Newport," p. 297.

49. See Appendix B, table 2.

50. Petitions of Long Wharf Proprietors to Town Meeting, Oct. 1739, box 123, folder 18A, Newport Historical Society; Minutes of Long Wharf Proprietors, 1739–1768, also NHS.

51. George C. Mason, *Annals of the Redwood Library* (Philadelphia, Evans Printing Co., 1891), pp. 2, 12–25, 31–57. The library was open to nonmembers, who could borrow books at the rate of two to five shillings a week.

52. "Newport, Rhode Island in 1730," painting in the possession of Trinity Church, Newport. Reproduced, 1975, for the Bicentennial Commission of Trinity Church.

53. Even after the final division of Providence in 1765, when North Providence split off to become a separate town, the heavily settled part of Providence remained very small, and the majority of the town's area was devoted to farms. Moses Brown owned a 300-acre farm within the town limits. Based on the census of 1774, Providence had only 617 persons per square mile, compared with 1,158 in Newport. John H. Cady, *Rhode Island Boundaries, 1636–1936* (Providence, Rhode Island Tercentenary Commission 1914), and Henry R. Chace, *Owners and Occupants of the Lots, Houses and Shops in the Town of Providence, Rhode Island, in 1798* (Providence, 1914).

54. Hedges, *The Browns*, pp. xviii, 2–8; Bigelow, "Commerce of Rhode Island," pt. 1, chap. 5, pp. 5–10.

55. Hedges, *The Browns*, pp. 8–9, 175–76.

Chapter 3

1. Remonstrance of the Colony of Rhode Island to the Lords Commissioners of Trade and Plantations, Jan. 24, 1764, John Bartlett, ed., Records of the Colony of Rhode Island and Providence Plantations in New England (Providence, Knowles, Anthony & Co. 1859), vol. 7, p. 379 (hereafter cited as RCRI).

2. Ibid., 380–81. In reality, the Rhode Islanders objected not so much to the tax as to the fact that it was to be strictly enforced.

3. Governor of Rhode Island to Lords of Trade and Plantations, Nov. 19, 1765, RCRI, vol. 6, p. 476.

4. James B. Hedges, *The Browns of Providence Plantations*, vol. 1 (Cambridge, Mass., Harvard University Press, 1952) pp. 25–26.

5. See Appendix B, table 3.

6. The four brothers, who worked together as the firm of Nicholas Brown & Co., were following the precedent of their uncle Obadiah who had traded with London in the 1750's. Obadiah, however, never became heavily involved in direct trade and dropped it altogether in 1759. At the time that his nephews reopened the trade, a few other merchants were also engaged in this trade, or preparing to become involved in it. Hedges, *The Browns*, 175–78; John Turner & Son (Amsterdam) to Nicholas Cook, June 25, 1764, Cooke Papers, vol. 1, Rhode Island Historical Society (hereafter cited as RIHS). There is little specific evidence on other merchants in Providence before the Revolution.

7. There is no way of knowing precisely how many men were involved in European trade, because papers do not survive for most of them. But at least Samuel and William Vernon, and Christopher Champlin became active in the trade, and it seems likely that there were several others as well.

8. A complete list of European correspondents of Newport merchants in this period appears in Lynne Withey, "Population Change, Economic Development, and the Revolution: Newport, RI As A Case Study" (Ph.D. diss., Univ. of Calif., Berkeley, 1976), Appendix 5, Table 1. See also Hedges, *The Browns*, 179–80. Various Newport merchants traded with at least four other London firms in this period.

9. These general problems of trade appear again and again in the letters of Newport merchants. The major collections of letters are those of Aaron Lopez, Christopher Champlin, William and Samuel Vernon, RIHS; The Wetmore Collection, Massachusetts Historical Society, most of which has been published as "The Commerce of Rhode Island," volumes 69 and 70 of the *Massachusetts Historical Society Collections* (Boston, 1914 and 1915) (hereafter cited as *MHS Coll.*). For discussions of

trade between other American cities and Europe, see Arthur L. Jensen, *The Maritime Commerce of Colonial Philadelphia* (Madison, Wis., 1963), pp. 95–97; W. T. Baxter, *The House of Hancock, Business in Boston, 1724–1775* (Cambridge, Mass., Harvard University Press, 1945), pp. 197–202; Philip L. White, *The Beekmans of New York* (New York: New York Historical Society), 288–31, 537–49; and Hedges, *The Browns*, 175–188.

10. Aaron Lopez-William Stead correspondence, 1763–73, esp. 1763–66. Aaron Lopez Papers, Newport Historical Society (hereafter cited as NHS).

11. Aaron Lopez to William Stead, Nov. 19, 1764, Lopez Papers, NHS; Lopez and Jacob R. Rivera to George Hayley, Dec. 21, 1767, Aaron Lopez Letter Book, 1767, NHS. Apparently this scheme did not work, since three years later Lopez wrote with Jacob R. Rivera to his London correspondent, George Hayley, proposing a similar plan.

12. Aaron Lopez to Gabriel Ludlow, Nov. 20, 1767; to Henry Cruger Sr., Nov. 21, 1764, Lopez Papers, box 52, NHS. Lopez-Henry Cruger Jr. correspondence, 1765–75, Lopez Papers, NHS. A few months after formally beginning trade with Henry Cruger Jr., Lopez wrote to Henry Sr. asking him in a polite way not to introduce any other potential business contacts to his son, since the Bristol trade was not sufficiently lucrative to support more than one person. Lopez to Cruger Sr., Aug. 14, 1765, Lopez Papers, box 52, NHS.

13. See Appendix B, table 5.

14. Not surprisingly, Boston was second in degree of involvement in the slave trade. Appendix B, table B-5.

15. See Appendix B, table B-4, on commodities exported. This and the information on exports which follows is from James F. Shepherd, "Commodity Exports from the British North American Colonies to Overseas Areas, 1768–1772: Magnitudes and Patterns of Trade," *Explorations in Economic History*, vol. 8 (1970), 14–49. This importance of New Bedford in supplying whale products is indicated in the correspondence between Aaron Lopez and Joseph Rotch & Son, New Bedford's leading whaling family. Lopez-Rotch & Son correspondence, 1767–69, Lopez Papers and Letter Book No. 72, NHS; Lopez-Leonard Jarvis correspondence, 1773, and Lopez-Francis Rotch correspondence, 1773, Lopez Papers, NHS. Relevant also is the Lopez-Henry Lloyd correspondence, 1756–57, Lopez Papers, NHS; 1755–56, 1768–71, Boston Merchants' Letters, Cambridge, Baker Library; 1765–67, Henry Lloyd Letter Book, Cambridge, Baker Library; Lopez-Obed Nye & Co. (Dartmouth) correspondence, 1767, Lopez Papers, NHS. Potash manufacturing is mentioned in Joseph and William Russell to Aaron Lopez, Nov. 20, 1769; April 6, 1770; June 18, 19, 22, 1770; July 11, 1770; July 16, 1770. Lopez Papers NHS. On the Boston potash trade, see Baxter, *House of Hancock*, 162–66.

16. Rhode Island and Boston were the largest importers of molasses. Richard Pares, *Yankees and Creoles: The Trade Between North America and the West Indies Before the Revolution* (Cambridge, Harvard University Press, 1956), p. 26–27.

17. Export information from Appendix B, table B-5. See, for example, Felix O'Hara to Aaron Lopez, Gaspee (Quebec), June 8, 1774, where he points out that fish served as currency there; and Aaron Lopez to Thomas Earnshey & Co., April 22, 1771, Lopez Papers, NHS. Lopez employed them to fish for cod. He supplied the ship and all equipment; they provided two fishing boats. Christopher Champlin to William Barron, Nov. 24, 1774 and to Stocker & Wharton (at Philadelphia), Nov. 25, 1774 are typical of arrangements made to pick up Pennsylvania flour for re-

export. Christopher Champlin Letter Book, 1774–81, NHS. Carl R. Woodward, *Plantation in Yankeeland* (Chester, Conn.: Pequot Press, 1971), pp. 60–63, discusses the export of Rhode Island horses.

18. Reports sent to England in 1768 listed Rhode Island manufacturing establishments, including ten forges to make iron, two furnaces to process the iron, six spermaceti candle works, twelve potash works, three rope walks, a paper mill, and twenty distilleries. Governor Josias Lyndon to Earl of Hillsborough, June 17, 1768, RCRI, vol. 6, 548. On the general development of Rhode Island manufacturing from about 1730 to 1770, see Richard Rudolph, "The Merchants of Newport, Rhode Island, 1763–1786" (Ph.D. diss., University of Connecticut, 1975), pp. 194–95; Sheila Skemp, "A Social and Cultural History of Newport 1740–1765," (Ph.D. diss., University of Iowa, 1974), pp. 308–11.

19. William Borden of Newport first petitioned for a subsidy for cloth manufacturing in 1723; his request was supported by over forty Newport merchants. In response to his petition, he was loaned £3,000 interest-free, in return for manufacturing 150 bolts of duck annually. In 1731, however, he asked for another subsidy, arguing that his was a new business and that he did not yet have enough knowledge to be able to manufacture high-quality duck cheaply. There was apparently criticism of his use of the subsidy and of the quality of his material, however, and this petition was denied. A group of prominent Newporters then tried their luck at petitioning for support to continue the business after Borden's failure. Among their justifications were the need for manufacturing to provide a medium of exchange and alleviate Rhode Island's currency problems by stemming the flow of currency out of the colony. They would also provide employment for the poor. Their petition, too was rejected. Petitions of William Borden to General Assembly, Jan. 2, 1723, Petitions, vol. 1; June 1731 and June 11, 1733, Petitions, vol. 2; Jahleel Brenton, Joseph Whipple, Henry Bull, Godfrey Malbone, Daniel Updike, and Benjamin Ellery, June 11, 1733, Petitions, vol. 2, Providence, Rhode Island State Archives (hereafter cited as RISA). Boston also experimented with linen manufacturing, motivated primarily by the need to create employment for the poor; see Gary B. Nash, *The Urban Crucible: Social Change, Political Consciousness, and the Origins of the American Revolution* (Cambridge, Mass.: Harvard Univ. Press, 1979), 189–93.

20. The earliest known candle-manufacturing operation was located in Rehoboth, Mass., in 1749. There were several Boston men involved in the business, but Rhode Island by the 1770's dominated the industry, exporting five times as many candles as Boston. Hedges, *The Browns,* 89; Pares, *Yankees and Creoles,* 25.

21. Hedges, *The Browns,* 89. Lopez's correspondence with Henry Lloyd of Boston indicates that he was manufacturing candles as early as 1755. Lopez-Lloyd letters, 1756–57, Lopez Papers, Newport Historical Society; Boston Merchants' Letters 1755–56, 1768–71, Baker Library, Harvard; and Henry Lloyd Letter Book, 1765–67, Baker Library. On the importance of New Bedford in supplying whale products, see note 15 above.

22. Jacob Rodrigues Rivera-Nicholas Brown & Co. correspondence, 1765–68; Obadiah Brown & Co. to John Brown, Oct. 8, 1761; John Collins, Jacob R. Rivera, Naphtali Hart & Co. and Aaron Lopez to Robert Cranch & Co., July 29, 1762; Nicholas Brown & Co. to the Spermaceti Manufacturers of Newport, April 5, 1763; Report of Committee . . . for United Company of Spermaceti Manufacturers, May 13, 1763; Agreements Among Spermaceti Manufacturers, to fix minimum prices, July 6, 1763; Spermaceti Manufacturers of Newport to Nicholas Brown & Co., Aug.

6, 1764; Articles of Agreement of Spermaceti Manufacturers, adopted at Newport, May 2, 1765 and May 6, 1766; all in *John Brown Papers,* Providence, John Carter Brown Library, Brown University. Indenture between Peter R. Livingston and Robert Jenkins (n.d.) in "The Commerce of Rhode Island," *MHS Coll,* vol. 69, p. 137. For a comprehensive account of the Brown family's activities in this industry, see Hedges, *The Browns,* 86–112. Despite the Association's problems, however, Hedges attributes the relative stability of this industry in the 1760's to the working of the Association.

23. Hedges, *The Browns,* 103–12.

24. Ibid., xiii, 123–54.

25. Franklin S. Coyle, "Welcome Arnold: Providence Merchant" (Ph.D. diss., Brown University, 1972). Lime, manufactured by burning limestone at high heat, was used primarily in the building trades, in making mortar and plaster, but was also used in manufacturing raw sugar and spermaceti candles. On the general importance of lime in the colonial New England economy, see Coyle, 22–26. Limestone deposits had been discovered in Smithfield—then part of Providence—in the mid-seventeenth century, and the first lime kiln was established there in 1648; Coyle, 27–28.

26. Ibid., 32.

27. Ibid., 38–43.

28. Moses Lopez petition Oct. 1753, Petitions, vol. 8, offered the usual justification for his enterprise that potash could be a source of remittances to Britain. His petition was granted by the General Assembly: RCRI, vol. 5 pp. 375–76. James Rogers petition, Feb. 1754, Petitions, vol. 8, and RCRI, vol. 5, 380. James Lucena Petition, Feb. 23, 1761, Petitions, vol. 10; RCRI, vol. 6, 267–68. His petition cited reasons similar to those of Lopez, and also argued that his enterprise would help employ the poor, a persistent theme.

29. Coyle, "Welcome Arnold", 32–35.

30. Newport marriage records show that 81% of congregationalists married other Newport residents, and 8%, residents of neighboring towns; the figures for Baptists were 91% and 7%, and for Quakers, 45% and 34%. Only 3% of Congregationalists and Quakers and fewer than 1% of Baptists chose mates from Providence and its neighboring towns. Number of cases = 397 Congregationalists (1740–75), 541 Baptists (1759–75), 292 Quakers (1700–75). Providence marriage records are scanty, and those which do exist do not list residence often enough to draw any conclusions. James N. Arnold, *Vital Records of Rhode Island 1636–1850,* vol. 7 (1895), pp. 1–40; vol. 8 (1898), pp. 412–29; *Magazine of New England History* 1 (1891), pp. 51–55, 124–28, 150–53, 243–49.

31. Hedges, *The Browns,* 157. Moses Brown, for example, corresponded with several Newport merchants, obtaining tobacco, dairy products, fish, lime, and even candles for them. In return he bought molasses, sugar, and parts for the Browns' iron furnace, among other things. Moses Brown correspondence with Thomas Robinson, 1756–57 and 1770–71; Jonathan Clarke Jr., 1758; Robert Mumford, Oct. 21, 1763; William Mumford, 1764; Benjamin Mason, 1763; and Joseph and William Wanton, 1765 and 1768, Moses Brown Papers, RIHS.

32. Samuel Nightingale correspondence with Aaron Lopez, 1767; Benjamin Mason, 1766–67; Joseph Bennet, Dec. 20, 1760. He also traded with Samuel Gibbs (Feb. 18, 1767); John Mawdsley (Feb. 13, 1767); and Francis and Jacob Pollock (April 9, June 1, and June 8, 1767). He obtained goods from Boston merchants as well. Correspondence with Lewis DeBlois, 1767; Thomas Lee, 1768; Jonathan and

John Amory, 1766–68; and Joshua Gardner, 1766–68. Nightingale-Jenckes Papers, RIHS.

33. Joseph Nightingale to Samuel Nightingale, May 27, 1767, Nightingale-Jenckes Papers, RIHS.

34. Hedges, *The Browns,* 31–36, 80–81.

35. See Appendix A for complete population figures.

36. John O. Austin, *Genealogical Directory of Rhode Island*, 2nd ed. (Baltimore: Genealogical Publishing Co., 1969) 258–61.

37. The Hopkins were descended from Thomas Hopkins, who settled in Providence by 1640; the Jenckes were descended from Joseph Jenckes, who came to Providence in the 1660's. Ibid., 324–25, 112–13.

38. They also preferred the more recently established religions—the Nightingales and Jonathan Russell were Congregationalists, and Joseph Russell was an Anglican.

39. Austin, *Genealogical Dictionary,* 402–03.

40. Ibid., 274–77.

41. Ibid., 254–55, 49, 292–95.

42. Ibid., 290–91, 18.

43. The figures are as follows: of 52 men from old families, 4 were Congregationalist, 9 Baptist, 9 Quaker, 12 Anglcian, and 19 unknown. Of other men, 13 were Congregationalists, 3 Baptists, 12 Quaker, 46 Anglican, 9 Jewish, and 20 unknown. Several of the Quakers in this latter group were descended from early North or South Kingstown families, where Quakerism was particularly strong. Another 4 were members of the Redwood family.

44. Only 21 percent of the wealthiest tenth of Newport taxpayers held any office at all, compared with 59 percent in Providence.

45. Stephen Innes, "Land Tenancy and Social Order in Springfield, Massachusetts, 1652 to 1702," *William and Mary Quarterly* 35 (1978), pp. 33–56; Bruce C. Daniels, "Family Dynasties in Connecticut's Largest Towns, 1700–1760," *Canadian Journal of History* 8 (1973), pp. 99–110, and *The Connecticut Town: Growth and Development, 1635–1790* (Middletown, Conn., 1979); Edward M. Cook, Jr., *The Fathers of the Towns: Leadership and Community Structure in Eighteenth-Century New England* (Baltimore: Johns Hopkins University Press, 1976), pp. 174–77. On political elites in New York and Philadelphia, see Eric Foner, *Tom Paine and Revolutionary America* (New York: Oxford University Press, 1976); Gary B. Nash, *Quakers and Politics: Pennsylvania, 1681–1726* (Princeton: Princeton University Press, 1968); Thomas Archdeacon, *New York City 1664–1710: Conquest and Change* (Ithaca, N.Y.: Cornell University Press, 1976); and Patricia U. Bonomi, *A Factious People: Politics and Society in Colonial New York* (New York: Columbia University Press, 1971).

46. David Lovejoy, *Rhode Island Politics and the Revolution* (Providence: Brown University Press, 1958), pp. 6–7, 11.

47. Ibid., 9–11, 20–21, 52–55, 151–53.

48. Reuben Aldrige Guild, *Early History of Brown University* (Providence: Snow & Farnham, 1897), 175–76.

49. Ibid., 187–88, 197–201; Lovejoy, *Rhode Island Politics,* 147–48.

50. Lovejoy, *Rhode Island Politics,* 148. James Manning, President of the College, himself wanted the school to be located at Providence and suggested the construction cost tactic to Moses Brown as a way of influencing the decision. Guild, *History of Brown,* 194–95.

Chapter 4

1. Gary B. Nash documents this process in detail for Boston, New York, and Philadelphia in *The Urban Crucible: Social Change, Political Consciousness, and the Origins of the American Revolution* (Cambridge, Mass.: Harvard University Press, 1979). See also Allan Kulikoff, "The Progress of Inequality in Revolutionary Boston," *William and Mary Quarterly* 28 (1971), pp. 375–412; Edward M. Cook, Jr. *The Fathers of the Towns: Leadership and Community Structure in Eighteenth Century New England* (Baltimore: Johns Hopkins University Press, 1976), pp. 165–74; and Bruce Daniels, *The Connecticut Town: Growth and Development, 1635–1790* (Middletown, Conn.: Wesleyan University Press, 1979), 165–70. More detail on the specific social characteristics of Newport and Providence's population appears in Appendix C.

2. Nash, *Urban Crucible,* 117–27, 184–87, 253–63, 395–404; and "Up from the Bottom in Franklin's Philadelphia, *Past and Present* 77 (1977), pp. 62–64.

3. Tax lists for Providence, 1705, in *Early Records of the Town of Providence,* vol. 17 (Providence, 1903), pp. 209–13; 1749–75, Rhode Island Historical Society (hereafter cited as RIHS). Tax lists for Newport, 1760, Rhode Island State Archives (hereafter cited as RISA); 1775, Newport Historical Society (hereafter cited as NHS). Tax lists are an imperfect means of measuring wealth distribution because of possible differences in the basis of assessment from one year to the next, and because they invariably underassessed the wealth of the rich. Nevertheless, they permit some analysis of the trends in wealth distribution over time, although the figures given here should be taken as a low estimate of the degree of concentration of wealth. For good discussions of the problems of measuring wealth distribution, see Gary B. Nash and James T. Lemon, "The Distribution of Wealth in Eighteenth Century America: A Century of Change in Chester County, Pennsylvania," *Journal of Social History* 2 (1968): 2–7; and Cook, *Fathers of the Towns,* 65. For figures on wealth distribution in other areas, see Bruce C. Daniels, "Long Range Trends of Wealth Distribution in Eighteenth Century New England," *Explorations in Economic History* 11 (1973–74), pp. 123–35; James Henretta, "Economic Development and Social Structure in Colonial Boston," *William and Mary Quarterly* 22 (1965), pp. 79–82; Kulikoff, "Progress of Inequality in Boston," pp. 380–82; Gary B. Nash, "Urban Wealth and Poverty in Pre-Revolutionary America," *Journal of Interdisciplinary History* 6 (1976); Nash and Lemon, "Distribution of Wealth in Eighteenth Century America," p. 11; Alice Hanson Jones, "Wealth Estimates for the New England Colonies about 1770," *Journal of Economic History* 32 (1972), pp. 98–127; Linda Auwers Bissell, "From One Generation to Another: Mobility in Seventeenth Century Windsor, Connecticut," *William and Mary Quarterly* 31 (1974), pp. 79–110; Jackson Turner Main, *The Social Structure of Revolutionary America* (Princeton: Princeton University Press, 1965), pp. 18, 20, 31, 35; Daniel Scott Smith, "Population, Family, and Society in Hingham, Massachusetts, 1636–1880," (PhD. diss., University of California, Berkeley, 1973), chap. 3; and Cook, *Fathers of the Towns,* 66–74.

4. There were two types of people affected by poor relief laws: legal residents, who were entitled to public assistance, and transients, who could be questioned by town authorities and sent back to their towns of legal residence. The latter were not necessarily in need of poor relief, but were usually laborers or servants looking for work; if there was any question of their ability to support themselves, however, town officials ordered them to leave, as a means of controlling future poor relief expenses. All colonies handled poor relief in much the same way; their laws were based on

English poor laws. See David J. Rothman, *The Discovery of the Asylum: Social Order and Disorder in the New Republic* (Boston: Little, Brown, 1971), pp. 20–25, 46–48; Gary B. Nash, "Poverty and Poor Relief in Pre-Revolutionary Philadelphia," *William and Mary Quarterly* 33 (1976), pp. 3–30; Douglas L. Jones, "The Strolling Poor: Transiency in Eighteenth Century Massachusetts," *Journal of Social History* 8 (1975), pp. 28–54; Stephen Foster, *Their Solitary Way: The Puritan Social Ethic in the First Century of Settlement in New England* (New Haven: Yale University Press, 1971), pp. 127–52.

5. Foster noted that, in the seventeenth century, people recognized only two types of poverty—those who couldn't work and those who wouldn't. Only in Boston, towards the end of the seventeenth century, was there recognition of a third group: those who couldn't find work. Foster, *Their Solitary Way,* 134–36, 144–47.

6. Transients were customarily questioned by Town Councils to determine their legal residences. The records of examination of such transients are reasonably complete for Providence, but incomplete for Newport, both because of a more haphazard system of recording the examinations, and because the Newport town records are incomplete and in very bad condition. Nevertheless, the number of transients coming to Newport gives a rough indication of the magnitude of the transient problem there, but it is necessary to keep in mind that these numbers represent a minimum and were probably considerably higher. It is also impossible to determine trends in the numbers of transients examined in Newport, because of the sporadic nature of the records. Newport Town Council Records, NHS; Providence Town Council Records, Providence City Hall.

7. See Appendix D, tables D-4–D-6.

8. Poor relief records also appear in the Town Council Records cited above, note 6. The fragmentary nature of Newport's records precludes reliable estimates of the actual number of cases, but the general trend toward an increase in poverty is unmistakable.

9. These figures do not add up to equal those in the table, because some individuals received aid in more than one decade; in addition, not everyone's identity could be determined, especially in Newport where people were sometimes identified by first or last name only.

10. See Appendix D, tables D-4 and D-7, for complete figures.

11. See Appendix C, table C-1.

12. See Rothman, *Discovery of the Asylum,* 20–25, 46–48.

13. See Appendix D, tables D-1 and D-2.

14. The Rhode Island General Assembly first authorized Town Councils to take bonds from strangers in a law passed March 1, 1662. The Providence Town Meeting instigated further discussion of this issue in November, 1680, and December, 1681. In response to Providence's requests, the General Assembly authorized Town Councils to examine all strangers and remove them bodily, if necessary. *Acts and Laws of His Majesties Colony of Rhode-Island, and Providence-Plantations in America, 1719* (Providence, 1895), p. 12 (hereafter cited as *Laws 1719*); *Early Records of the Town of Providence,* vol. 8 (Providence, 1895), pp. 86, 104; vol. 15 (1899), p. 235; John R. Bartlett, ed., *Records of the Colony of Rhode Island and Providence Plantations in New England* (Providence, 1859), vol. 3, 116–17 (hereafter cited as RCRI).

15. Law passed February 1727, *Acts and Laws of His Majesty's Colony of Rhode-Island, and Providence-Plantations, in America* (Newport, 1730), pp. 150–51; compilation of laws passed in 1727, 1741, 1748, and 1765, *Acts and Laws of the English Colony of Rhode-Island and Providence-Plantations, in New England, in*

America (Newport, 1767), 228–32 (hereafter cited as *Laws 1730* and *Laws 1767*).
16. Ibid.

17. The General Assembly passed a law May 6, 1702, ordering that residents could not "entertain" anyone from outside the colony for more than a week without giving notice to town authorities; RCRI, vol. 3, 357–59; the provision was reiterated in the 1765 settlement law cited above, note 15. The Town Council's concerns were recorded in their meetings of July 6, 1728; Jan. 14, 1758; Sept. 28, 1770; and June 18, 1773; Town Council Records, vols. 3 and 4.

18. Petition of Feb. 1729, in Petitions, vol. 2; *Laws 1730*, 214–15.

19. *Laws 1730*, 185–86. (Law passed June 1729.)

20. Laws passed 1752, 1755, and 1753, in *Laws 1767*, 17–19; 201; 197.

21. Town meeting, Aug. 29, 1758, Town Meeting Records, vol. 5. Unfortunately, the list, if actually made, does not survive.

22. Town Council meeting, Oct. 6, 1770, Town Council Records, vol. 4.

23. Town meeting, Oct. 1760, Town Meeting Records, vol. 2.

24. Case of Naomi Mumford, March 2, 1752, Newport Town Council Records, vol. 2.

25. Town Council meeting, Feb. 6, 1716/7, Newport Town Council Records, 1714–19.

26. Newport Town meeting, Aug. 1759 or 1760, Town Meeting Records, vol. 2; Court of Justices, June 21, 1736, Providence Town Papers, 2nd ser., vol. 3, p. 24, RIHS; Providence Town Council meeting, Jan. 2, 1776, Town Council Records, vol. 5; Newport Town Council meeting, Feb. 1756 and May 2, 1768, Newport Town Council Records, vol. 12 and 15.

27. This type of case usually originated in local justices' courts, and appeals were heard by the county Courts of General Sessions of the peace.

28. Rothman, *Discovery of the Asylum,* discusses the rarity of institutional poor relief before the nineteenth century, pp. 30–31, 35–36. On the beginnings of institutional poor relief in Philadelphia and Boston, see Nash, "Poverty in Pre-Revolutionary Philadelphia," and "War, Widowhood and Poverty: The Failure of Female Factory Labor in Boston" (paper presented at the Annual Meeting of the Organization of American Historians, April 1978).

29. Newport town meeting, July 31, 1723, Town Meeting Records, vol. 1; act to establish workhouse in Providence, 1753, *Laws 1767,* 8–10; petitions of Feb. 1762 and Feb. 1764, Petitions, vol. 11, pt. 1; and Sept. 1769, vol. 13, pt. 1.

30. Providence Town meeting, July 27, 1737, Town Meeting Records, vol. 4; July 4, 1750, and April 18, 1753, vol. 5.

31. Newport town meeting, April 15, 1752; n.d., [sometime in 1762]; and Oct. 13, 1770, Town Meeting Records, vol. 2.

32. Laws re workhouse, 1745 and 1765, *Laws 1767,* 197–99.

33. Providence town meeting, April 18, 1759; June 4, 1764; June 1768; June 1771; Town Meeting Records, vol. 5; Town Council meetings, Nov. 4 and Dec. 17, 1768; Sept. 30, 1773; Town Council Records, vol. 4; April 10, 1776, Town Council Records, vol 5; and Town Meeting, Aug. 27, 1776, Town Meeting Records, vol. 6; Newport town meeting, April 15, 1752, and n.d. [sometime in 1762], Town Meeting Records, vol. 2.

34. Rothman argues that eighteenth century workhouses were largely an extension of family-centered relief in *Discovery of the Asylum,* 42–43.

35. Town Meeting, January 19, 1774, Providence Town Papers, vol. 2, 82.

36. In the 1760's and 1770's, about 20 percent of transients examined were black. See Appendix D, table D-5.

37. See Appendix D, tables D-6 and D-7. Cf. A. L. Beier, "Vagrants and the Social Order in Elizabethan England," *Past and Present* 64 (1974), pp. 6–7, 12–13; and Douglas L. Jones, "Poverty and Vagabondage: The Process of Survival in Eighteenth Century Massachusetts," (Paper presented at the Annual Meeting of the Organization of American Historians, April 1978), pp. 18–19, and *Village and Seaport: Migration and Society in Eighteenth Century Massachusetts* (Hanover, N.H., University Press of New England, 1981), pp. 51–54; they found similar characteristics among transients in rural Massachusetts and England.

38. Based on 93 cases. The proportions were even lower after the Revolution—9 percent and 14 percent, respectively.

39. See Appendix D, table D-8. Beier also found that English transients traveled erratically and were generally arrested not more than 50 miles from their place of origin. "Vagrants and the Social Order," 18–19.

40. Jan. 15, 1781, Providence Town Council Records, vol. 5.

41. April 8, 1787, ibid., vol. 6.

42. Jan. 30, 1767, Providence Town Papers, vol. 2.

43. July 5, 1769, ibid.

44. Nov. 1774, Town Council Records, vol. 5.

45. July 20, 1785, ibid.

46. July 30, 1764, Providence Town Papers, vol. 2.

47. Dec. 31, 1757, Town Council Records, vol. 4; Sept. 26, 1799, vol. 7.

48. Feb. 25, 1757, ibid., vol. 4.

49. Aug. 7, 1786, ibid., vol. 5.

50. Oct. 30, 1735; Sept. 23, 1738; Oct. 10, 1738; Feb. 3 and Feb. 5, 1738/9; Town Council Records, vol. 3.

51. Petition of Christopher Stocker to Town Council, Oct. 1, 1787, Providence Town Papers, vol. 10.

52. Petition of Robert Gray to Town Council, Dec. 15, 1751, ibid., vol. 3.

53. Town clerk of Cambridge to Town Council of Cranston, Dec. 11, 1787, ibid., vol. 11.

54. April 10, 1776; Nov. 1, 1776, Town Council Records, vol. 5; State of Rhode Island to Town Sergeant of Providence and Overseers of the Poor of Rehoboth, May 18, 1778; Justices of the Peace of Rehoboth to constable of Rehoboth, May 18, 1778, Providence Town Papers, vol. 4; Providence Town Council to Rehoboth Town Council, Oct. 5, 1778, Town Council Records, vol. 5.

55. Petition of Christopher Stocker to Town Council, Oct. 1, 1787, Providence Town Papers, vol. 10.

56. For the proportion of blacks living in the northern colonies, see Lorenzo Greene, *The Negro in Colonial New England* (New York: Columbia University Press, 1942), pp. 74, 76. See Appendix A for complete figures and citations on Rhode Island blacks from colony censuses.

57. The white population increased 195 percent and the black population, 433 percent, in this period. For complete figures on the white population, see Appendix A, table A-2.

58. In Newport, 18 percent of adult males were black servants, and 9 percent white; in Providence, 9 percent were black servants and 19 percent white. Figures on white servants are estimates. For complete figures, see Appendix C, table C-2.

59. Calculated from 1774 census.

60. Jan 4, 1703/4, *Laws 1719*, 58: 1750, in *Laws 1767*, 151–53: Aug. 31, 1756, Newport Town Meeting records, vol. 2; and "An Act for the more effectual governing of Indian, Mulatto, and Negro Servants and slaves, in the Town of Newport," *Acts and Resolves,* Sept. 1770, 56.

61. Oct. 27, 1714, *Laws 1719,* 70–71; General Assembly, June 13, 1757, RCRI, 6, 64–65.

62. Feb. 1728/9, *Laws 1730,* 62–3; *Acts and Resolves,* Sept. 1770, 57–58.

63. *Newport Mercury,* January 4, 1768.

64. July 5, 1715, June 1719, and June 1729, *Laws 1730,* 78–79, 219–185.

65. Report from James Honeyman, June 13, 1743, to SPG, in Mason, *Annals of Trinity Church*; Second Congregational Church Records, 1728, pp. 122–23, and Records, 1733–1834, p. 37.

66. These figures are based on the total group, not just those runaways from Newport and Providence. This is necessary because of the small numbers involved. All examples, however, are taken from the two towns. Of the blacks, 9 were slaves, 6 were servants, and 2, indentured servants. Among mulattos, 3 were slaves, 6 servants, and 2 indentured. Indians included 1 slave, 3 servants, and 3 indentured. Mustees included 8 slaves, 1 servant, 2 indentured. The term "servant" may have been used to mean servant for life, as opposed to an indentured servant, who had a fixed term. Or it may have been simply a euphemism for slave.

67. *Newport Mercury,* Oct. 8, 1770. There were seven women runaways, four of them from Newport.

68. Thirty-eight were aged 12 to 19; fifty-six, 20 to 29; nineteen, 30 to 39; one was 40, one 55. The ages of the remainder were not given.

69. But most birthplaces were not given. Thirty-two were born in America; five were listed as specifically born in Rhode Island.

70. See Gerald Mullin, *Flight and Rebellion: Slave Resistance in Eighteenth Century Virginia* (New York: Oxford University Press, 1972), pp. 39–47, 89–98, 103–12, 128–30; and Peter Wood, *Black Majority: Negroes in Colonial South Carolina from 1670 Through the Stono Rebellion* (New York: Oxford University Press, 1974), pp. 239–68.

71. *Newport Mercury,* Nov. 3, 1761, and March 27, 1775.

72. Ibid., Aug. 15, 1774; May 22, 1775; Oct. 2, 1769; Sept. 28, 1772; *Boston Gazette,* July 1, 1769.

73. *Boston Gazette,* July 21, 1770.

74. *Newport Mercury,* Sept. 10, 1764.

75. *Boston Gazette,* June 10, 1775; *Newport Mercury,* Sept. 14, 1767.

76. Occupations: 9 were sailors, 7 sailors on whaling ships, 11 artisans, 2 coachmen, 2 "gentlemen's gentlemen," 2 gardeners, 2 farmers, 1 did needlework, 1 could draw, 1 was a peddler. Of those whose English ability was mentioned, 11 were poor, 22 good, 9 very good. Physical deformities: 5 were branded, 7 had broken teeth, 2 had swellings, 2 stooped when they walked, 3 had eye problems, 1 had been kicked in the jaw by a horse, and 14 had various kinds of scars.

77. It seems that such a culture was stronger in Newport than in Providence, where the number of blacks was considerably smaller; most legislation attempting to control slaves was written with Newport in mind.

Chapter 5

1. To Jacob Greene, Dec. 20, 1775, in William Johnson, *Sketches of the Life and Correspondence of Nathanael Greene* (Charleston, 1822), vol. 1, p. 50.

2. Richard Rudolph notes that the lack of any popular leadership in Newport pushing nonimportation was a major reason for its lack of success. "The Merchants of Newport, Rhode Island, 1763–1786" (Ph.D. diss., University of Connecticut, 1975), pp. 174–75.

3. Ibid., 169, 177–78; Sydney V. James, *Colonial Rhode Island: A History* (New York: Scribners, 1975), pp. 335–36; Providence Town Meeting, Oct. 24, 1769, in Town Meeting Records, vol. 5, Providence City Hall.

4. Town Meeting, May 31, 1770, Town Meeting Records, vol. 5; James, *Colonial Rhode Island,* 336. The other members of the committee were Darius Sessions, Ephraim Bowen, Nicholas Cook, and Job Sweeting.

5. Town Meeting, June 6, 1770, Town Meeting Records, vol. 5.

6. Town Meeting, August 1770, ibid.; Moses Brown to Committee of Merchants in Boston, May 23, 1770; to Joseph Wanton Jr., July 6, 1770; Wanton to Brown, July 10, 1770; all in Moses Brown Papers, Rhode Island Historical Society (hereafter cited as RIHS); Rudolph, "Merchants of Newport," 181–83.

7. November 24, 1774, Christopher Champlin Letter Book 1774–81, Newport Historical Society (hereafter cited as NHS).

8. May 23, 1774, William Vernon Letter Book 1751–76, NHS.

9. John Collins to Samuel Ward, Jan. 4, 1774; Feb. 7, 1774; Ward to Collins, Jan. 17, 1774; Ward Papers, RIHS. Collins also accused the Russells of Providence of noncompliance. According to Rudolph, Lopez never honored the nonimportation agreements. Rudolph, "Merchants of Newport," 178–79.

10. Rudolph, "Merchants of Newport," 215–16; Newport Town Meeting, Dec. 16, 1774, Newport Town Meeting Records, vol. 2, NHS.

11. William Vernon to Hayley & Hopkins, May 23, 1774, William Vernon Letter Book 1751–76; Memorial to Continental Congress, n.d.; Joseph Hewes to Vernon, Philadelphia, Jan. 6, and Jan. 27, 1776; all in Vernon Papers, Box 49, NHS. Vernon's position as a patriot was complicated by the fact that his cousin, Thomas, was a noted loyalist; Thomas to William, Sept. 30, 1776, Vernon Papers, Box 79, NHS.

12. "Address of the Colony of Rhode Island, to the Congress, relative to its Condition," Jan. 15, 1776, in John R. Bartlett, ed., *Records of the Colony of Rhode Island and Providence Plantations in New England* (Providence, 1858), vol. 7, p. 425 (hereafter cited as RCRI.)

13. RCRI, vol. 7, 439; Edmund S. Morgan, *The Gentle Puritan, A Life of Ezra Stiles* (New Haven: Yale University Press, 1962), pp. 278–79; Samuel Ward and Stephen Hopkins, Philadelphia, to Governor Nicholas Cooke, Oct. 9, 1775; Ward to Isabel Marchant and Betsy Ward, April 23, 1775; to Evan and Francis Malbone, April 23, 1775; Ward Papers, RIHS.

14. Petition of Newport Town Council to General Assembly, Oct. 1775, Petitions, vol. 16, Rhode Island State Archives (hereafter cited as RISA); RCRI, 7, 383–84; copy of truce, Nov. 14, 1775, and renewal of truce, Dec. 14, 1775, in Petitions, vol. 16. See also Rudolph, "Merchants of Newport," 221–23, 186–89.

15. Petitions from Newport Town Meeting to General Assembly, Dec. 12 and 14, 1775, Petitions, vol. 16; Nicholas Cooke to Esek Hopkins, Oct. 21, 1775, Cooke Papers, vol. 2, RIHS, with copy of Newport Town Council proceedings for Oct. 12, 1775. Wallace threatened to destroy the town if the truce was not renewed in December 1775.

16. Nicholas Cooke to Esek Hopkins, ibid.; Ambrose Page to Nicholas Cooke, Providence, Oct. 19, 1775, ibid.

17. William Ellery to Henry Marchant, Nov. 6, 1775, William Ellery Papers, RIHS; Samuel Fowler to his wife, Nov. 1775, H. Audley Clarke Papers, RIHS.

18. RCRI, 7, 61; Thomas W. Bicknell, *The History of the State of Rhode Island and Providence Plantations* (New York: American Historical Society, 1920), vol. 2, p. 753.

19. Information about Newport's inhabitants during the British occupation comes from a list of houses drawn up during this period, of which only part survives. Of the 147 houses counted, 21 were vacant; half the remainder were occupied by their owners, and half by tenants. Seventeen of the owners and 15 of the tenants were widows. Of the 94 male household heads still in the town, 21 were known to be loyalists; a few others were Quaker pacifists. Ezra Stiles, *Literary Diary,* ed. Franklin B. Dexter (New York: Scribners, 1901), vol. 2, pp. 131–34; list of owners and occupants of Newport houses during the Revolution, compiled by Francis Brinley, ms., box 123, folder 2, Newport Historical Society (hereafter cited as NHS); Elisha Anthony to his brother, March 7, 1779, Essex Institute.

20. Appeal of Newport Town Meeting to General Assembly, Aug. 27, 1776, Newport Town Meeting Records, vol. 2; Providence Town Meeting, Nov. 21, 1778, Providence Town Meeting Records, vol. 5; RCRI, vol. 8, 474–75.

21. Newport Town Meeting, March 14, 1775, Town Meeting Records, vol. 2; Providence Town Council, Dec. 7, 1778, Town Council Records, vol. 5. The Council estimated that 300 residents of the island were living in Providence and required public assistance; a list of people from the island receiving relief from the Providence Town Council, December 1778, appears in Providence Town Papers, 2nd ser., vol. 3.

22. Mary Callender to Moses Brown, Jan. 24, 1776, Moses Brown Papers, RIHS; Samuel Vernon to Isabel Marchant, March 20, 1776, Vernon Papers, box 49, NHS.

23. RCRI, 8, 474-75; Philip Wanton to Moses Brown, Jan. 24, 1776; Mary Callender to Moses Brown, Feb. 1, 1776; Edmund Townsend to Moses Brown, Feb. 29, 1776; Moses Brown Papers, RIHS. On Quaker poor relief in general, see also Henry J. Cadbury, "Quaker Relief during the Siege of Boston," *Transactions of the Colonial Society of Massachusetts,* 34 (1937–42): 39–179; and Sydney V. James, *A People Among Peoples: Quaker Benevolence in Eighteenth Century America* (Cambridge: Harvard University Press, 1963), pp. 258–67.

24. Providence Town Council, Jan. 23, 1779, town Council Records, vol. 5; James Manning to Moses Brown, March 15, 1779, Moses Brown Papers, RIHS.

25. When Newport was invaded, Providence thought it might be next; Town Meeting, Dec. 8, 1776, Town Meeting Records, vol. 6. In 1778, another wave of fear swept the town; Solomon Drown to Betsey Drown, June 18, 1778, and July 17, 1778; Sarah Drown to Elizabeth Drown, June 13, 1778, Drown Papers, boxes 4 and 5, Providence, John Hay Library, Brown University. It was estimated that 130 taxpayers had left Providence by 1777; Town Meeting, Sept. 6, 1777.

26. Petition of Providence to General Assembly, Jan. 30, 1778, Providence Town Papers, 2nd ser., vol. 3.

27. Solomon Drown to Jacob Nash, July 3, 1782, Drown Papers, box 5; James Manning to Rev. Samuel Jones, March 9, 1777, Samuel Jones Papers, Providence. John Hay Library, Brown University.

28. William H. Vernon went to France in 1778, with the idea of entering a French countinghouse for a time to learn the trade of that country. He chose Bordeaux because it was a major port, and close enough to Spain to allow him to learn something about Spanish commerce as well. As a result of his efforts, the family began trading with Bordeaux by 1779. William H. Vernon to William Vernon, Oct. 12, 1779, Vernon Papers, box 49; correspondence between Samuel and William Vernon, 1780–81, Vernon Papers, box 79; John Bondfield to William Vernon, March 1, 1783, Vernon Papers, box 656.

29. Christopher Champlin to Capt. Ebenezer Shearman, March 5, 1783; to Charles Soderstrom, March 5, 1783; to Mary Hayley, May 10, 1783, and Feb. 4, 1782; to Henry Grieg, May 10, 1780; to Charles Soderstrom & Co., April 1, 1781; to John deNeufrille & Son, April 17, 1780, April 1, 1781, and Nov. 26, 1781; Christopher Champlin Letter Books, 1774–81 and 1781–85, NHS; see also Rudolph, "Merchants of Newport," 300–301.

30. Rudolph, "Merchants of Newport," 300–301.

31. See above, note 29.

32. Rudolph, "Merchants of Newport, 307.

33. Franklin S. Coyle, "Welcome Arnold (1745–1798), Providence Merchant: The Founding of an Enterprise," (PhD. diss., Brown University, 1972), pp. 60, 85–90, 96–127.

34. James B. Hedges, *The Browns of Providence Plantations,* vol. 1, (Cambridge, Mass.: Harvard University Press, 1952) pp. 241–56.

35. See Appendix A, table A-2 for complete population statistics.

36. The town also barred loyalists from participating in town meetings; RCRI, vol. 8, 605–06; *Acts and Resolves,* Oct. 1779, 24–28; July 1780, 19–20; Feb. 1783, 73 (facsimile edition, Providence, 1936). Forty-four of the fifty-four loyalists from Rhode Island who made claims to the British government were from Newport; Rudolph, "Merchants of Newport," 227.

37. The General Assembly heard other similar petitions as well, and they were generally granted; RCRI vol. 9, 728–31.

38. For complete statistics on persistence of Newport residents before and after the Revolution, see Lynne Withey, "Population Change, Economic Development, and the Revolution: Newport, Rhode Island, As A Case Study, 1760–1800" (Ph.D. diss., University of California, Berkeley, 1976), pp. 40–41.

39. Of 55 men in the top 5 percent in 1790, 22 had been in the top 5 in 1775; 13 in second 5; 15 ranked lower; 5 were not present. Of 51 men in the second 5 percent in 1790, 27 had moved up from lower positions.

40. Joseph Russell was fourth in 1775, eleventh in 1790; William was seventh and twelfth; Angell was fifth and ninth. Joseph Brown, alone among the Brown brothers, slipped from the top; he ranked eighth in 1775, and farther down but still within the top 5 percent in 1790.

41. Of 32 men in the top 5 percent in 1789, 15 had been in the top 5 in 1775, 5 in second 5 percent, 2 in lower ranks, and 9 not present.

42. To George Wright, Nov. 20, 1782, Champlin Letter Book, 1781–85, NHS.
43. See Appendix B, table B-1.

Chapter 6

1. See Appendix B, table B-2, for figures. Charles R. Ritcheson, *Aftermath of Revolution: British Policy Toward the United States, 1783–1795* (Dallas: Southern Methodist University Press, 1969), pp. 128–29; James B. Hedges, *The Browns of Providence Plantations* (Cambridge, Mass.: Harvard University Press, 1952), pp. 287–88, 306.

2. See Stuart Bruchey, *Robert Oliver, Merchant of Baltimore, 1783–1819* (Baltimore, Johns Hopkins University Press, 1956), especially pp. 31–51; and Edward Papenfuse, *In Pursuit of Profit: The Annapolis Merchants in the Era of the American Revolution, 1763–1805* (Baltimore: Johns Hopkins University Press, 1975), for an analysis of Annapolis's decline in the face of Baltimore's rise to commercial dominance. Gary Nash discusses the importance of a rich agricultural hinterland in the growth of New York and Philadelphia, as compared with Boston, before the Revolution, in *The Urban Crucible: Social Change, Political Consciousness, and the Origins of the American Revolution* (Cambridge, Mass.: Harvard University Press, 1979), pp. 54–55, 127–28.

3. Robert Albion, *The Rise of New York Port, 1815–1860* (New York: Scribners, 1939), pp. 10–15.

4. Carl Bridenbaugh, *Cities in Revolt: Urban Life in America, 1743–1776* (New York: Knopf, 1955).

5. Robert East calls this change the growth of a metropolitan economy; he argues that the upheaval of the war years worked to the advantage of wealthier merchants and certain seaports, by weeding out the weaker businessmen and allowing those in better financial condition—who also tended to gravitate to the larger cities—to expand and consolidate their activities. *Business Enterprise in the American Revolutionary Era* (New York: Columbia University Press, 1938), p. 231 and passim.

6. Hedges, *The Browns*, 293–98.

7. Jay Coughtry, *The Notorious Triangle: Rhode Island and the African Slave Trade, 1700–1807* (Philadelphia: Temple University Press, 1981), pp. 17–18, 39–42.

8. Hedges, *The Browns*, 287. This depression was not confined to Rhode Island.

9. Ibid., 288–89; Franklin S. Coyle, "Welcome Arnold: Providence Merchant," (Ph.D. diss., Brown University, 1972), pp. 132, 143–44, 148–55, 158–60, 172, 191–93; Christopher Champlin to Gouverneur & Kimble, May 20, 1786; to Lane Son & Fraser, May 30, 1787; to Protero & Claxton, Dec. 10, 1787; Champlin Letter Book, 1786–88, Newport Historical Society (hereafter cited as NHS).

10. Christopher Champlin to Lane Son & Fraser, May 30, 1787, Champlin Letter Book, 1786–88, NHS.

11. See Appendix B. table B-2.

12. Christopher Champlin and Samuel Fowler correspondence with Reuben Harvey at Cork, 1783–85; with Edward Forbes at Dublin, 1785–87; with Conally, McCausland, and Campbell at Londonderry, 1785; with William Willcocks at Cork, 1788; to Thompson and Gordon at Newry, Jan. 21, 1790; to Ross Thompson & Sons at Newry, Feb. 18, 1791, and Jan. 21, 1793; to Capt. Aaron Sheffield, Dec. 24, 1783; to Capt. Benjamin Pierce, Aug. 14, 1784; to Mary Hayley, Dec. 4, 1783, and

Jan. 19, 1784; to Lane Son & Fraser, Dec. 28, 1786; Christopher Champlin Letter Books, 1781–85 and 1786–88, NHS.

13. For example, Christopher Champlin to Ross Thompson & Sons, Jan. 29, 1793, Christopher Champlin Letter Book, 1792–99, NHS.

14. Christopher Champlin to Henry Grieg, May 10, 1780; to Charles Soderstrom, April 1, 1781; Christopher Champlin Letter Books, 1774–81 and 1781–85, NHS.

15. Christopher Champlin to Charles Soderstrom, May 12, 1783; Jan. 18, 1784; May 7, 1784; Champlin et al. to Capt. Ebenezer Shearman, May 12, 1783; to Capt. John Green, May 7, 1784; to Caspar Voght & Co., April 5, 1785; Champlin to J. J. Frolich & Co., April 20, 1785; Champlin, George Champlin, Samuel Fowler & Son to Capt. Benjamin Pierce, April 19, 1785; Christopher Champlin Letter Book, 1781–85; Caspar Voght & Co. to Champlin, June 3, 1785, *Massachusetts Historical Society Collections,* vol. 70 (1915), pp. 252–54.

16. Christopher Champlin to Nicholas Ryberg & Co., April 16, 1786, and Dec. 28, 1787; to Capt. Benjamin Pierce, April 16, 1786; Christopher Champlin Letter Book, 1786–88, NHS.

17. Christopher Champlin to [?] Grant, Nov. 10, 1787; Christopher and George Champlin to Hazard & Robinson, March 12, 1795, and Dec. 28, 1795; Christopher Champlin to Moses Hays, April 26, 1787, and April 30, 1788; Christopher and George Champlin to William Minturn, May 24, 1794; to Joseph Anthony, May 24, 1794; Christopher Champlin correspondence with Nicholas Ryberg & Co., 1787–98; with Edward James Smith, 1787–95; Christopher and George Champlin to Capt. Benjamin Pierce, April 22, 1788; to Capt. Benjamin Bayley, June 10, 1789; May 6, 1791; and May 22, 1792; to Capt. Robert Robinson, March 1795 and Jan. 17, 1798; Christopher Champlin Letter Books, 1786–88, 1788–92, 1792–99, NHS; Robert Robinson to Christopher and George Champlin, May 23, 1796, Champlin Papers, Rhode Island Historical Society (hereafter cited as RIHS); Edward James Smith and Co. to Christopher and George Champlin, Sept. 5, 1788; Nov. 28, 1788; and Feb. 16, 1789; *MHS Coll.,* 70, 390–98.

18. Christopher and George Champlin to George Washington, Dec. 27, 1789; to Rudolph Saaby, Dec. 30, 1789; Christopher Champlin Letter Book, 1788–92, NHS.

19. See note 10 above.

20. Christopher Champlin to Francis Rotch, Jan. 1, 1787; to Brothers DeBauque, April 6, 1787; to Sarmeto & Co., April 19, 1790, and Dec. 10, 1790; to Lanchon Bros., May 8, 1790; May 17, 1790; and May 26, 1791; to Luething Brothers & Co., May 8, 1790; to Capt. Benjamin Bayley, May 17, 1790; to Fenwick Mason & Co., May 24, 1791; to Capt. Robert Robinson, June 13, 1797; Christopher Champlin Letter Books, 1788–92, 1792–99, NHS. Ritcheson, *Aftermath of Revolution,* 23–25; Hedges, *The Browns,* 259.

21. Articles of Agreement between Christopher Champlin and William Green of London, May 1, 1784; Memorial to the Continental Congress, July 1784; sailing orders to William Green, Aug. 1784, *MHS Coll.,* 10, 202, 216, 222–23; Champlin to William Green, May 24, 1784, and June 25, 1785, Champlin Papers, Box 52, NHS; agreement between Christopher Champlin and Capt. Jeremiah Clarke, Oct. 6, 1786, *MHS Coll.,* 70, 290–91; to Jeremiah Clarke, Oct. 19, 1786; to William Green, Oct. 12, 1786; Christopher, George and Christopher Grant Champlin to Capt. William Wood, Jan. 23, 1793; to John C. Jones, March 3, 1794; Christopher Champlin to Nathaniel Prime, Aug. 1, 1797; Christopher Champlin Letter Books, 1786–88, 1792–99, NHS.

22. Hedges, *The Browns,* vol. 2, 2, 118.

23. Coyle, "Welcome Arnold," 192; Brown and Francis power of attorney to William Megee, Jan. 2, 1792; William Megee to Samuel Nightingale Jr., Feb. 12, 1794; to Ebenezer Jenckes, March 26, 1797; Clarke and Nightingale to Megee, Feb. 26, 1796; John Innes Clark to Lydia Clark, Canton, March 22, May 8, and May 18, 1797, all in Nightingale-Jenckes Papers, RIHS. Megee was supercargo for the Browns and for Clarke and Nightingale. These letters discuss voyages to Canton, Ile de France, Manila, and Batavia.

24. Act prohibiting the slave trade, Oct. 1787, in John Bartlett, ed., *Records of the Colony of Rhode Island and Providence Plantations in New England* (Providence, 1859) (hereafter cited as RCRI) vol. 10, p. 262. This act was preceded by one in February 1784, which stated that slaves shipped to the West Indies in Rhode Island ships could no longer be brought to Rhode Island; RCRS, vol. 10, 8.

25. See Appendix B, table B-3; Coughtry, *The Notorious Triangle,* 27–28.

26. Petition to General Assembly, Jan. 1790, Petitions, vol. 25; Act confirming the corporation called the River Machine Co., n.d.; Obadiah Brown to Theodore Foster, Aug. 2, 1790, both in Foster Papers, vols. 1 and 2, RIHS.

27. Peter Coleman, *The Transformation of Rhode Island, 1790–1860* (Providence: Brown University Press, 1963), pp. 166–69; Providence and Norwich Turnpike Society ms., Dec. 18, 1794 and July 7, 1796, John Hay Library. The initial subscribers to this company included Brown & Francis, Clarke & Nightingale, Brown, Benson & Ives, Welcome Arnold, Moses Brown, Jabez Bowen, Joseph and William Russell, Nicholas Power & Co.

28. Coleman, *Transformation of RI,* 171–72. An example of trade with eastern Connecticut after the Revolution appears in the letters of Elijah Williams, who established a shop in Woodstock, to various members of his family in Providence and to other Providence businessmen in the years 1790–98; Jason Williams Papers, RIHS.

29. John Brown to Moses Brown, Aug. 14, 1791, and Sept. 1, 1791, Moses Brown Papers, RIHS.

30. Act incorporating Providence Bank, Nov. 5, 1791; incorporation of Bank of Rhode Island, Newport, Oct. 28, 1795, *The Public Laws of the State of Rhode-Island and Providence Plantations* (Providence, 1798), pp. 447–56; 456–65. (Hereafter cited as *Laws 1798.*) See also Hedges, *The Browns,* vol. 1, 187, 203; and Coleman, *Transformation of RI,* 186–87.

31. $332,000 in Providence, $100,000 in Newport. Coleman, *Transformation of RI,* 185.

32. Coleman, *Transformation of RI,* 33–38.

33. "Exhibit of the Products of Industry in Providence, from January 1, 1790, to October 10, 1791," reprinted in *Mechanics' Festival: An Account of the 71st Anniversary of the Providence Association of Mechanics and Manufacturers* (Providence: Knowles, Anthony & Co., 1860), pp. 99–104. See also Moses Brown's account of Rhode Island manufacturing in a letter to William Ellery, Nov. 19, 1791, Moses Brown Papers, vol. 7, RIHS.

34. Coleman, *Transformation of RI,* 80.

35. Hedges, *The Browns,* vol. 2, 161–65.

36. Ibid., 135, 174–79; Coleman, *Transformation of RI,* 77–79; *Mechanics' Festival,* 103. The other factories were run by William Potter, Lewis Peck, Andrew Dexter, and James McKenis. Other members of the Brown family who invested in cotton manufacturing did it only as a sideline to their commercial interests until after

1815, when the general decline of trade made the whole family shift their interests almost entirely to manufacturing.

37. Coleman, *Transformation of RI,* 79–80.

38. Ibid., 85–88.

39. Ibid., 71–73.

40. *Mechanics' Festival,* 99–104.

41. Coleman, *Transformation of RI,* 95.

42. Ibid., 83.

43. *Newport Mercury* advertisements, 1794–99.

44. Gary Kornblith, "From Artisans to Businessmen: Master Mechanics in New England, 1789–1850," (Ph.D. diss., Princeton University, 1983). See also Eric Foner, *Tom Paine and Revolutionary America* (New York: Oxford University Press, 1976), chap. 2; Alfred Young, "The Mechanics and the Jeffersonians: New York, 1789–1801," and Staughton Lynd, "The Mechanics in New York Politics, 1774–1788," both in *Labor History* vol. 5 (1964), pp. 247–76 and 225–46; and Gary Nash, *The Urban Crucible: Social Change, Political Consciousness, and the Origins of the American Revolution* (Cambridge, Mass.: Harvard University Press, 1979), pp. 323–27, 359–82.

45. Bylaws passed June 15, 1789, Records of the Providence Association of Mechanics and Manufacturers, vol. 1, RIHS (hereafter cited as PAMMR).

46. Kornblith, "Artisans to Businessmen."

47. Membership lists, PAMMR, vol. 1, and *Records of Newport Association of Mechanics and Manufacturers,* box 141 (hereafter cited as NAMMR).

48. Biographical information from *Mechanics' Festival,* 40–43, 48–49; list of first officers from PAMMR, vol. 1.

49. Providence Association to Boston Association, July 21, 1790, to Trenton, N. J., Mechanics, May 4, 1790, both in PAMMR, vol. 1.

50. Providence Association to Newport Association, March 5, 1792, PAMMR, vol. 1.

51. This issue first came up in Newport in 1785, before the formation of the Association, when the town meeting voted approval of a petition to the General Assembly to establish import duties. April 20, 1785, Newport Town Meeting Records, 1779, NHS. The Providence Association began to write to other organizations in 1790 to urge them to cooperate in petitioning Congress; minutes of meeting, July 12, 1790; letter to Boston Association, July 21, 1790; PAMMR, vol. 1. In 1799 a committee was appointed to draw up a petition to Congress; Nov. 18, 1799, PAMMR, vol. 2. The Newport Association also supported this effort. Robert Taylor, president of Newport Association, to Providence Association, March 6, 1800, NAMMR, box 141.

52. Petition to General Assembly, approved Oct. 22, 1790; meetings, March 30 and Oct. 12, 1789, all in PAMMR, vol. 1.

53. Providence Association to Newport Association, March 5, 1792, PAMMR, vol. 1.

54. Bylaws, March 30, 1789, PAMMR, vol. 1.

55. Providence Association to Newport Association, March 5, 1792, PAMMR, vol. 1; petition adopted Feb. 4, 1799, PAMMR, vol. 2, and Petitions, vol. 32.

56. Jan. 10, 1798, PAMMR, vol. 2.

57. Newport Association to Norfolk, Virginia, Association, June 10, 1794, NAMMR, vol. 1.

58. April 30, 1789, PAMMR, vol. 1.

Chapter 7

1. Frederick D. Stone, "The Struggle for Delaware: Philadelphia Under Howe and Under Arnold," in *Narrative and Critical History of America,* Justin Winsor, ed., vol. 6 (Boston and New York: Houghton Mifflin, 1887), pp. 384–97; Robert A. East, *Business Enterprise in the American Revolutionary Era* (New York: Columbia University Press, 1938), pp. 49, 149–51; Oscar Barck, *New York City During the War for Independence* (New York: Columbia University Press, 1931), pp. 48, 74, 120–30, 143, 226; Wilbur C. Abbott, *New York in the American Revolution* (New York: Scribners, 1929), p. 214.

2. Carville Earle and Ronald Hoffman, "Urban Development in the Eighteenth Century South," *Perspectives in American History,* 10 (1976), p. 42; James B. Hedges, *The Browns of Providence Plantations,* vol. 1 (Cambridge, Mass.: Harvard University Press, 1952), pp. 260–61.

3. James W. Livingood, *The Philadelphia-Baltimore Trade Rivalry, 1780–1860* (Harrisburg, Pa., Pennsylvania Historical and Museum Commission, 1947), p. 13. The richness of the agricultural produce of this area ensured that Baltimore's expansion would be much greater than Providence's; by 1800, Baltimore was the country's third largest city.

4. Edward C. Papenfuse, *In Pursuit of Profit: The Annapolis Merchants in the Era of the American Revolution, 1763–1805* (Baltimore: Johns Hopkins University Press, 1975), pp. 101, 131, 133.

5. John Brown to James Brown, Nov. 26, 1782 and Feb. 9, 1783, John Brown Papers, Rhode Island Historical Society (hereafter cited as RIHS).

6. Newport and Norfolk both suffered from their dependence on the West Indian trade, and Annapolis, from its specializing in importing luxury goods. Papenfuse, *In Pursuit of Profit,* 131. On the problem of the distance between urban centers, see Earle and Hoffman, "Urban Development in the South," 67.

7. East, *Business Enterprise,* 231. This trend became even stronger after 1815, when New York began to monopolize the lion's share of American commerce. See Robert Albion, *The Rise of New York Port* (New York, Scribners, 1939).

8. Richard D. Brown, "The Emergence of Urban Society in Rural Massachusetts, 1760–1820," *Journal of American History* 61 (1974): 29–51; Richard Wade, *The Urban Frontier: The Rise of Western Cities, 1790–1830* (Cambridge, Mass.: Harvard University Press, 1959), pp. 30–35; John Modell, "Family and Fertility on the Indiana Frontier," *American Quarterly* 23 (1971): 615–34.

Appendix A

1. Estimates of the population of all colonies appear in U.S. Bureau of the Census, *Historical Statistics of the United States: Colonial Times to 1957* (Washington, 1960), p. 756.

2. Bridenbaugh's estimates appear in *Cities in the Wilderness* (New York: Ronald Press, 1938), pp. 6n, 143, 303; and *Cities in Revolt* (New York, Knopf, 1955), pp. 5, 216.

Appendix B

1. Lists for 1720–39 were published in the *Boston Gazette*; 1762–84, in the *Newport Mercury*; post–1784 statistics for Newport, in the *Newport Mercury*; and for Providence, in the *Providence Gazette*.

2. Customs 16:1, Public Record Office, London; I used copies in the possession of Lawrence Harper, University of California, Berkeley.

3. Richard Beale and John Nicoll to the Commissioners of the Board of Trade, Feb. 16, 1768, Customs House Letters 1767–75, Newport Historical Society. They reported the number of ships clearing only, for one year: 218 from Newport, 100 from Providence, 34 from Taunton River, 10 from Bristol, 18 from Warren, and 7 from East Greenwich.

4. Shipping lists, *Providence Gazette,* 1774. These lists recorded 148 ships entering, and 129 ships clearing Providence from March to September. Clearances were not always recorded, however, so the best estimate can be made by comparing entries.

5. "List of Vessels Paying Port Tax at Newport in 1744 and 1745," Rhode Island Historical Society *Collections,* vol. 16 (1923), pp. 84–89.

Appendix C

1. Newport tax list, 1760, Rhode Island State Archives; 1775, Newport Historical Society. Providence tax lists, 1760 and 1775, Rhode Island Historical Society. In the case of Newport, these are the only extant tax lists for the pre-Revolutionary period. More lists are available for Providence, but these years were chosen to correspond with Newport.

2. David Lovejoy, *Rhode Island Politics and the Revolution* (Providence, Brown University Press, 1958), note 32 to chap. 1, pp. 197–98.

3. There is no single list of occupations for either town, making it necessary to piece together this information from several sources. The best source for Newport is a notebook kept by George Richardson; it is in the Newport Historical Society, with a photostat copy in the Rhode Island Historical Society. For Providence, the best source is the list compiled by Franklin S. Coyle, in "The Survival of Providence Business Enterprise after the Revolution," (M.A. thesis, Brown University, 1960). More occupations can be pieced together from tax lists and censuses, which occasionally listed occupations, and from court records, which also gave the occupations of litigants; and from newspaper advertisements.

4. Information on religion from Ezra Stiles' lists of church members made in 1763, in his "Miscellanies," vol. 1, Beinecke Library, Yale University. No comparable information is available for Providence.

5. Sydney V. James, *Colonial Rhode Island* (New York: Scribners, 1975), p. 211.

6. In making distinctions between major and minor town officials, I have followed Edward M. Cook Jr., in *The Fathers of the Towns* (Baltimore: Johns Hopkins University Press, 1976). Town officials and representatives to the General Assembly were elected annually and noted in the town meeting records. Sometimes they were also published in the newspapers. The fragmentary nature of the Newport records makes its listings incomplete; but the fact that most people held the same offices for many years makes this not a serious problem.

Bibliography

PRIMARY SOURCES
Manuscripts

Providence, Rhode Island Historical Society

James Brown Papers.
John Brown Papers.
Moses Brown Papers.
Carter-Danforth Papers.
Christopher Champlin Papers.
John Innes Clark Papers.
H. Audley Clarke Papers.
Cooke Papers.
William Ellery Papers.
First Baptist Church Records (Providence).
First Congregational Church Records (Providence).
Theodore Foster Papers.
Friends Records: Smithfield Men's and Women's Monthly Meetings; Rhode Island Men's and Women's Monthly Meetings.
Aaron Lopez Papers.
Malbone Papers.
Henry Marchant Papers.
Record Book, Newport County Court of General Sessions of the Peace, 1746–70.
Registry of Newport Vessels, 1785–90.
Nightingale-Jenckes Papers.
Records of the Providence Association of Mechanics and Manufacturers.
Providence tax lists, 1749, 1760, 1775, 1790, 1800.
Providence Town Papers.
Stillwell Papers.
"Sundry Letters of the Church and Nicholas Eyre and the Church offer to the Separated Men."
Tillinghast Papers.

Ward Manuscripts.
Jason Williams Papers.
Letters and Papers of Roger Williams, 1629–82. Photostat.

Newport Historical Society

Christopher Champlin Letter Books, 1774–1805; Invoice Books, 1757–64, 1769–1804.
Customs House Letters, 1767–1775.
First Baptist Church Records (Newport).
First Congregational Church Records (Newport).
"A List of House Owners and Occupants during the Revolution, compiled by Francis Brinley."
Aaron Lopez Papers; Letter Books, 1751–67, 1767; Ships Books, 1763–5, 1765–71; Shipping Book, 1771–3.
Records of Newport Association of Mechanics and Manufacturers, Box 141 and bound record books.
Newport Marine Society Records (also called "Fellowship Club").
Newport tax lists, 1775, 1786, 1789, 1800.
Newport Town Council Records.
Newport Town Meeting Records.
Records of Proprietors of Long Wharf, Record Book and Box 123.
Thomas Richardson Letter Books, 1710–15, 1715–19, 1716–41.
Second Baptist Church Records (Newport).
Second Congregational Church Records (Newport).
Seventh Day Baptist Church Records (Newport).
William Vernon Papers, Boxes 49, 79, 656; Letter Book, 1751–76.

Providence. John Carter Brown Library, Brown University
John Brown Papers.

Providence. John Hay Library, Brown University

Solomon Drown Papers.
Samuel Jones Papers.
Providence and Norwich Turnpike Society manuscripts.

New Haven. Beinecke Library, Yale University

Ezra Stiles, Itineraries.
Ezra Stiles, Miscellanies.

Boston. Baker Library, Harvard University Business School.

Peter Ayrault Letter Book.
Boston Merchants' Letters.
Hazard and Ayrault Invoice Book.
Hazard, Robinson & Co. Invoice Book.
Henry Lloyd Letter Book.

Providence City Hall

Providence Town Council Records.
Providence Town Meeting Records.

Providence State Records Center

File Papers, Providence County Inferior Court of Common Pleas, 1732, 1740, 1750, 1760, 1770.

Providence County Court House

Minute Books and Docket Books, Providence County Inferior Court of Common Pleas, 1730–75.
Minute Books, Providence County Court of General Sessions of the Peace, 1747–75.

Newport County Court House

Record Books, General Court of Trials, 1671–1715, 1715–24.
Record Books, Newport County Inferior Court of Common Pleas.

Providence. Rhode Island State Archives

Newport tax list, 1760.
Petitions to General Assembly.

Printed Sources

Government documents

Acts and Laws of His Majesty's Colony of Rhode-Island, and Providence-Plantations, In America. Newport, 1730.

Acts and Laws of the English Colony of Rhode-Island and Providence-Plantations, in New-England, in America. Newport, 1767.

Arnold, James N. *Vital Records of Rhode Island, 1636–1850,* vols. 7 and 10. Providence, 1895, 1898.

Bartlett, John R. ed., *Records of the Colony of Rhode Island and Providence Plantations in New England.* 10 vols. Providence, 1859.

Census of the Inhabitants of the Colony of Rhode Island and Providence Plantations, 1774. Providence, 1858.

Census of 1782, reprinted in *New England Historical and Genealogical Society Register,* vol. 127 (1972), 5–17; vol. 128 (1973), 138–42.

Census of 1800. Washington, D.C., 1801.

The Charter and the Acts and Laws of His Majesties Colony of Rhode-Island, and Providence-Plantations in America, 1719. Providence, 1895.

The Early Records of the Town of Providence, 21 vols. Providence, 1892–1909.

Heads of Families, at the First Census of the United States, Taken in 1790. Washington, 1907–1908.

Laws and Acts of Her Majesties Colony of Rhode Island, and Providence Plantations made from the First Settlement in 1636 to 1705. Providence, 1896.

The Public Laws of the State of Rhode-Island and Providence Plantations. Providence, 1798.

Records of the General Court of Trials of the Colony of Providence Plantations, 2 vols. Providence, 1920, 1922.

A Supplement to the Digest of the Laws . . . 1798. Providence, 1810.

Newspapers

Boston Gazette, 1720–1750.
Newport Mercury, 1758–1800.
Providence Gazette, 1762–1800.

Other

Barrows, C. Edwin, ed. "The Diary of John Comer." *Collections of the Rhode Island Historical Society,* vol. 8 1893.

Bigelow, Bruce M., ed. "The Walter Newbury Shipping Book." *Collections of the Rhode Island Historical Society,* vol. 24, 1931, pp. 73–91.

Bridenbaugh, Carl, ed. *Gentlemen's Progress: The Itinerarium of Dr. Alexander Hamilton, 1744.* Chapel Hill: University of North Carolina Press, 1948.

Chace, Henry R. *Maps of Providence, Rhode Island, 1650–1765–1770.* Providence, 1914.

———. *Owners and Occupants of the Lots, Houses, and Shops in the Town of Providence, Rhode Island, in 1798.* Providence, 1914.

Chapin, Howard M. *Documentary History of Rhode Island.* 2 vols. Providence: Preston & Rounds 1916, 1919.

Claggett, William. *A Looking-Glass for Elder Clarke and Elder Wightman, and the Church Under Their Care.* Boston: James Franklin, 1721.

"The Commerce of Rhode Island," *Collections of the Massachusetts Historical Society.* vols. 69 and 70. 1914, 1915.

John Hammett's Vindication and Relation. Newport: James Franklin 1727.

"Harris Papers," *Collections of the Rhode Island Historical Society.* vol. 10. 1902.

[James Honeyman], *Faults on All Sides, The Case of Religion Consider'd.* Newport: James Franklin, 1728.

Hopkins, Samuel. *The Life and Character of Miss Susanna Anthony.* Hartford: Hudson & Goodwin, 1799.

———. *Memoirs of Mrs. Sarah Osborn.* Worcester: Leonard Worcester, 1799.

The Letter Book of Peleg Sanford of Newport, Merchant, 1666–1668. Providence: R.I. Historical Society. 1928.

A Letter From Sundry Members belonging to A Church of Jesus Christ, in Newport on Rhode-Island Under the Pastoral Care of Timothy Packcom, To the several Baptist Churches in New-England. Newport, 1742.

Mechanics Festival, An Account of the 71st Anniversary of the Providence Association of Mechanics and Manufacturers. Providence: Knowles, Anthony & Co., 1860.

Mr. Samuel Gorton's Ghost, broadside. Newport, 1728.

Rowland, David. *Catholicism: or, Christian Charity.* Providence: John Carter, 1772.

Stiles, Ezra. *A Discourse on the Christian Union.* Boston: Edes & Gill, 1761.

———. *Extracts from the Itineraries and Miscellanies,* ed. Franklin B. Dexter. New Haven, 1916.

———. *Literary Diary,* ed. Franklin B. Dexter, 3 vols. New York: Scribners, 1901.

Survey of Federal Archives, *Ships Registers and Enrollments.* Providence, 1938–41.

The Complete Writings of Roger Williams. New York: Russell & Russell, 1963.

"Winthrop Papers," *Collections of the Massachusetts Historical Society,* ser. 4, vols. 6, 7 (1863, 1865); ser. 5, vol. 1 (1871).

SECONDARY SOURCES
Works Relating to Rhode Island

Austin, John O. *Genealogical Dictionary of Rhode Island.* Albany, 1887.

Bayles, Richard M. *History of Newport County, Rhode Island.* New York, 1888.

———. *History of Providence County, Rhode Island.* New York: W. W. Preston, 1891.

Bicknell, Thomas W. *The History of the State of Rhode Island and Providence Plantations,* 4 vols. New York: American Historical Society 1920.

Bigelow, Bruce M. "The Commerce of Rhode Island with the West Indies, Before the American Revolution." Ph.D. diss., Brown University, 1930.

Bridenbaugh, Carl. *Fat Mutton and Liberty of Conscience: Society in Rhode Island, 1636–1690.* Providence: Brown University Press, 1974.

———. *Peter Harrison, First American Architect.* Chapel Hill: University of North Carolina Press, 1949.

Cady, John H. *The Civic and Architectural Development of Providence, 1636–1950.* Providence: The Book Shop, 1957.

———. *Rhode Island Boundaries, 1636–1936.* Providence: Rhode Island Tercentenary Commission, 1936.

Coleman, Peter. *The Transformation of Rhode Island, 1790–1860*. Providence: Brown University Press, 1963.

Conley, Patrick T. "Rhode Island Constitutional Development, 1636–1775: A Survey," *Rhode Island History* vol. 27, pp. 49–63, 74–94.

Coyle, Franklin S. "The Survival of Providence Business Enterprise in the Revolutionary Era (1770–1785)." M.A. thesis, Brown University, 1960.

———, "Welcome Arnold: Providence Merchant." Ph.D. diss., Brown University, 1972.

Crane, Elaine. "'The First Wheel of Commerce': Newport, Rhode Island, and the Slave Trade 1760–1776," *Slavery and Abolition*, vol. 1 (1980).

Dorr, Henry C. "The Proprietors of Providence, and Their Controversies with the Freeholders." *Collections of the Rhode Island Historical Society*, vol. 9, 1897.

Downing, Antoinette. *Early Homes of Rhode Island*. Richmond, Va.: Garrett & Massie, 1937.

———. and Vincent Sculley, *The Architectural Heritage of Newport, Rhode Island, 1640–1915*. Cambridge, Mass.: Harvard University Press, 1952.

Farrell, John T. "The Early History of Rhode Island's Court System," *Rhode Island History* 9 (1950); 14–25, 65–71, 103–17.

Guild, Reuben Aldridge. *Early History of Brown University*. Providence: Snow & Farnham, 1897).

Hedges, James B. *The Browns of Providence Plantations*, vol. 1. Cambridge, Mass.: Harvard University Press, 1952); vol. 2 Providence: Brown University Press, 1968.

James, Sydney V. *Colonial Rhode Island: A History*. New York: Scribners, 1975.

Lowther, Lawrence L. "Rhode Island Colonial Government, 1732." Ph.D. diss., University of Washington, 1964.

Mason, George C. *Annals of the Redwood Library*. Philadelphia: Evans Printing Co., 1891.

———. *Annals of Trinity Church*. Newport: V. M. Francis, 1894.

Morgan, Edmund S. *The Gentle Puritan: A Life of Ezra Stiles*. New Haven: Yale University Press, 1962.

Platt, Virginia. "'And Don't Forget the Guinea Voyage': The Slave Trade of Aaron Lopez of Newport," *William and Mary Quarterly* 32 (1975): 601–18.

Rudolph, Richard. "The Merchants of Newport, Rhode Island, 1763–1786," Ph.D. diss., University of Connecticut, 1975.

Skemp, Sheila. "A Social and Cultural History of Newport, 1740–1765." Ph.D. diss., University of Iowa, 1974.

Withey, Lynne E. "Household Composition in Urban and Rural Areas: The Case of Rhode Island," *Journal of Family History*, 3 (1978): 37–50.

————. "Population Change, Economic Development, and the Revolution: Newport, Rhode Island, as a Case Study." Ph.D. diss., University of California, Berkeley, 1976.

Woodward, Carl R. *Plantation in Yankeeland.* Chester, Conn.: Pequot Press, 1971.

Other works

Abbott, Wilbur C. *New York in the American Revolution.* New York: Scribners, 1929.

Albion, Robert. *The Rise of New York Port.* New York: Scribners, 1939.

Archdeacon, Thomas *New York City, 1664–1710: Conquest and Change.* Ithaca: Cornell University Press, 1976.

Bailyn, Bernard. *New England Merchants in the Seventeenth Century.* Cambridge, Mass.: Harvard University Press, 1945.

Barck, Oscar. *New York City During the War for Independence.* New York: Columbia University Press, 1931.

Beier, A. L. "Vagrants and the Social Order in Elizabethan England," Past and Present 64 (1974): 3–29.

Bissell, Linda Auwers. "From One Generation to Another: Mobility in Seventeenth Century Windsor, Connecticut," *William and Mary Quarterly* 31 (1974): 79–110.

Bonomi, Patricia U. *A Factious People: Politics and Society in Colonial New York.* New York: Columbia University Press, 1971.

Breen, T. H. "Persistent Localism: English Social Change and the Shaping of New England Institutions," *William and Mary Quarterly* 32 (1975): 3–28.

————. "Transfer of Culture: Chance and Design in Shaping Massachusetts Bay, 1636–1660." *New England Historical and Genealogical Register,* vol. 132 (1978), pp. 3–17.

————. and Stephen Foster, "The Puritans' Greatest Achievement: A Study of Social Cohesion in Seventeenth-Century Massachusetts," *Journal of American History* 60 (1973): 5–22.

Bridenbaugh, Carl. *Cities in Revolt.* New York: Ronald Press, 1955.

————. *Cities in the Wilderness.* New York: Knopf, 1938.

Brown, Richard D. "The Emergence of Urban Society in Rural Massachusetts, 1760–1820," *Journal of American History* 61 (1974): 29–51.

Bruchey, Stuart. *The Colonial Merchant.* New York: Harcourt, Brace & Worth, 1966.

————. *Robert Oliver, Merchant of Baltimore, 1783–1819.* Baltimore: Johns Hopkins University Press, 1956.

————. *The Roots of American Economic Growth, 1607–1861.* New York: Harper & Row, 1965.

Bushman, Richard. *From Puritan to Yankee: Character and the Social Order in Connecticut, 1690–1760.* Cambridge, Mass.: Harvard University Press, 1967.

Cadbury, Henry J. "Quaker Relief During the Siege of Boston," *Transactions of the Colonial Society of Massachusetts,* vol. 34 (1937–42), pp. 39–179.

Cook, Jr., Edward M. *The Fathers of the Towns: Leadership and Community Structure in Eighteenth Century New England.* Baltimore: Johns Hopkins University Press, 1976.

Coughtry, Jay. *The Notorious Triangle: Rhode Island and The African Slave Trade, 1700–1807.* Philadelphia, Temple University Press, 1981.

Daniels, Bruce. *The Connecticut Town: Growth and Development, 1635–1790.* Middletown, Conn.: Wesleyan University Press, 1979.

Demos, John. *A Little Commonwealth: Family Life in Plymouth Colony.* New York: Oxford University Press, 1970.

Earle, Carville, and Ronald Hoffman, "Urban Development in the Eighteenth Century South," *Perspectives in American History,* vol. 1 (1976), pp. 7–78.

East, Robert A. *Business Enterprise in the American Revolutionary Era.* New York: Columbia University Press, 1938.

Egnal, Mark. "The Economic Development of the Thirteen Continental Colonies, 1720 to 1775," *William and Mary Quarterly* 32 (1975): 191–222.

Ernst, Joseph A. and H. Roy Merrens. " 'Camden's turrets pierce the skies!' The Urban Process in the Southern Colonies during the Eighteenth Century," *William and Mary Quarterly* 30 (1973): 549–74.

Foner, Eric. *Tom Paine and Revolutionary America.* New York: Oxford University Press, 1976.

Foster Stephen. *Their Solitary Way: The Puritan Social Ethic in the First Century of Settlement in New England.* New Haven: Yale University Press, 1971.

Green, Lorenzo. *The Negro in Colonial New England.* New York: Columbia University Press, 1942.

Greven, Philip. *Four Generations: Land, Population and Family in Colonial Andover, Massachusetts.* Ithaca, N. Y.: Cornell University Press, 1970.

Gross, Robert. *The Minutemen and Their World.* New York, 1976.

Henretta, James A. Economic Development and Social Structure in Colonial Boston," *William and Mary Quarterly* 22 (1965): 75–92.

———. "Families and Farms: Mentalité in Pre-Industrial America," *William and Mary Quarterly* 35 (1978): 3–32.

Innes, Stephen. "Land Tenancy and Social Order in Springfield, Massachusetts, 1652 to 1702," *William and Mary Quarterly* 35 (1978): 33–56.

James, Sydney V. *A People Among Peoples: Quaker Benevolence in Eighteenth-Century America.* Cambridge, Mass.: Harvard University Press, 1963.

Jensen, Arthur L. *The Maritime Commerce of Colonial Philadelphia*. Madison, Wisconsin: University of Wisconsin Press, 1963).

Jones, Alice Hanson. "Wealth Estimates for the New England Colonies About 1770," *Journal of Economic History* 32 (1972): 98–127.

Jones, Douglas L. "Poverty and Vagabondage: The Process of Survival in Eighteenth Century Massachusetts." Paper presented at the Annual Meeting of the Organization of American Historians, April 1978.

————. "The Strolling Poor: Transiency in Eighteenth Century Massachusetts," *Journal of Social History* 8 (1975): 28–54.

————. *Village and Seaport: Migration and Society in Eighteenth Century Massachusetts*. Hanover, N.H.: University Press of New England, 1981.

Kornblith, Gary. "From Artisans to Businessmen: Master Mechanics in New England, 1789–1850." Ph.D. diss., Princeton University, 1983.

Kulikoff, Allan. "The Progress of Inequality in Revolutionary Boston," *William and Mary Quarterly,* 28 (1971): 375–412.

Lemon, James. *The Best Poor Man's Country*. Baltimore: Johns Hopkins University Press, 1972.

————. "Urbanization and the Development of Eighteenth Century Southeastern Pennsylvania and Adjacent Delaware," *William and Mary Quarterly* 24 (1967): 501–42.

Livingood, James W. *The Philadelphia-Baltimore Trade Rivalry, 1780–1860*. Harrisburg, Pa.: Pennsylvania Historical and Museum Commission, 1947.

Lockridge, Kenneth. "Land, Population, and the Evolution of New England Society, 1630–1790," *Past and Present* 39 (1968): 62–80.

————. *A New England Town: The First Hundred Years*. New York: Norton, 1970.

Lynd, Staughton. "The Mechanics in New York Politics, 1774–1788," *Labor History* 5 (1964): 225–46.

Main, Jackson Turner. *The Social Structure of Revolutionary America*. Princeton: Princeton University Press, 1965.

Modell, John. "Family and Fertility on the Indiana Frontier, 1820," *American Quarterly* 23 (1971): 615–34.

Morgan, Edmund S. "New England Puritanism: Another Approach," *William and Mary Quarterly* 18 (1961): 236–42.

————. and Helen M. Morgan, *The Stamp Act Crisis*. Chapel Hill: University of North Carolina Press, 1953.

Mullin, Gerald. *Flight and Rebellion: Slave Resistance in Eighteenth Century Virginia*. New York: Oxford University Press, 1972.

Nash, Gary B. "Poverty and Poor Relief in Pre-Revolutionary Philadelphia," *William and Mary Quarterly* 33 (1976: 3–30.

————. *Quakers and Politics: Pennsylvania 1681–1726*. Princeton, 1968.

————. "Up from the Bottom in Franklin's Philadelphia," *Past and Present* 77 (1977): 62–64.

————. "Urban Wealth and Poverty in Pre-Revolutionary America," *Journal of Interdisciplinary History* 6 (1976): 545–84.

————. *The Urban Crucible: Social Change, Political Consciousness, and the Origins of the American Revolution*. Cambridge, Mass: Harvard University Press, 1979.

————. "War, Widowhood and Poverty: The Failure of Female Factory Labor in Boston." Paper presented at the Annual Meeting of the Organization of American Historians, April 1978.

————, and James Lemon. "The Distribution of Wealth in Eighteenth Century America: A Century of Change in Chester County, Pennsylvania," *Journal of Social History* 2 (1968): 1–24.

Ostrander, Gilman M. "The Colonial Molasses Trade," *Agricultural History*, 30 (1956): 77–84.

————. "The Making of the Triangular Trade Myth," *William and Mary Quarterly* 30 (1973): 635–44.

Papenfuse, Edward C. *In Pursuit of Profit: The Annapolis Merchants in the Era of the American Revolution, 1763–1805*. Baltimore: Johns Hopkins University Press, 1975.

ᵖares, Richard. *Yankees and Creoles: The Trade Between North America and the West Indies Before the Revolution*. Cambridge, Mass.: Harvard University Press, 1956.

Pope, Robert. *The Halfway Covenant: Church Membership in Puritan New England*. Princeton: Princeton University Press, 1969.

Price, Jacob. "Economic Function and the Growth of American Port Towns in the Eighteenth Century," *Perspectives in American History* 8 (1974): 123–86.

Ritcheson, Charles R. *Aftermath of Revolution: British Policy Toward the United States, 1783–1795*. Dallas: Southern Methodist University Press, 1969.

Rothman, David J. *Discovery of the Asylum: Social Order and Disorder in the New Republic*. Boston: Little, Brown, 1971.

Rutman, Darrett. "People in Process: The New Hampshire Towns of the Eighteenth Century," *Journal of Urban History* 1 (1975): 268–92.

Shy, John. *A People Numerous and Armed*. New York: Oxford University Press, 1976.

Smith, Daniel Scott. "Population, Family and Society in Hingham, Massachusetts, 1636–1880." Ph.D. diss., University of California, Berkeley, 1973.

Stone, Frederick D. "The Struggle for Delaware: Philadelphia under Howe and under Arnold." In *Narrative and Critical History of America*, ed. Justin Winsor, vol. 6. Boston and New York: Houghton Mifflin, 1887.

Wade, Richard. *The Urban Frontier: The Rise of Western Cities, 1790–1830*. Cambridge, Mass: Harvard University Press, 1959.

Warden, G. B. *Boston, 1689–1776*. Boston: Little, Brown, 1970.

Waters, John. "The Traditional World of the New England Peasants: A View from Seventeenth Century Barnstable." *New England Historical and Genealogical Register,* vol. 130 (1976), pp. 3–21.

White, Philip L. *The Beekmans of New York in Politics and Commerce, 1646–1877*. New York: New York Historical Society, 1956.

Wood, Peter. *Black Majority: Negroes in Colonial South Carolina from 1670 Through the Stono Rebellion*. New York: Oxford University Press, 1974.

Young, Alfred. "The Mechanics and the Jeffersonians: New York, 1789–1801," *Labor History* 5 (1964); 247–76.

Index

URBAN GROWTH IN COLONIAL RHODE ISLAND
Newport and Providence in the Eighteenth Century

LYNNE WITHEY

By the early decades of the eighteenth century, Rhode Island had developed a commercial economy with not one, but two centers. *Urban Growth in Colonial Rhode Island* is the tale of these two cities: Newport, fifth largest city in the colonies, and the much smaller Providence. This absorbing history of two interdependent cities in a restricted rēgion shows how they developed, competed with each other, and eventually traded places as major and secondary economic centers within the region.

The book has drawn upon the substantial body of local and regional history of colonial America. Unlike other studies, which concentrate on the social structure and family life of rural communities, *Urban Growth in Colonial Rhode Island* explores the relationship between economic development and social structure in an urban setting. The book concludes with a discussion of the impact of the Revolution on the two cities, and the ways in which the war, combined with general economic trends, transformed Providence into Rhode Island's major city.

"This is more than a study of colonial cities; it is a study in regionalism and in urbanization"—Virginia Yans-McLaughlin, Associate Professor of History, Rutgers University.

State University of New York Press
State University Plaza
Albany, New York 12246

ISBN 0-87395-752-0